AF744405

Theoretical Studies in Islamic Banking and Finance

Theoretical Studies in Islamic Banking and Finance

Edited by: Mohsin S. Khan
Abbas Mirakhor

The Institute for Research and Islamic Studies

For information contact: The Institute for Research and Islamic Studies
P.O. Box 35844, Houston, Texas 77235 U.S.A.

First published 1987
Published in the United States of America by IRIS Books, a division of FIL, Inc.

Library of Congress Cataloging-in-Publication Data

Theoretical Studies in Islamic Banking and Finance.

Bibliography: p.
Includes index.
1. Banks and banking—Islamic countries. 2. Economics—Religious aspects—Islam. 3. Interest (Islamic law)
I. Khan, Mohsin S. II. Mirakhor, Abbas.
HG3368.A6T47 1987 332.1′0917′4927 86-83221
ISBN 0-932625-07-X
ISBN 0-932625-06-1 (pbk.)
IR3-4MRE0787-1

Cover design by Hossein Ava

Contents

Transliteration

Letter	Transliteration
ء	'
ب	b
ت	t
ث	th
ج	j
ح	ḥ
خ	kh
د	d
ذ	dh
ر	r
ز	z
س	s
ش	sh
ص	ṣ
ض	ḍ
ط	ṭ
ظ	ẓ
ع	‘
غ	gh
ف	f
ق	q
ک	k
ل	l
م	m
ن	n
و	w
ه	h
ى	y-i
ة	t

Short Vowels	
ـَ	a
ـُ	u
ـِ	i

Long Vowels	
آ	ā
وُ	ū
يِ	ī

Diphthongs	
ـَوْ	aw
ـَىْ	ay
ـِيّ	iyy
ـُوّ	uww

Persian Letters	
پ	p
چ	ch
ژ	zh
گ	g
و	v

Persian Short Vowels	
ـِ	e

Persian Diphthongs	
ـَوْ	ow
ـِىْ	ey

A Note from the Institute

The contemporary Islamic movement not only challenges the political structures of Muslim societies, but also aims at the transformation of their economies. Although Islam has its own economic doctrines, these doctrines have not been put into practice for centuries. The reform movement in the Muslim world has brought economic issues to the fore. A number of well researched studies have already been published which open the way to further inquiry in Islamic economics, but many unresolved questions remain.

Islam is a faith which has social and political dimensions, and as such economics is essential to it. In the West, the political face of the Islamic movement has generated considerable interest, although relatively little attention has been paid to the development of Islamic economic theory. The members of The Institute for Research and Islamic Studies hope that through the publication of several volumes on Islamic economics, the principles of Islamic economics will become more widely understood, and research in this field will be stimulated.

The first volume in this series has been edited by our colleagues, Mohsin Khan and Abbas Mirakhor. Both of these economists are well known among those who are familiar with the literatures of the IMF, the World Bank, and Islamic economics journals. We hereby express our gratitude to them for compiling and editing this volume. The members of IRIS would also like to thank Prof. Khurshid Ahmad for granting us permission to reprint one of the articles of his valuable book, the International Monetary Fund and the Pakistan Journal of Applied Economics for their permission to reprint some of their research, and Waqar Massood Khan, Shahrukh Rafi Khan, Ali M. Al-Jarhi and Nadeem ul-Haque for their contributions to this volume. We are also thankful to those who encouraged the initiation of this project, especially Ahassem Salehkhou, member of the executive board of the IMF. We are grateful to Jack Schriver, Gary Legenhausen and Khalil Yazdi for detailed copy-editing and for suggestions regarding grammar and usage. We owe our appreciation to Abbas Mirakhor and Mehdi Abedi for the bibliography.

It is our hope that scholars and students of economics will send us suggestions and research proposals in Islamic economics, as well as other areas of Islamic studies. We pray that God may help us and accept this endeavor.

Mehdi Noorbaksh
Director, IRIS
March 1987

Introduction

A central tenet of Islam, and thus of an economic system based on Islamic principles, is the unequivocal prohibition against the payment and receipt of interest. The Quran explicitly states that the charging of interest will draw a declaration of war from Allah and His Messenger and promises total destruction of an economy which allows interest-based transactions. Banking and financial operations must, therefore, be conducted in the absence of interest, and Islam suggests ways and means by which interest and the economic institutions that accompany it can be replaced.

Historical research has shown that early Islamic societies were able to develop financial instruments and institutions that were consistent with religious strictures. These developments facilitated the economic operations of Islamic systems for nearly a millenium. The growth in power of European nations, however, which brought Muslim countries under the direct and indirect control of the West, led to a period of neglect of Islamic rules and norms regarding economic relations that lasted some four hundred years. By the middle of the present century almost all of the economies of Muslim countries had been transformed into capitalistic systems in which interest played a central role.

The decades of the second half of this century, which also marked the beginning of the 15th century of the Islamic era, witnessed a truly impressive upsurge in the desire to return to fundamental Islamic values in many parts of the Muslim world. In this process Islam's views on how individuals and nations must behave in the economic arena have not been ignored. A number of Islamic countries, notably the Islamic Republics of Iran and Pakistan, have moved towards transforming their economic systems to conform more closely with the precepts and conditions of Islam. Because of the uncompromising stance of Islam against interest, this transformation process has begun in these countries with the eradication of the institution of interest from banking and financial transactions. In the last ten years there has also been a rapid expansion of financial institutions that can be characterized as Islamic, in that they do not conduct interest-based transactions. At present, about 45 countries, encompassing most of the Muslim world, have some type of Islamic banking or financial institution.

Islam proposes that the banking systems that operate on the basis of an ex ante fixed rate of interest be replaced by a profit-sharing system in which the rate of return to the financial resources is not known and is not fixed prior to the undertaking of the transaction. While in Islam interest is forbidden, trade and profits are permissible and in fact encouraged. An uncertain rate of return based on profits would thus be consistent with the Shariah. From this distinction between a certain rate of interest and an uncertain rate of return it follows that, if a banking structure could be evolved in which the return for the use of financial resources would fluctuate according to actual profits made from such use, the resulting system would be in conformity with Islamic rules and guidelines.

The replacement of an interest-based system by an alternative profit-sharing system raises a number of fundamental theoretical, practical, and policy questions. It would be fair to argue that the interest-free banking aspect of Islamic economics has received the most attention by economists, and most of the research conducted has focused on this subject. Even though such research is in many respects in its infancy, it is still possible to detect certain patterns and trends. The earlier papers were concerned primarily with historical-doctrinal issues and with questions of what the system was and how it could be implemented. In the second stage we are seeing the emergence of papers that delve more deeply into the theoretical aspects of the system. Such work, which is designed to complement the writings of Islamic scholars, brings to bear modern analytical tools and concepts on questions such as:

a. What is the theoretical framework underlying Islamic banking and finance?

b. Will the Islamic system be more or less stable than the traditional interest-based system?

c. What will be the effect of the adoption of an interest-free Islamic system on important macroeconomic variables like saving and investment? and

d. Will monetary policy have a role to play in such a system?

The papers in this volume all address one or more of these basic questions at the theoretical level. As experience with the practice of Islamic banking grows, we will undoubtedly see studies where the empirical properties of the system will be examined. The papers here represent a start in the attempt to introduce rigor into the analysis of Islamic banking and finance, thereby clarifying the nature of the basic relationships underlying the system.

In the first paper, *Mohsin Khan* and *Abbas Mirakhor* present a brief overview of the structure and practice of Islamic banking. The authors start by stressing that the abolition of interest is only one aspect of Islamic economics. Islam provides precise guidelines and rules governing individual rights, property rights, contracts, work, the accumulation and distribution of wealth, and the role of the State. Islamic banking has to operate within the overall framework of the system defined by these codes, in addition to respecting the injunction against interest. The authors discuss reasons why interest is prohibited, specifically using the argument that interest represents an unjustified creation of instantaneous property rights. The paper then goes on to describe how the financial system would be expected to function in an Islamic setting, dealing specifically with the sources of funds and lending operations of banks, the role of the central bank, and the conduct of monetary policy. The final part of the paper covers the practice of Islamic banking around the world, with special emphasis being given to the examples of Pakistan and the Islamic Republic of Iran. The authors are careful to highlight the problems that policymakers and banks face in these countries, and the attempts that are being made to overcome them.

The next four papers examine the underlying theoretical framework and stability of the Islamic system, namely questions a and b. *Mohsin Khan* takes the view that the replacement of interest by some type of profit-sharing arrangement makes the Islamic system an equity-based system, as opposed to a traditional interest-based system. Using this concept of equity participation, a relatively simple theoretical model is developed in the paper to examine the workings of the Islamic banking system. It is shown that the Islamic system may well turn out to be better suited than the interest-based banking system to adjust to shocks that can lead to banking crises. In an equity-based system, shocks to the asset positions of banks are immediately absorbed by changes in the nominal values of shares (deposits) held by the public in banks. Therefore, the real values of assets and liabilities would be equal at all points in time. In the traditional banking system, since the nominal value of deposits is guaranteed, such shocks can cause a divergence between real assets and real liabilities, and it is not clear how this disequilibrium would be corrected and how long the process of adjustment would take. On the basis of the analysis, the paper yields the important insight that from an economic standpoint the principal difference between the Islamic and traditional banking systems is not that one allows interest payments and the other does not. The more relevant distinction is that the Islamic system treats deposits as shares and accordingly does not guarantee their nominal value, whereas in the traditional system such deposits are guaranteed either by the banks or by the government.

In his paper, *Mabid Al-Jarhi* investigates the theoretical implications of introducing information and transaction costs into the classical model of supply and demand for fiat means of exchange (defined as assets that yield no direct real rate of return). The paper derives behavior rules for the government, producers, households, and the banking system under varying postulates about the production, pricing, and distribution of fiat money. The main conclusion of the paper is that, among the alternative institutional configurations considered, the "optimal" arrangement is one in which: (i) the government produces fiat money and provides it to the economy at no cost; (ii) there is no interest charged on borrowing; and (iii) the government imposes a 100 percent reserve requirement on banks. The last feature has been considered somewhat controversial, since the introduction of a 100 percent reserve requirement eliminates bank multiple creation of money.

Waqar Masood Khan uses the theory of contracts to compare the Islamic banking system with the alternative interest-based system. The paper shows that because the Islamic system spreads the risk of an economic enterprise it is superior to the traditional system if both investors and lenders have the same information. If the assumption of symmetric information between investor and lender is relaxed, the traditional debt contract then becomes superior because it reduces the cost of monitoring. These costs of monitoring can be sufficiently reduced, however, if the possibility of dishonest behavior on the part of either parties is excluded. The author's argument that dishonesty is a function of the incentive structures existing in society is particularly meaningful. The driving force of a truly Islamic society is the existence of a strong ideological consensus that the success of the society and its members depends on how closely the rules of the Shariah are followed. Honesty and faithfulness to the terms of one's contracts are indispensable ingredients of Islamic behavior. In a full Islamic system, therefore, the costs of monitoring would be insignificant and the equity-participation arrangement would be superior to the interest-based system.

The paper by *Shahrukh Rafi Khan* discusses the implications of introducing a profit-sharing system to replace an interest-based system, for portfolio behavior. A model of profit and loss sharing is developed and various comparative static exercises are conducted to illustrate its workings. The principal conclusions are that: (i) expectations-based profit-sharing ratios can serve as a pricing mechanism to bring the loanable funds market into equilibrium; (ii) the elimination of a risk-free asset with positive returns will leave lenders worse off; (iii) profit-sharing ratios are relatively inefficient instruments of monetary policy; and (iv) the introduction of interest-free banking does not necessarily lead to a situation where all profitable projects will be financed irrespective of their rate of return. Caution must be expressed about these conclusions since they are conditional on the model and the specific assumptions under which the results are obtained. For example, as the author himself notes, in interpreting the second conclusion the welfare implications of implementing an Islamic banking system have to be evaluated within the context of changed preferences once society decides to adopt such a system. Traditional welfare comparisons are incorrect because the welfare function itself will change with Islamization of the economy.

The next two papers by *Nadeem Ul Haque* and *Abbas Mirakhor* take up the question of the effects of the adoption of an interest-free system on savings and investment behavior. In the first paper they address the assertion often made that elimination of a predetermined rate of interest will result in a decline in savings due to increased uncertainty. The authors develop a model which permits variations in the rate of returns as well as in risk and derive an unambiguous condition which has to be met in order for savings to decrease as risk increases. Basically this condition requires that the rate of return must not be higher after the increase in uncertainty than it was before it if savings are to fall. If the rate of return also increases as risk increases, then savings may in fact rise. It is suggested that the structural changes accompanying the implementation of an Islamic financial system may produce favorable effects on the rate of return on financial assets. As such, there is no *a priori* reason for believing that savings in an Islamic system will necessarily be lower than in an interest-based system.

The second paper by Haque and Mirakhor analyzes the issue of investment in an Islamic system. The adoption of a profit-sharing arrangement between the lender and investor may raise monitoring costs that could have an adverse effect on the supply of credit, and thus on investment. The problem they address is thus similar to the one considered by Waqar Masood Khan. The paper models investment in the Islamic system as a principal-agent problem and investigates the relevant issues under conditions of uncertainty and moral hazard. It is shown that individual contracts can be designed to take into account the moral hazard problem that arises when the lender and the investor have different information on the profits from the investment. To avoid an adverse effect on investment requires, therefore, the implementation of a legal and institutional framework that facilitates contracting. The Islamic law of contracts provides for such a framework, but it has not yet been fully adopted in countries where an Islamic banking system is being established. In the absence of this framework, monitoring costs could be prohibitive and investment could consequently be discouraged. On the other hand, the analysis shows that if legal measures are present to safeguard the terms of contracts, the level of investment may increase.

Mohsin Khan and *Abbas Mirakhor* examine the functioning of the Islamic financial system and the role of monetary policy through a simple theoretical model. This model explicitly incorporates the main characteristics of Islamic banking and finance by replacing interest-based transactions with partnership arrangements on both the lending and borrowing sides. It is shown that there is no fundamental change in the way monetary policy operates. The central bank can achieve the same effects on the rates of return in the economy, and national income, through the control of profit-based lending as they can through variations in the money supply in the context of a traditional interest-based banking system. What the central bank loses in the process is the ability to directly set financial rates of return, which is common practice in developing countries. The paper underscores the fact that Islamization of the economy makes the financial system relatively more market oriented.

The last paper in this volume by *Abbas Mirakhor* deals with an observed tendency among banks in Pakistan and the Islamic Republic of Iran to concentrate on short-term assets. In this paper Mirakhor argues that because of their concerns for the safety of deposits and their attempts to avoid or minimize the risk of default, the monetary authorities in these countries may, through various policy actions, be discouraging the banks from engaging in risk-return sharing. The paper uses a simple portfolio model to show that, apart from considerations of social benefits which can be derived from adopting Islamic risk- and profit-sharing modes of financial transactions, the policy of restricting banks' risk-sharing activities may be a sub-optimal policy.

The papers collected in this volume are intended to provide answers to some fundamental theoretical questions that arise in discussions regarding the impact of the adoption and implementation of an Islamic financial system. The papers represent attempts by a new generation of Muslim economists, trained in the West and well-versed in analytical and quantitative techniques, to apply modern economic techniques to answer these questions. Although these and numerous other studies have been made in the theoretical study of Islamic banking and finance, the authors would be the first to admit that their work has only scratched the surface. Many of the important issues are as yet unresolved. These include, among others, the respective roles of monetary and fiscal policies, exchange rate policies, and the effects of changes in the system on financial intermediation, economic growth, and development. Even in the specific topics already addressed there is large room for further work. Economists will have to deal with issues of uncertainty, expectations, and dynamics that characterize individual and financial market behavior.

In conclusion, theoretical studies on Islamic banking and finance, including those considered here, have not dealt with full-fledged Islamic models. The mathematical functions and behavioral assumptions of the models developed so far have only tangentially picked up Islamic characteristics. For the most part the main question has been the consideration of what happens to selected economic variables if the rate of interest is eliminated and replaced by some type of profit-sharing mechanism. Indeed, it could be argued that removing the term "Islamic" would not materially affect the analysis or the conclusions of many of these papers. To correctly analyze the Islamic system, all behavioral assumptions, axioms, hypotheses, theorems, utility and production functions must bear distinctly Islamic imprints. However, this is no easy task. Considerably more theoretical analysis and actual experimentation is required to reconcile the rules and codes of economic behavior that have evolved over fourteen hundred years with the functioning of a modern-day economy. That so much progress has been achieved already in implementing Islamic values and ideals in the economic sphere is a tribute to Muslim scholars and policymakers in Muslim countries. However, it will take time before such rules of behavior can be explicitly built into economic models. Only when that happens can economists working with Islamic concepts truly lay claim to a totally new paradigm.

Mohsin S. Khan and Abbas Mirakhor

Mohsin S. Khan is Assistant Director, Research Department, International Monetary Fund. He was previously on the staff of the World Bank and has taught at the London School of Economics. He received his PhD from the London School of Economics and has published widely in the fields of macroeconomics, money and banking, and international economics.

Abbas Mirakhor is an economist in the Research Department of the International Monetary Fund. He was formerly Professor of Economics at the Florida Institute of Technology. He received his PhD from Kansas State University, and has published in a variety of areas, including microeconomic theory, mathematical economics, and Islamic economics.

1

The Framework and Practice of Islamic Banking

Mohsin S. Khan and Abbas Mirakhor

Reprinted from *Finance and Development* (September, 1986). Mohsin S. Khan is Assistant Director, Research Department, International Monetary Fund; Abbas Mirakhor is Economist, Research Department, International Monetary Fund.

The resurgence of fundamental Islamic values in many parts of the world has manifested itself on the economic front as well, with a number of Muslim countries moving toward the transformation of their economic systems—especially the banking systems—to conform more closely with the precepts of Islam. Developments in the Islamic Republic of Iran and Pakistan have been particularly intensive and have attracted wide interest, both in other Muslim countries and elsewhere.

The popular conception of the Islamic economic and financial system is that it differs from other systems only in that it proscribes interest. Since the elimination of interest has generally been the first step in the Islamization of the economy, it is perhaps only natural that the institution of interest-free banking has received the most attention. While the abolition of interest-based transactions is a central tenet of the Islamic economic system, it is by no means an adequate description of the system as a whole.

Broadly speaking, "Islamic economics" defines a complete system that prescribes specific patterns of economic behavior for all individuals and society within an Islamic way of life. This article briefly describes the main characteristics of the Islamic economic system, shows how a financial system that fits into the framework of that system is likely to function, and describes some attempts at its implementation.

ISLAMIC ECONOMIC SYSTEM

At the core of the Islamic economic system lies a collection of immutable and universal rules that affect economic behavior and relationships. These rules are specified by the *Sharī'ah,* namely, the codification of injunctions given in the Qur'an, and the traditions of the Prophet Mohammed. On the periphery there are also rules and institutions which affect economic behavior, but which are subject to change depending on circumstances. Economic policy, designed by legitimate authorities, may vary from one Muslim society to another only with respect to the periphery of the system. Such policies must, nevertheless, be compatible with the *Sharī'ah.*

Some of the key elements of the core of the Islamic economic system are the following:

- *Individual rights.* In Islam individual rights are a consequence of human obligations and not an antecedent to them. When these obligations are fulfilled, certain rights are gained. Islam stresses the need to respect the obligations as well as the rights of individuals; among them is first the duty, and then the right, of the individual to pursue his economic interests, within the framework of the *Sharī'ah.*
- *Property rights.* Property rights in Islam are the result of three basic principles. The first asserts that God is the ultimate owner of all property; for man to become materially able to perform his duties, he has been given the right of possession as a trust. Second, property is only a means of achieving higher objectives and not an end in itself, and all members of the society share the natural resources at man's disposal. The third principle, called the principle of invariance of ownership, is derived from the first two. This establishes the rights of society and of other individuals in the final product. These rights are protected by the *Sharī'ah* through the limitations imposed on the disposition of property and the wealth resulting from it.
- *Contracts.* Islam places all economic relations, including exchange, on the firm footing of contracts. The freedom to enter into contracts, designed within the framework of the *Sharī'ah,* and the

obligation to remain faithful to their stipulations has been deeply emphasized in Islam.

• *Prohibition of interest.* The Qur'an forcefully prohibits the payment and receipt of interest, or *ribā*. Strictly speaking, the term *ribā* refers to the addition to the amount of principal of a loan on the basis of time for which it is loaned, or of the time for which the payment is deferred. In accordance with Islamic jurisprudence it signifies the additional money charged in a money-money type exchange or the uncompensated increase in a commodity-commodity transaction. There is now a consensus of opinion among Muslim scholars that this prohibition extends to any and all forms of interest.

• *Work and wealth.* Islam exalts work and considers it as an inseparable dimension of faith itself. Conversely, idleness is viewed as a manifestation of unbelief in the religion. All persons are exhorted to work in order to earn their living, and no one who is physically and mentally able is allowed to become a liability to his family or the state through idleness and voluntary unemployment.

Wealth itself is considered as an important means by which man can pave the way for the attainment of his ultimate objective. It is considered among the highest blessings bestowed on man and everyone is encouraged to strive for it. However, the methods of earning, possessing, and disposing of wealth are defined by the *Sharī'ah.* Among these rules are those relating to extravagance in consumption, waste, the obligation of sharing (through mandatory levies); and those on inheritance. These rules are aimed at modifying patterns of income and wealth distribution.

• *Role of the state.* The state's role in the Islamic economy relates to ensuring, first, that everyone has equal access to natural resources and means of livelihood; second, that each individual has equal opportunity, including education, skills, and technology, to use these resources; third, that markets are supervised to ensure justice in exchange (Islam places great emphasis on the market and its efficient operation, and the *Sharī'ah* has provided a network of ethical and moral rules of behavior which cover all market participants); fourth, that transfer takes place from those more able to use the economy's resources to those less able, according to the rules of the *Sharī'ah;* and, finally, that distributive justice is assured for the next generation through the implementation of the laws of inheritance.

The state is empowered, within the framework of the *Shariah,* to design any specific economic policy that is required in order to guarantee the attainment of these objectives and to meet the necessary expenditure associated with the performance of its duties through taxation and utilization of national resources.

ISLAMIC BANKING

Islamic banking is intended to operate within an economic system some of whose features have been briefly described above. The principal restriction under which the financial system must work is the injunction against interest. However, what is forbidden is the fixed or predetermined return on financial transactions and not an uncertain rate of return, represented, for example, by profits.

Prohibition of Interest

Although the fact of prohibition against interest in Islamic banking is axiomatic, a variety of arguments have been provided by Islamic scholars to explain and justify its application. One argument which has not received any attention in the literature on Islamic banking, and which goes a long way in justifying the prohibition, is based on Islam's position on property rights and obligations and its conception of economic justice.

Money represents the monetized claim of its owner to property rights created by assets that were obtained through work or transfer. Lending money, in effect, is a transfer of this right, and all that can be claimed in return is its equivalent and no more. Thus, interest on money is regarded as representing unjustified creation of instantaneous property rights: unjustified, because interest is a property right claimed outside the legitimate framework of recognized property rights; instantaneous, because as soon as the contract for lending upon interest is concluded, a right to the borrower's property is created for the lender. On the other hand, when the financial capital of the lender is used in partnership with the human capital and labor of the entrepreneur, the lender's right to his property is not transferred and he shares, as co-owner, the final product his money has helped to create. He will be remunerated in proportion to his financial investment in the ensuing incremental wealth. This emphasis on profit-sharing provides the basis for the development of an Islamic financial system.

In broad terms, the transformation of banking from an interest-based system to one that relies on profit- and loss-sharing makes an Islamic banking system essentially an equity-based system. In such a system depositors are treated as if they were the shareholders of the bank, and consequently are not guaranteed a nominal value, or a predetermined rate of return, on their deposits. If the bank makes a profit, the shareholder (depositor) is entitled to receive a certain share of it; on the other hand, if the bank incurs a loss, the depositor is expected to share in it and thus receive a negative rate of return. From the depositors' perspective, then, an Islamic bank is in most respects identical to a mutual fund or an investment trust. Furthermore, to remain consistent with religious strictures, banks cannot charge interest on their lending operations, but have to use special modes of investment and financing that are also based on profit and loss sharing.

Sources of Funds

Besides its own capital and equity, the main sources of funds for Islamic banks would be two forms of deposits—transaction deposits and investment deposits.

Transaction deposits are directly related to transactions and payments, and can be regarded as equivalent to demand deposits in a conventional banking system. Although a bank would guarantee the nominal value of the deposit, it would pay no return on this type of liability. Generally speaking, funds mobilized through this source cannot be used for profitable investment by banks. As such, banks would presumably have to levy a service charge on deposit holders to cover the cost of administering this type of account.

Investment deposits constitute the principal source of funds for banks and they more closely resemble shares in a firm, rather than time and saving deposits of the customary sort. The bank offering investment deposits would provide no guarantee on their nominal value, and would not pay a fixed rate of return. Depositors, instead, would be treated as if they were shareholders and therefore entitled to a share of the profits or losses made by the bank. The only contractual agreement between the depositor and the bank is the proportion in which profits and losses are to be distributed. The profit- or loss-sharing ratio has to be agreed in advance of the transaction between the bank and the depositors, and cannot be altered during the life of the contract, except by mutual consent.

Lending Operations of Banks

Islamic banks also are required by the *Sharī'ah* to apply the same principles of profit- and loss-sharing in their loan operations. The two methods that fully satisfy the requirements of the law on the lending side are *Muḍārabah* and *Mushārakah* arrangements.

Under *Muḍārabah* arrangements surplus funds are made available by the owner to the entrepreneur to be invested in a productive economic activity in return for a predetermined share of the profits earned. Financial losses are borne exclusively by the lender. The borrower, as such, loses only the time and effort invested in the venture. This arrangement, therefore, effectively places human capital on par with financial capital.

A *Mushārakah* transaction is one in which there is more than a single contributor of funds. All parties invest in varying proportions and the profits and losses are shared strictly in relation to their respective capital contributions. The essential difference between the two forms of financing is the number of parties involved in the transaction and, indeed, *Mushārakah* financing corresponds closely to an equity market in which shares can be acquired by the public, banks, and even the central bank and the government. For example, firms desiring to raise funds for investment could use this mechanism and offer *Mushārakah* certificates in the market. Such certificates would be, in effect, transferable corporate instruments secured by the assets of the company. Their price, and the implicit rate of return, would be determined by the market.

Other Modes of Financing

In cases where profit-loss sharing cannot be implemented, for example, in the case of small-scale borrowers or for consumption loans, a number of alternative instruments for investment and financing are available to banks. These include deferred payment sales or "mark-up," purchase with deferred delivery (known as *Bay' salam*), lease-purchase, beneficence loans, and the levying of a service charge.

Role of the Central Bank

Under an Islamic system, operations are undoubtedly more varied and complex than in a traditional banking system. In terms of profit-sharing activities, the criterion of creditworthiness of the borrower that underlies the conventional banking system has to be changed to place more emphasis on the viability and profitability of projects. In addition to a term structure of rates of return, there has to be a structure of returns from different economic activities that banks have to consider. Project evaluation and appraisal, determination of profit-sharing ratios, and the establishment of a procedural framework for the processing, monitoring, supervision, and auditing of various projects create new demands on commercial banks.

The monetary authorities operating in an Islamic framework continue to have the power to regulate banking and financial operations in the economy, both to allocate resources in conformity with the priorities of the society, and to direct monetary policy toward specific goals. To achieve its policy objectives, the central bank has control over the supply of "high-powered" money (that is, currency plus deposit liabilities of the central bank to commercial banks), the reserve ratios on different types of liabilities, and the maximum amounts of assets that banks can allocate to their profit-sharing activities. A further control is available to the central bank through its purchases of equity shares of banks and other financial intermediaries. Through performance of its regulatory, supervisory, and control functions, as well as its lender-of-last-resort role, the central bank can continue to exert substantial influence on the financial system. Moreover, opportunities may exist for direct investing in the real sector on a profit-sharing basis, as well as taking equity positions in joint ventures along with other banks. The ability to buy and sell securities representing real assets in the financial market, that is, open market operations, would still be permitted as long as these securities do not have par value features and a non-zero coupon rate.

Additionally, the suggestion has been made that the central bank could regulate profit-sharing ratios between the banks and borrowers on the one hand, and the banks and depositors on the other. Variations in these ratios would alter the rates of return and could have the same impact as changes in interest rates on the overall and sectoral flows of financial resources.

Impact of Monetary Policy

The main accounting relationships that can be expected to exist in an Islamic financial system are summarized in the accompanying table.

In this stylized system the public's financial assets would be invest-

Flow of Funds Accounts of the Islamic Financial System

	Public		Banks		Central Bank	
	Uses	Sources	Uses	Sources	Uses	Sources
Investment deposits	ΔD_p			ΔD_b		
Mudarabah credit		ΔF_p	ΔF_b			
Musharakah credit		ΔF_p^m	ΔF_b^m			
Equity of banks				ΔE_b	ΔE_c	
Reserves			ΔR_b			ΔR_c

Definition of symbols: D_p = public's investment deposits in the banking system, D_b = banks' deposit liabilities, F_p = public's *Muḍārabah* liabilities to the banking system, F_b = banks' *Muḍarabah* financing of investment projects, F_p^m = public's *Mushārakah* liabilities to the banking system, F_b^m = bank's *Mushārakah* financing of investment projects, E_b = banks' sale of equity shares to the central bank, E_c = central bank's purchase of equity shares in the banking system; R_b = banking system's reserves with the central bank, and R_c = central bank's holding of the reserves of the banking system.

ment deposits, and its liabilities would be loans obtained under *Muḍārabah* and *Mushārakah* arrangements. The rates of return on both deposits and loans would be entirely market determined. The assets of commercial banks are credit extended to the public, and reserves held at the central bank. These reserves can be either legally imposed by the central bank or voluntary. The banking sector's liabilities are investment deposits and the equity of banks held by the central bank. The latter essentially represents the tool through which the central bank changes reserves, and thereby the flow of credit and rates of return, in the system.

In the literature, macroeconomic models that explicitly incorporate the flow of funds accounts presented in the table have been developed to show how an Islamic financial system would function and how it would interact with the real side of the economy. An analysis of such models indicates that there is apparently no fundamental change in the way monetary policy affects economic variables in an Islamic economy. The authorities can achieve the same results through controlling the supply of profit-based bank lending as they can through variations in the total money supply. While institutions and financial instruments may be quite different in an Islamic economy, the standard macroeconomic result, for example, that an expansionary monetary policy would reduce rates of return and increase output in the short run, carries through. What the authorities do lose in the process is the ability to set directly financial rates of return, a practice that is fairly common in developing countries; in this sense the financial system is more market-oriented in an Islamic economy.

PRACTICAL APPLICATIONS

At present, about 45 countries, encompassing most of the Muslim world, have some form of Islamic banking or financial institution. Most of these have been established since the second half of the 1970s. This development has basically taken two forms. The first has been an attempt to establish Islamic financial institutions side by side with traditional banking. In such attempts, two types of institutions have evolved, Islamic commercial banks established mostly in Muslim countries, and Islamic investment and holding companies operating in some Muslim, but mostly in non-Muslim, countries. In both cases, generally, the banking operations of Islamic banks are subject to the specific regulations that apply to all banks. Examples of the first category are Faisal Islamic Banks in Egypt and Sudan, the Dubai Islamic Bank, and the Jordan Islamic Bank. Examples of the second—that is, investment holding companies having either a national or international mandate—include the Dārul Māl Al-Islāmī (Geneva), the Islamic Investment Company (Bahamas), and the Bahrain Islamic Investment Bank. These institutions compete with conventional banks to attract deposits from Muslims who wish to avoid interest and invest these funds wherever they find profitable investment opportunities. The majority of these institutions were established through private initiatives.

The second form has involved an attempt to restructure the whole financial system of the economy to accord with Islamic precepts. This has taken two approaches: one in which the entire economy and its institutions, including financial, are transformed into Islamic ones, as in the Islamic Republic of Iran; and the other where total Islamization of the economy is undertaken through a gradual process beginning with the banking sector, as in Pakistan.

PAKISTAN

The process of Islamization of the banking system in Pakistan was initiated in 1979–80, when banks were allowed to accept deposits on a profit-loss sharing (PLS) basis. In June 1984 the Government announced a program for phased transformation of the entire financial system, including commercial and specialized banks as well as nonbank financial institutions, to non-interest-bearing Islamic financial modes during 1984–85. As of July 1, 1984, all financial institutions were allowed to carry out transactions on the basis of either Islamic or interest-based modes, on condition that interest-based accommodation for working capital would not be provided or renewed for more than six months. Since January 1, 1985, all transactions with the Federal and Provincial Governments, public sector corporations, and public or private joint stock companies have been based on Islamic modes and, from April 1, 1985, all financing to all entities and individuals was required to be on an Islamic basis. The State Bank of Pakistan (the central bank) is empowered to determine for each permissible mode of Islamic financing the maximum and minimum rates of return to financial institutions. However, the specific instrument and the terms of any financial arrangements are to be agreed upon between the institution and its clients.

Even though a wide variety of banking modes is permitted, ranging from service fees to equity participation on the PLS basis, over 90 percent of bank lending has, up to now, been done on the basis of mark-up, mainly because of operational convenience. Mark-ups can vary according to the type of transaction or expected profit of the client, but only within a range of 10–20 percent, as prescribed by the State Bank of Pakistan. Depositors are assured of the security of their deposits and a share in the bank's earnings on the PLS basis.

The early experience of Pakistan has shown that the implementation of Islamic banking has not impaired the effectiveness of monetary policy. In fact, it is believed that the new system, by permitting variations in the range of mark-up rates as well as profit-sharing ratios, has enhanced the ability of the monetary authorities to affect allocation of financial resources. The effectiveness of the primary instrument of monetary policy, namely credit allocation, has remained unaffected. It is expected that through the gradual process of Islamization some significant changes will take place in the legal and institutional framework, which will enhance the transformation of the total system. Among these are: changes in the attitude of banks toward medium- and long-term lending on *Muḍārabah* and *Mushārakah* basis; comprehensive retraining of staff to enable them to evaluate and appraise investment projects; reform of the auditing and monitoring system; establishment of an efficient equity market and development of a secondary market; and the establishment of an efficient judicial arbitration system and legal framework to allow for settlement of disputes.

ISLAMIC REPUBLIC OF IRAN

The most comprehensive implementation of the Islamic financial system to date has taken place in Iran. This is only natural in that the Islamic Revolution was meant to transform the total society. Because banking in Iran is an integral part of the much broader Islamic system, it should provide the most far reaching test of the effectiveness of Islamic banking within its natural framework of a total Islamic system.

Immediately following the Revolution steps were taken to transform the banking system by first nationalizing and then streamlining the system. The Bank Nationalization Act of 1979 reduced the number of banks from 36 to 9 and the total number of bank branches or offices were reduced by nearly 2,000. After this reorganization, interest was eliminated from banking operations and replaced by a service charge and minimum rates of profit, while the Law of Usury (Interest)-Free Banking was being developed for submission to the Parliament. The law was passed in late 1983 and implemented beginning March 21, 1984.

This law established 14 different modes of approved transactions and financing and 4 modes of transactions on the liability side. It required that all transactions be based on these specified modes of finance, that existing transactions be converted to the prescribed method within a year for deposits, and that all banking operations be carried out in accordance with the new law within three years after its enactment. While no returns are to be paid on current or saving deposits, the latter will be eligible for variable prizes and bonuses. The investment deposits can be utilized in two ways. The bank can either employ the funds on behalf of the depositor (as a trustee) to invest in profitable projects, in which case the depositor receives all the profits earned and the bank receives a commission; alternatively, the bank can use the depositor's funds along with its own resources and pay the depositor a predetermined portion of the profits earned.

The deposits of all banks were transformed into Islamic modes well before the legislated deadline. At present, the asset side of banks' balance sheets is being transformed into Islamic modes and it is expected that this transformation will be completed well before the legislated deadline. Because of a de-emphasis of collateral and creditworthiness of the borrower, and reliance on the viability and profitability of projects, the banks' clients, particularly in manufacturing, industrial, and agricultural sectors, have been encouraged to submit new investment projects for financing on a profit-sharing basis. A significant innovation by the banks has been their willingness to combine a variety of financing modes in order to provide the most financially advantageous package for their clients. The most serious difficulty faced by the banks has been the lack of trained and skilled staff (in the *Sharī'ah* as well as banking) to appraise and monitor investment projects.

PROBLEMS OF TRANSITION

A distinction has been made between the concept of Islamic banking implmented as a profit-making enterprise operating in an interest-based system and Islamic banking implemented as an integral part of a complete Islamic system. Each will face different sets of problems. In most of the Muslim world (and in some Western countries) Islamic banks compete with conventional banks. The problems faced by these banks will be of the type experienced by all attempts at transplanting parts of one system into another. Aside from problems of contradictions and conflict in basic values, these institutions will have to meet the challenges emanating from the legal and regulatory framework of the environments in which they wish to operate, as well as those generated by the requirements of security, viability, and profitability which conventional banking systems have tried to meet. In the meantime they will serve as a channel for mobilization of funds from interest-averting clients to profitable projects wherever they are found.

As for attempts of the second type, their success will depend on how intent these societies are in transforming their total system into an Islamic one in which not only the prerequisites of the Islamic economic system are implemented but also those of a successful and sound Islamic financial system are met. The provision of markets (in financial and real assets), which operate on the basis of the *Sharī'ah;* the development of a legal framework which can implement the property rights structure of the Islamic system as well as Islamic laws of contracts; the necessary change of attitudes among the providers and users of surplus funds; and finally the provision of trained personnel for financial institutions seem to be the minimum requirements for operation of a banking system which will not only be sound but also meet the objectives and requirements of Islam.

In conclusion, policy makers in Islamic countries face a number of difficult problems as they move toward transforming their economies to be consistent with religious principles. There are many macroeconomic and financial issues that are as yet unresolved. These include, among others, the respective roles of monetary, fiscal, and exchange rate policies; the effects of changes in the system on financial intermediation, savings, and investment; and the impact of the change in financial institutions on growth and development. During the transition many seemingly ad hoc and second-best policies have needed to be adopted, but this is only natural as Islamization represents an attempt to apply Islamic rules and codes of economic behavior in countries in which economic and financial systems of largely foreign provenance have become well established.

2

*Islamic Interest-Free Banking A Theoretical Analysis**

Mohsin S. Khan

Reprinted from *IMF Staff Papers* (March, 1986). Mohsin S. Khan is Assistant Director, Research Department, International Monetary Fund.

The general resurgence of fundamental Islamic values in many parts of the world has manifested itself on the economic front as well, with a number of countries having moved toward the transformation of their economic systems to accord more closely with the precepts and conditions of Islam. The most far-reaching attempts in that direction have taken place in the Islamic Republic of Iran and in Pakistan, although this phenomenon can be observed to varying degree in most Islamic countries. More significantly, the process of Islamization of these economic systems appears to be gaining momentum over time.

This shift toward the institution of an Islamic economic system has generated widespread interest not only on the part of economists in the countries directly involved, but also in the economic profession at large. The recent outpouring of papers dealing with a variety of aspects of the structure and operation of the Islamic economy attests to the importance being attached to the subject. Whereas until the mid- to late 1970s writings on the Islamic economic system were relatively scarce,[1] the picture has changed quite dramatically in the 1980s. In the past four or five years there has been a remarkable increase in the number of papers and books,[2] conferences and seminars devoted solely to Islamic economics—even the production of a journal, the *Journal of Research in Islamic Economics* (Jeddah, Saudi Arabia).

Because this material is still relatively new, considerable misunderstanding still exists about what Islamic economics is and how an economic system based on Islamic criteria differs from other economic systems. The popular perception is that it is the concept of an interest-free financial structure that in essence characterizes the Islamic economic system, and discussions of the subject often tend to treat Islamic economics and interest-free banking as one and the same thing. Because the elimination of interest is perhaps the most controversial of the policy proposals contained in Islamic economics and has typically been the first step in the Islamization of the economy, it is perhaps only natural that the issue of an interest-free economy has received the most attention. However, although the elimination of interest is certainly a central tenet of the Islamic economic system, it is by no means an adequate description of the system as a whole or, for that matter, even of Islamic banking.

Broadly speaking, the term "Islamic economics" defines a complete system that prescribes specific patterns of social and economic behavior for all individuals. It deals with a wide-ranging set of issues, such as property rights, the incentive system, allocation of resources, types of economic freedom, the system of economic decision making, and the proper role of the government.[3] The overriding objective of the system is social justice and specific patterns of income and wealth distribution, and consequently economic policies are to be designed to achieve these ends. Aside from the issue of a zero interest rate, Islamic economics also offers fairly precise guidelines on, for example, tax policy and the orientation of government expenditures. Islamic banking is expected to participate actively in achieving the goals and objectives of an Islamic economy; consequently, Islamic banking is to be conducted "in consonance with the ethos of the value system of Islam" (Ahmad (1984, p. 1)). Even though the terms "Islamic banking" and "interest-free banking" have been used interchangeably, it has been stressed by several writers that the former is a more normative concept whereas the latter is the actual practice or mode of banking.[4]

Despite the increased study and discussion of the theory and practice of Islamic banking, the subject still presents several puzzles for academics and policymakers alike. Whether a system that forbids the payment or receipt of interest can be viable in a modern economy is a question often raised by economists, especially those trained in the Western economic tradition.[5] The writings of Muslim scholars have helped to broaden understanding somewhat, but there still exists substantial confusion on the main issues. In this paper an attempt is made to answer some of the basic questions that arise by providing, with the tools and concepts of modern Western economics, a formal analysis of the main features of Islamic banking. By doing so it is hoped that the gap between Muslim scholars and the profession at large will be narrowed.

In more specific terms, the paper presents a theoretical model of an interest-free banking system that is considered to be broadly consistent with the principles of Islam. The purpose of the exercise is fourfold: first, to show that the Islamic banking system can be rationalized in a neoclassical framework; second, to demonstrate that, when cast in this formal way, the model underlying Islamic banking is not totally alien to Western economic thinking (indeed, it is pointed out that variants of such a system have appeared in the writings of a number of eminent economists, such as Fisher (1945), Simons (1948), and Friedman (1969)); third, to argue that there may be circumstances in which an Islamic banking system would be relatively more stable than the traditional, or interest-based, banking system in the face of certain types of shocks;[6] finally, to propose how the Islamic banking system should be implemented so as to maximize its inherent benefits.

To define the scope of the study it is necessary to point out the limitations that have been placed on the analysis. First, a complete and detailed description of Islamic banking, or of how it is expected to work in the countries that have adopted such a system, is not attempted. Rather, this paper focuses exclusively on the analytical features of Islamic banking. Second, and following from this limitation, the model developed here is a simple one that incorporates only those elements of Islamic-type banking that are considered essential to the argument. Although it is not intended to be a fully realistic representation of the complete Islamic banking system, the model nevertheless is able to highlight the principal issues of concern. Last, the paper does not try to imply that the Islamic system is always more stable, or that the traditional banking systems are necessarily unstable; all it suggests is that there may be situations in which an Islamic financial system can adjust relatively faster to shocks than would the traditional system.

The remainder of the paper proceeds as follows. In Section I the background for the policy of elimination of interest in an Islamic economy is described, as well as the expected mode of operation of such an economy. This discussion sets the stage for the formulation of the model in Section II. In this section the dynamic properties of the model are examined under the assumptions of both fixed and flexible prices. It is shown here that the results do not depend on what is assumed about prices; more generally, the results turn out to be equally applicable whether one has a Keynesian or a classical view of how the economy works. The concluding section brings together the main findings of the exercise and attempts to draw some policy implications.

I. GENERAL ASPECTS OF AN ISLAMIC INTEREST-FREE FINANCIAL SYSTEM

It is useful to begin examining the Islamic banking system by first defining some basic terminology. *Ribā* is the Arabic word for the predetermined return on the use of money. In the past there has been dispute about whether *Ribā* refers to interest or usury, but there is now consensus among Muslim scholars that the term covers all forms of interest, and not only "excessive" interest.[7] Thus, in the ensuing discussion the terms *Ribā* and "interest" will be used interchangeably, and an Islamic banking system will be one in which the payment or receipt of interest is forbidden. An interest-based, or traditional, banking system is defined as symmetrical, with interest being paid and charged for the use of funds.

The Islamic restriction against interest is quite explicit and has to be taken as axiomatic. Transactions based on *Ribā* are strictly prohibited in the Qur'an, as the following verse forcefully states:[8]

> Those who devour *Ribā* will not stand except as stands one whom the devil hath driven to madness by [his] touch. (II:275)

To see that there can be no doubt of the condemnation of the system of interest, and the penalties that would be imposed if the rule were not observed, consider the following verse:

> O ye who believe! Observe your duty to Allah and give up what remains [due to you] from *Ribā*, if ye are [in truth] believers. And if ye do not, then be warned of war [against you] from Allah and His Messenger. And if ye repent then ye have your principal [without *Ribā*]. Wrong not, and ye shall not be wronged. (II:278–79)

Although there have been discussions among Muslim scholars on the reasons for this prohibition against interest, it is obvious from the above quotations that there is no real room for differences in interpretation about whether interest can or cannot be paid in an Islamic economy. It is the general view that it is considerations of equity and protection of the poor that lie behind the strong condemnation of interest-based transactions.[9] In any case, the Islamic economic system, and of course the corresponding banking system, has to operate within the prescribed framework, which does not permit interest.

The concept of an economy in which interest is not allowed appears quite counterintuitive to many observers. Arguments that such a system is unlikely to work efficiently in the short run, and in the long run will result in an eventual drying up of savings and investment, have frequently been made in this connection.[10] This view, however, tends to reflect a basic confusion between the terms "rate of interest" and "rate of return." Whereas Islam clearly forbids the former, it not only permits, but rather encourages, trade and therefore profits. For example, consider this verse from the Qur'an:

> That is, because they say: Trade is just like *Ribā;* whereas Allah permitteth trading and forbiddeth *Ribā*. (II:275)

Intangible rewards are also permitted; using the Arabic term *Ṣadaqāt,* for charity or alms, the next verse from the Qur'an says that

> Allah has blighted *Ribā* and made *Ṣadaqāt* fruitful. (II:276).

In essence, what is forbidden in Islam is the fixed or predetermined return on financial transactions and not an uncertain rate of return, such as that represented by profits. From this distinction it follows that, if a banking structure could evolve in which the return for the use of money would fluctuate according to actual profits made from such use, the resultant system would be consistent with the guidelines of Islam.

The view that profits are perfectly legitimate has provided the foundation for the development and implementation of Islamic banking. In this system profits and losses are to be shared between banks and economic agents according to certain predefined rules.[11] Specifically, the depositor would not be guaranteed a predetermined return on the nominal value of this deposit by the bank, but would be treated as if he were a shareholder of the bank and would thus be entitled to a share of the profits made by the bank. The system is symmetrical, so that if the bank incurs losses the depositor would share in these as well, and the nominal value of his desposit would be reduced. On the other side of the balance sheet the bank could also not charge a fixed rate of interest on its loans but instead would have to engage in some type of a profit- and loss-sharing arrangement. At the simplest level the Islamic system can be considered as an equity-based, rather than an interest-based, system. The depositor in essence purchases equity in the bank, and the bank in turn has an equity position in whatever activity the borrower uses the funds for. (This does raise some interesting issues, yet to be resolved, regarding consumption loans.) The distinction between equity-based and interest-based systems is crucial and will be used in the remainder of the analysis.

The earliest modern example of a bank established along the principles of profit and loss sharing was the Myt Gamt Savings Bank in Egypt in the early 1960s. The 1970s saw the emergence of similar banks in Kuwait, the United Arab Emirates, Jordan, Sudan, and Pakistan (see Khan (1983) for a detailed discussion). Two such banks were also established in Luxembourg and Switzerland, and with the active encouragement of the Kingdom of Saudi Arabia, an international development bank—The Islamic Development Bank—was set up in Jeddah in 1975. In most Muslim countries Islamic banks operate side-by-side with traditional banks, but certain governments have taken steps to eliminate the latter over time. For example, the Government of Pakistan in 1978 started a gradual process of eliminating interest-based transactions entirely from its banking system; as of July 1, 1985, all transactions by banks were required by law to be conducted solely on an equity-participation basis (see Pakistan (1984)). Similar steps have been announced by the government authorities of the Islamic Republic of Iran (see Bank Markazi Jomhouri Islami Iran (1983)).

That the process of establishing Islamic banking appears to be well entrenched, at least in Pakistan and the Islamic Republic of Iran, raises two related questions. Does such a system make theoretical sense, and can it work in a modern setting? The first of these questions has been examined in a number of papers that show that it is indeed possible to rationalize the profit- and loss-sharing system through the use of risk and uncertainty analysis (for example, Naqvi (1982) and Khan (1984)). Basically these papers replace a certain, or predetermined, rate of interest with an expected rate of return and go through the usual procedures to show that this change does not affect the conclusions about standard banking and macroeconomic behavior in any fundamental sense. With respect to the second question, however, because the experience with an economy-wide profit- and loss-sharing system is relatively recent it is not possible to state with confidence that such a system will function as well, or better, than the traditional banking system. There are, of course, those who argue on mostly a priori grounds that it will (see Ahmad (1984)), but clearly, in the absence of empirical analysis, the issue is far from settled.

Once one gets past the terminology and the interest-free and interest-based distinction and recognizes that Islamic banking is really a particular variant of equity-participation systems, it can be seen that proposals for reform of the traditional banking system along similar lines have been made at various times in the United States. These times have in general corresponded with episodes of banking crisis, and the most ardent proponent of an equity-based financial system was Henry Simons (1948).[12] Arguing in the context of bank collapses in the 1930s that the fractional-reserve banking system was "inherently unstable," Simons proposed that traditional banks should be replaced by two separate financial institutions:

> First, there would be deposit banks which, maintaining 100 percent reserves, simply could not fail, so far as depositors were concerned, and could not create or destroy effective money. These institutions would accept deposits just as a warehouse accepts goods. . . . A second type of institution, substantially in the form of an investment trust, would perform the lending functions of existing banks. Such companies would obtain funds for lending by sale of their own stock, and their ability to make loans would be limited by the amount of funds so obtained. (Simons (1948, pp. 64–65))

Although Simons's call for a sharp distinction between the payments and portfolio functions of banks—and for a 100 percent reserve requirement on the former—were rejected in favor of official deposit insurance at that time,[13] interest in Simons's ideas has remained.[14] Friedman (1969) agreed with Simons on the idea of a 100 percent reserve requirement, but more on the grounds that such a system would reduce government interference with the lending and borrowing operations of banks and thus would increase economic freedom. In connection with bank failures in the United States during the 1980s, there has been a revival of proposals for the equity-based system that Simons advocated. Papers by Kindleberger (1985), Kareken (1985), and Golembe and Mingo (1985), presented at a conference organized by the Federal Reserve Bank of San Francisco, again raise the issue of the potential financial instability of a fractional-reserve banking system combined with official deposit insurance. Kareken and Golembe and Mingo argue that bank failures are special because, unlike bankruptcies of firms in general, they affect the payments mechanism of the economy. Consequently, what must be protected is the efficient functioning of the payments mechanism and not necessarily the overall lending and borrowing operations of banks. These authors would, therefore, have the government separate the provision of payments services from lending services and in effect create the two types of banks that Simons had in mind.[15] The payments side of banking (that is, transaction balances) would be backed 100 percent by some safe security (say, U.S. Treasury bills), whereas the portfolio activities would be effectively unregulated. Neither of these schemes, nor the one proposed by Simons, are significantly different from the Islamic banking systems being implemented in several countries, at least on the deposit side.[16] At the same time, however, it should be stressed that the Islamic banking system goes further and requires that loans and advances made by banks also be based on equity participation.

There are many reasons advanced in the literature for the possible instability of the traditional banking system. In Simons's view the basic flaw in the traditional system is that, as a crisis developed and earnings fell, banks would seek to contract loans to increase reserves. Each bank could do so, however, only at the expense of other banks, and in the process some banks would become insolvent and be forced to close. Alternatively, Mayer (1974) contends that banks tend to switch from techniques of asset management to those of liability management in the face of a crisis, and that this practice has increased in the U.S. banking system. In other words, if banks raise interest rates to attract or retain deposits in problem situations, and if the total stock of deposits is fixed in the short run, the process would clearly be unstable and would eventually lead to bankruptcies. In such circumstances any system that guaranteed the transaction-balances component of deposits and eliminated the need or incentives for liability management would likely stabilize the process.

In the following section it is shown formally how an equity-based banking system of the Islamic type would operate and how it would be stable in the context of real shocks.

II. A FORMAL MODEL OF ISLAMIC BANKING

The framework used here to represent the Islamic banking system is based on an aggregate macroeconomic model developed by Meltzer (1951) and extended by Fernandez (1984). The model is quite simple, and, although it incorporates some fairly restrictive assumptions, it turns out to be a very useful device for the purpose at hand. In this section two versions of the basic model are considered. The first takes prices as fixed, or predetermined, and real output as endogenous; in the second version the price level is assumed to be flexible, and output in turn is assumed to be exogenous. These two versions can also be respectively interpreted as the Keynesian or classical representations of the basic model.

The Basic Model with Fixed Prices

The macroeconomic model contains a capital market, a money market, and a market for goods. For simplicity it is assumed that all real income goes to capital rather than being divided between capital and labor, as is more customary. Meltzer (1951), for example, assumes that capital receives a constant proportion of national income, and his approach could easily be followed without affecting the analysis.[17] The three markets in the model are described in turn below.

Capital Market

Consider an economy in which banks are the only intermediaries that connect saving and investment. These banks are treated as if they were simply firms that issue shares (deposits) and derive their earnings from investments. Economic agents hold their savings in the form of deposits whose nominal value is not guaranteed, and the rate of return they receive from these deposits (that is, the yield on shares) is also not predetermined and can vary. Indeed, there is no restriction preventing the rate of return from becoming negative, since this would only imply that the value of shares falls. All investments in the economy are also assumed to be undertaken by borrowing from banks.

Because the price level is given, one can use the simple discounting formula suggested by Meltzer (1951) to relate the real value of the banks' shares to the capitalized value of the future real earnings of the banks:[18]

$$S/P = s = y/r, \tag{1}$$

where

S = nominal value of shares
P = price level
s = real value of shares
y = real income
r = real yield or real rate of return on shares.

If banks are assumed not to hold any reserves and to have zero net worth, then equation (1) defines the balance sheet of the banking system. The assumption that banks cannot absorb losses through reserves or net capital is also not crucial, since the concern here is with the issue of bankruptcies. Basically, ignoring the reserves or the net capital of banks is tantamount to assuming that the potential losses that would occur in the event of a failure exceed the provisions that a bank can reasonably be expected to make against them.

The balance sheet of the simplified aggregate banking system in real terms would therefore be

Banking System	
Assets	Liabilities
y/r	S/P

Money Market

Money is the asset in the model and is considered to consist solely of currency, assumed to be exogenously supplied by the government. In other words, all money in the model is "outside" money. Total real wealth w is defined as $w = m + s$, where m is the stock of real money balances ($m = M/P$) and M is the exogenously given nominal stock of money. Equilibrium in the money market is determined by the following:

$$m/s = g(r), \qquad g_r < 0, \tag{2}$$

where the proportion of wealth held in the form of money depends negatively on the real rate of return on shares. From equation (1), $s = y/r$; therefore the equilibrium condition in the money market can be rewritten as

$$m = g(r) \cdot y/r. \tag{3}$$

Goods Market

The goods market is assumed to be characterized by slow adjustment, and output is assumed to respond to variations in excess aggregate demand. This formulation is not difficult to justify for the case in which prices are fixed. (The alternative case of flexible prices is taken up later.) Specifically, the relationship between real income, or output, and excess aggregate demand can be derived using a standard Keynesian-type framework, with the assumption that the economy is closed and there is no explicit government sector. Real aggregate demand (y^d) is defined as

$$y^d = C(r, w) + I(r)$$
$$C_r < 0, \qquad C_w > 0, \qquad I_r < 0, \tag{4}$$

where $C(r, w)$ is a standard consumption function, with wealth as the relevant scale variable, and $I(r)$ is the investment function. Note that from equation (1), total wealth can be written as

$$w = m + y/r. \tag{5}$$

The assumption of slow adjustment in the goods markets can be represented by the following differential equation for output:

$$dy/dt = \dot{y} = \beta[C(r, m + y/r) + I(r) - y], \qquad \beta > 0, \tag{6}$$

where the expression inside the brackets is excess aggregate demand. This can be written as a reduced-form equation:

$$\dot{y} = f(r, y; m)$$
$$f_r < 0, \qquad f_y < 0, \qquad f_m > 0. \tag{7}$$

Equation (7) can be viewed as a dynamic form of the IS curve in which real income responds positively to excess aggregate demand, which in turn is a negative function of the real rate of return and (with marginal propensity to consume, $\partial C/\partial y$, assumed to be less than unity) of real income. The change in real income is a positive function of (exogenous) real money balances.

It will be noted that the model here is a dynamic variant of the standard IS-LM model, and no special factors have had to be introduced up to now. In analyzing the Islamic banking system, the crucial point to remember is that the nominal value of shares (S) is not guaranteed to the depositor and thus can be treated as perfectly flexible. In the model, equation (3) ensures that the capital and money markets are continuously in equilibrium, whereas from equation (7) real income adjusts slowly to any shocks to excess aggregate demand. From equation (3) for the money market and equation (7) for output, one can derive a standard IS-LM diagram to determine the equilibrium values of the real rate of return r^* and of real income y^*. Given r^* and y^*, it is a straightforward matter to obtain the equilibrium real value of shares, $s^* = y^*/r^*$. The basic system used to describe the Islamic banking system is depicted in Figure 1.[19]

To examine the dynamics of the system, consider the case of an

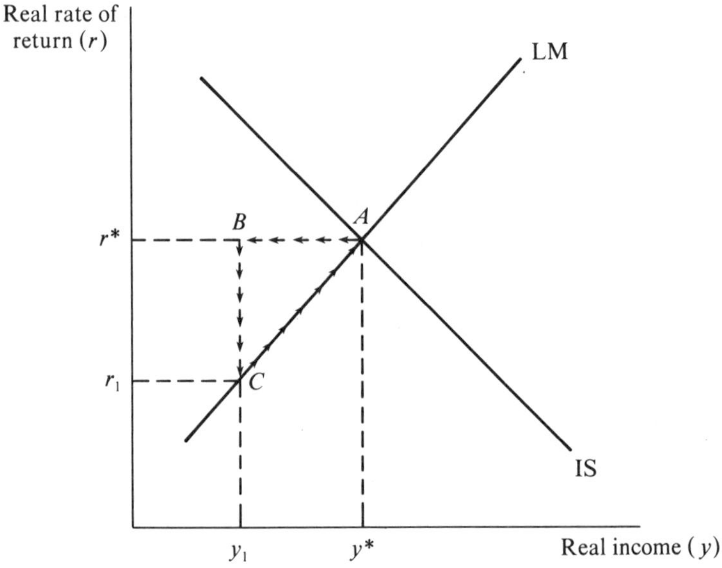

Figure 1

Islamic Banking System with Fixed Prices

exogenous fall in real income (real earnings) of banks from y^* to y_1 in Figure 1. At point B there is an excess supply of money that causes an instantaneous decline in the real rate of return on shares from r^* to r_1 (to point C).[20] At C, with real income at y_1 and the real rate of return at r_1, however, there is excess aggregate demand. This excess demand will move real income slowly back toward y^* to eliminate the disequilibrium in the goods market, and as real income grows the real rate of return will also rise toward r^*. Equilibrium will once again be reached at the original steady state—that is, at A with $r = r^*$ and $y = y^*$.

From Equation (1) one can trace what happens to the real value of shares during the process of adjustment. As the real rate of return declines, the real value of shares falls immediately from $s^* = y^*/r^*$ to $s_1 = y_1/r_1$ to maintain continuous equilibrium in the capital market. This result follows because the nominal value of shares is flexible and can thus adjust immediately to clear any disequilibrium in the capital market. This feature ensures that the system is dynamically stable.

By contrast, in the traditional banking system the nominal value of shares (deposits) is guaranteed to the depositor by the bank (if the price level is given, then the real value obviously is also guaranteed), and it is this guarantee that distinguishes the two systems. In standard banking systems the individual is assured of the nominal value of his deposit, and if the bank pays interest on these deposits, the rate of return that he will receive is also predetermined. In most countries there exists some form of official insurance scheme that backs the guarantee provided by banks; even if there is not, it is normally assumed that the government would step in should the need arise.

In the analysis developed here, the introduction of a guarantee for the nominal value of the shares simply means that the balance sheet of the banking system is now written as

$$\bar{S}/P = y/r, \tag{1a}$$

where $\bar{S}$ is the predetermined, or guaranteed, value of shares. Although it is possible to show that the introduction of a deposit guarantee—in other words, using equation (1a) in place of equation (1) in the model—does not change anything insofar as equilibrium behavior is concerned, important differences can emerge in the transition process. As discussed above, in the Islamic banking model any divergence between the real values of assets and liabilities would be immediately reflected in a corresponding adjustment in the nominal value of shares. In the traditional banking system, however, because the nominal value of shares is guaranteed and the interest rate is predetermined, changes in y will not necessarily cause immediate variations in the real values of shares. In the short run, therefore, one could have y/r not equal to S/P, and the fundamental question becomes how the system can be expected to adjust to this disequilibrium.

One way, of course, would be for banks to cover the discrepancy between assets and liabilities through a drawdown of reserves or a reduction in net capital. But if losses exceed available reserves, as has been assumed here, banks would presumably face the possibility of runs on deposits and of bankruptcy as net worth became negative (recall that the net worth of banks is assumed to be zero to start with). In general, in such circumstances the government would enter into the picture and would assume the liabilities of the banks, either in its capacity as the ultimate guarantor of deposits or, more important, to protect the payments mechanism. In any case, the depositors would be repaid by the government from resources obtained through taxes or borrowing.[21] If one ignores distributional complications, what the government has done is to reduce wealth by a capital levy on shareholders, either imposed now or in the future, that would be equal to the loss of assets of the banks. The end result of such an operation would be equivalent to that observed in the case of the Islamic banking model: the fall in real earnings of banks would be matched by a decline in real wealth, with the government intervening to ensure such an outcome.

Short-run differences between the two systems can, however, arise for a variety of reasons. For example, the public may not see through the "veil," may not believe that despite the government's actions real wealth has been reduced, and may thus not alter its behavior. The behavior of banks may also create short-run problems. Even though the liabilities of the banks may be insured directly or indirectly by the government, it has been argued by Mayer (1974) and Fernandez (1984), among others, that banks may try to postpone bankruptcy by resorting to liability-management techniques and raising interest rates to bid for deposits. Such actions, which reflect myopic behavior on the part of bankers, can easily lead to instability because attempts to increase interest rates would reduce y/r even further.[22] In the Islamic banking model the market immediately writes down the real value of shares, and these types of short-run phenomena cannot arise.

The Basic Model with Flexible Prices

The analysis can be extended to consider the alternative case in which output is exogenously given and prices adjust to excess aggregate demand. This model, in contrast to the Keynesian-type model of the previous subsection, therefore corresponds more to the classical system. In terms of real money balances, the adjustment function can be specified as

$$\dot{m} = -f(r, m; y^*)$$
$$f_r < 0, \qquad f_m > 0, \qquad f_{y^*} < 0, \tag{8}$$

where $\dot{m}$ is the change in real money balances and $f(r, m; y^*)$ is the excess demand function for an exogenously given level of (long-run) real income, y^*.[23] Equation (8) is now used in place of the output adjustment equation (7) that was specified in the case of rigid prices. Slow adjustment in the goods market has been maintained to highlight the dynamic properties of the system, although one could easily assume that prices adjusted instantaneously to clear the market. This would simply amount to specifying $f(r, m; y^*) = 0$ in equation (8).

In this system equations (1), (3), and (8) can be combined to determine the endogenous variables r, m, and s. The model is described by Figure 2, where $\dot{m}_{y^*} = 0$ represents the locus of points that clear the goods market and where $\dot{r}_{y^*} = 0$ is the corresponding locus of points that clear the money market, $m = g(r) \cdot y^*/r$. As before, once m^* and r^* are determined, one can derive the value of the real value of shares s^*, which equals $m^*/g(r^*)$.

In Figure 2, point A represents the steady-state equilibrium, yielding the values of m^* and r^*. Suppose that real income falls from y^* to y_1. The economy will now have to adjust to this lower level of (exogenously given) real income, and thus the $\dot{r}_{y^*} = 0$ schedule will shift downward to $\dot{r}_{y1} = 0$, and the $\dot{m}_{y^*} = 0$ schedule will shift up to $\dot{m}_{y1} = 0$. A new steady-state equilibrium will be reached at point C, with $r = r_2$ and $m = m_1$. The instantaneous short-run equilibrium obtains at point B because the real rate of return moves immediately from r^* to r_1 to preserve equilibrium in the assets market at r_1 and m^*. At B the real money supply remains constant at m^* because prices, which are allowed to change only gradually, cannot jump to the new steady state. At point B, however, there is an excess demand for goods that increases prices and lowers real money balances. As real money balances decline, the real rate of return starts to rise to maintain equilib-

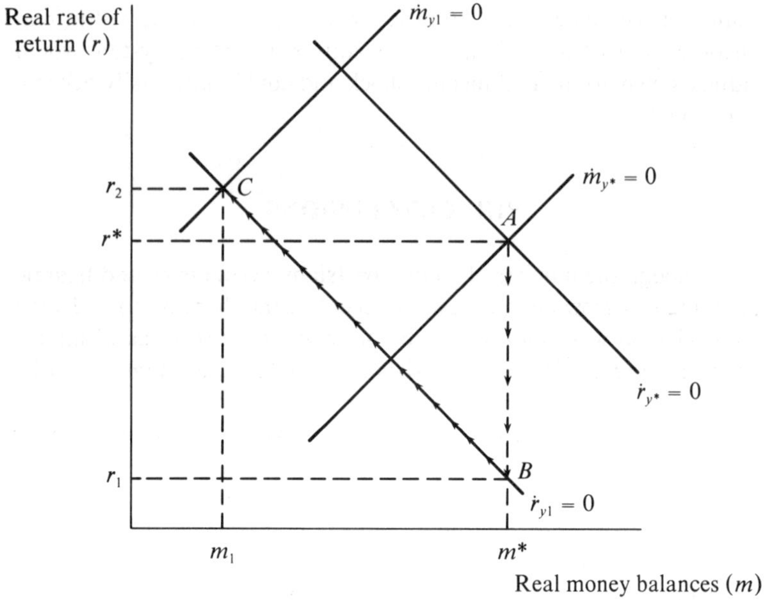

Figure 2
Islamic Banking System with Flexible Prices

rium in the money market, and this rise reduces excess aggregate demand. The process would continue until the new steady state (point C), where $r = r_2$ and $m = m_1$, is reached.

The real value of shares does not behave exactly the same way as it did in the case of fixed prices. Initially the real value of shares declines sharply, since at B

$$m^*/g(r_1) < m^*/g(r^*),$$

and then continues to fall as the system approaches the steady state at C. The path followed by the real value of shares is a consequence of the assumption of slow adjustment of prices; if instantaneous adjustment of the goods market were allowed, one would observe the economy moving directly from A to C, and the real value of shares would, as in the fixed-price case, move immediately from $s^* = y^*/r^*$ to $s_1 = y_1/r_2$.

Again the process can be replicated by the traditional banking model is both the public and bankers behave rationally in the short run, and if the government moves rapidly to correct the disequilibrium between assets and liabilities that results from the fall in real income from y^* to y_1. If not, the traditional banking system would adjust slowly to the real income shock and could quite easily become unstable.[24]

III. CONCLUSIONS

Although the number of studies on Islamic economics and Islamic banking has grown enormously in recent years, there is still a dearth of analytical work on the subject. In many ways the lack of understanding and confusion that exists about Islamic economics can be attributed to the virtual absence of formal descriptions of the theory underlying the proposed system. In this paper an attempt has been made to provide a theoretical description of the Islamic banking system by formulating a relatively simple model that explicitly incorporates the constraints imposed by religion on the conduct of financial transactions. As was shown in the paper, this model does provide a reasonable portrayal of the types of Islamic banking systems that have been put into practice in certain countries. The exercise further demonstrated that standard economic concepts and methods can be fruitfully employed to analyze issues in Islamic economics.

The model that has been developed in this paper also turns out to have many similarities with standard models used to analyze the behavior of banks at an aggregate level. Indeed, it is readily apparent that the Islamic model of banking, being based on principles of equity participation, bears a striking resemblance to proposals made in the literature on the reform of the banking systems in many countries, particularly in the United States. The paper demonstrates that the Islamic system may well prove to be better suited to adjusting to shocks that result in banking crises and disruption of the payments mechanism of the country. In an equity-based system that excludes predetermined interest rates and does not guarantee the nominal value of deposits, shocks to asset positions are immediately absorbed by changes in the values of shares (deposits) held by the public in the bank. Therefore, the real values of assets and liabilities of banks in such a system would be equal at all points in time. In the more traditional banking system, since the nominal value of deposits is fixed, such shocks can cause a divergence between real assets and real liabilities, and it is not clear a priori how this disequilibrium would be corrected and how long the process would take. In other words, there is a rigidity in the traditional banking system that prevents instantaneous adjustment, and this rigidity can lead to possible instability.

Thus, as argued in this paper, the principal difference between Islamic and traditional banking systems is *not* that one allows interest payments and the other does not. The difference stems from the fact that an Islamic system treats deposits as shares and accordingly does not guarantee their nominal value. In the traditional banking system such deposits are guaranteed either by the banks or by the government. This distinction has apparently not been generally appreciated in the literature. In essence, the interest rate issue is shown not to be central from an economic or analytical point of view, and one can argue that the debate in many ways has been misdirected.

It should be acknowledged, of course, that the scope of this paper has been fairly limited, and several interesting questions associated with Islamic banking remain as yet unanswered. The model specified was a somewhat stylized one, and certain restrictive assumptions were imposed to highlight the essential features of the Islamic financial system. Obvious generalizations of the approach here would have to examine in greater detail how both deposit and loan behavior can be theoretically modeled within an equity-based system. Moreover, the analysis here was restricted to the operation and practice of banking under the Islamic system. The effects that the adoption of this system would have on saving, investment, the level of financial development, and so forth—and, furthermore, the question of how monetary, fiscal, and exchange rate policies can be expected to operate in such an environment—were beyond the scope of the analysis presented here. In addition, at this stage it is not possible to say very much about the effects that the introduction of uncertainty created by the elimination of a predetermined rate of interest on financial transactions would have on basic economic behavior and on the efficiency of the financial system. Perhaps even more important is the question of whether the profit- and loss-sharing practice meets the fundamental objectives of Islamic economics relating to income and wealth distribution. Addressing these various issues will clearly require concerted efforts at both the theoretical and empirical levels.

Despite these caveats, it is still possible to draw certain policy implications from this study that relate to the practice of Islamic banking. The equity-based system being implemented in Muslim countries appears to have considerable merit from a purely economic standpoint, independent of its consistency with the strictures of Islam. From a policy perspective, one can argue from the analysis in the paper that banks should operate two windows for deposit transactions. One window would cover only transaction balances and would pay no interest on deposits. In other words, all deposits made through this window would be akin to existing demand deposits, with one important difference. Such deposits would have a 100 percent reserve requirement placed on them, and there would be no possibility of using these deposits as a basis for multiple credit creation. The backing for these deposits could be in the form of currency, foreign exchange, or suitable government securities. The reason for adopting a 100 percent reserve requirement is that these deposits would be made completely safe and thus would simultaneously satisfy the desires of risk-averse individuals and prevent the dangers of runs from interfering with the payments mechanism. If such deposits did not yield any return to the banks, then presumably a service charge could be levied on depositors that would correspond to the costs of administering this window.

The other window would be the profit-and-loss, or equity, account in which a depositor would be treated exactly as if he were a shareholder in the bank. There would be no guarantee provided of the rate of return or of the nominal value of the share. No official reserve requirement would be necessary for these investment deposits, although presumably for prudential reasons banks would maintain some minimum level of reserves. Since deposits through the profit-and-loss window would be treated as investments (as in a mutual fund or investment trust, for example), there would be no obvious reason for the government to impose legal reserve requirements. Regulations similar to those applying to public companies, such as equity-to-capital ratios, could of course still be imposed.

In conclusion, although the two-window scheme is in fact being implemented in Islamic countries, there has been no basic change in the reserve requirements on different types of deposits. To maximize the safety benefits that are inherent in the system, such a change clearly would seem advisable. Differential reserve requirements on deposits that are based on their terms to maturity are already commonplace, and a 100 percent reserve requirement on one particular subset of deposits is not that radical a proposal; furthermore, such a requirement would not be too difficult to implement within existing financial structures. If a clear distinction is to be made between the equity-related operations of banks and the payments process, then such a step is necessary.

NOTES

*The author is grateful to Willem Buiter, Roque Fernandez, Jacob Frenkel, Saul Lizondo, Abbas Mirakhor, Peter Montiel, and Nadeem Ul Haque; to Executive Directors of the IMF—Mohammed Finaish, Yusuf Nimatallah, and Ghassem Salehkhou; and to Dr. Ziauddin Ahmad and the staff of the International Institute of Islamic Economics, Islamabad, Pakistan, for their helpful comments. Those who commented on the paper are, of course, not responsible for all the views expressed therein.

1. The most often-quoted source on the subject is Ahmad (1952). For surveys of the earlier literature, see Siddiqi (1980) and Mirakhor (1986).

2. See, for example, Ahmad (1980) and the papers contained in Ariff (1982) and in Ahmad, Iqbal, and Khan (1983).

3. See Ahmad (1980) and Naqvi and others (1984). The Islamic system has also been examined in a recent comprehensive paper by Pryor (1985).

4. Islamic banking is discussed in detail in Qureshi (1967) and Ahmad (1984), as well as in the papers in Ahmad, Iqbal, and Khan (1983) and in Ariff (1982). A useful survey is also provided in Karstens (1982).

5. Pryor (1985), for example, is one who is quite skeptical about the feasibility of such a system.

6. Stability here is defined in the strict mathematical sense, rather than as a general description of the state of the world. The latter interpretation is adopted, for example, by Zarqa (1983).

7. There is still debate on whether *Ribā* is defined as the nominal or real rate of interest; in the latter interpretation, indexing of the principal would presumably be allowed. This distinction is not addressed here.

8. The Roman numerals refer to chapters, the Arabic to verses. The classic English translation of the Quran is by Mohammed Marmaduke Pickthall (1953).

9. The Quran itself provides no detailed rationale for the prohibition of interest. For a discussion of some of the possible reasons for this restriction, see Ahmad (1984).

10. Pryor (1985), for example, states quite categorically that "the simple story is that if there is no interest rate, aggregate saving would fall" (p. 208) and later that "elimination of a nominal interest rate would lead to a reduction of savings in an Islamic economic system, other things remaining the same" (p. 209).

11. In general, these rules are based on the concept of *Muḍārabah* (or *Qirāḍ*), which refers to transactions in which profits and losses are shared by the borrower and lender in some mutually agreed proportions.

12. Arguments for a profit- and loss-based system have also been made in the wake of bank failures in Latin America, particularly in Argentina; see Fernandez (1984).

13. Irving Fisher (1945) was also an early supporter of a 100 percent (cash) reserve requirement for banks. His view, too, was that the institution of this scheme would stop bank runs and thus banking failures.

14. Some Muslim writers also have suggested a 100 percent reserve requirement for the same reasons as Simons; see Kahf (1978) and Al-Jarhi (1983).

15. Alternatively, each bank would simply have its activities separated in this manner. The issue of "corporate separateness" naturally involves legal and regulatory questions that are discussed at length by Golembe and Mingo (1985).

16. The 100 percent reserve requirement, however, has not been considered seriously in these systems. This issue will be discussed later in this paper.

17. If y is national income, then one only has to assume that capital receives ωy, where ω is a constant, and that the remainder $(1 - \omega)y$ goes to labor.

18. Although this discounting formula is not exact, it nevertheless is convenient to use and helps to clarify the analysis that follows. The proper discounting formula would be an integral that took into account continuous changes in y and r. Such a formula converges in the steady state to the one used here.

19. Although Figure 1 is drawn for positive values of r, the real yield on shares could be negative without affecting the argument.

20. One can see from this relationship that Pryor's (1985) conclusion that adjustment of the money market would be slower and more complicated stems from his confusion of the real rate of interest and the real yield on shares. Although the commonly defined interest rate may be fixed at zero, as was pointed out in Section I, there is nothing in Islamic economics that requires the real yield on shares to be zero or constant.

21. One can argue that the choice between taxation and borrowing really represents a choice between present and future taxation, since any government debt created to pay depositors has to be retired at some point in the future.

22. It is formally demonstrated in the Appendix that the addition of a liability-management process to the basic model yields a saddle-point solution.

23. Equation (8) follows directly from equation (7). The adjustment equation (6) is now specified as $\dot{m} = -\beta[y^d - y^*]$; with the relevant substitutions, it yields equation (8).

24. As before, a liability-management equation in place of equations (1) and (3) would yield a saddle-point solution; see the Appendix.

3

The Relative Efficiency of Interest-Free Monetary Economies: The Fiat Money Case

Mabid Ali Muhamed Mahmoud Al-Jarhi

Reprinted from Khurshid Ahmad (ed.), *Studies in Islamic Economics* (London: The Islamic Foundation, 1981). Mabid Al-Jarhi is Senior Economist, Arab Monetary Fund.

I. GENERAL

Monetary theory, like the rest of macroeconomics, suffers from the logical ramifications of being built on a structure of perfect-market models. The assumptions underlying such models, *viz*, perfect information and zero transactions costs, give no reason for anyone to hold money. Nevertheless, economists have proceeded to impose the existence of money on such models as a first step to found an economic theory of money. Obviously, this is untenable. Among the consequences of such reasoning are the common misconceptions and erroneous policy recommendations in monetary literature.

Naturally, the first step in restoring some analytical consistency to monetary theory is to reconstruct the basic price-theoretic structure to include the necessary frictions which make transactions costly and thus make money necessary to hold. This, however, is beyond the scope of this paper and has been undertaken, from different angles and in different ways, by some economists.

The purpose of this paper is to challenge the traditional institutional arrangement of paying interest on money as an efficient monetary policy. Having done this elsewhere already for economies with commodity means of exchange, we will concentrate on fiat means of exchange. Both cases of government and privately-produced fiat money will be considered. Moreover, private borrowing and financial intermediation will be given analytical attention.

The paper introduces a set of fiat means of exchange into an economy and a few related questions. First, how much money should an individual use in order to spend his income? Second, how much should the government produce in order to provide for the optimal use of money, and how should it distribute its money? Third, given the volume of government money, how much would a private producer supply of his own money under conditions of imperfect information? Fourth, how do private concerns and financial intermediaries behave within our theoretical framework? The fifth and last question is, how much should the government produce of its own money, how should it distribute it among different individuals, and what regulations should it impose on the banking system and financial intermediaries, in order to provide for the optimal supply of monetary services?

The conclusions of this paper make it obvious that economies with no interest payments on borrowing and no bank multiple creation of money are most optimal between the different institutional arrangements considered. This means that it is most efficient if the government initially provides its own money free, lends it free, and imposes a 100% reserve ratio on banks.

We expect such conclusions to be more of a surprise to economists in Muslim countries than to the young economists of the Western world, who have grown skeptical about accepting the results of models which are devoid of viscosity. Nonetheless, we hope our conclusions will be an inspiration to the economists of the Muslim world to revamp the economies of their own countries and rid them of the traditions of old Western economics. We finally hope that this will be a first step towards constructing an Islamic economic theory.

II. INTRODUCTION

In a free market economy, interest is the price of money. It is the price at which the "producers" of money sell their "output." Since this price depends on the quantities of money supplied, its determination raises the question of the optimum supply of money.

The treatment of the optimal supply of money in the literature has been mostly traditional in nature, and we are using the word "traditional" in a special sense. The basic fault with the traditional approach is that it ignores the issue of the *raison d'etre* of money, namely, the existence of transactions costs. One class of the traditional approach contains no explicit treatment of transactions costs.[1] The other class, while it accounts for transactions costs in a fashion, presumes the existence of money from the very outset. This lends no particular usefulness to the treatment of those costs.[2]

Some economists have attempted to remedy the inadequacies of the traditional approach by introducing frictions explicitly in the standard perfect-market model. Those non-traditionalists have taken various approaches.

One group incorporated transactions costs in the standard Walrasian model while keeping exchange centralised.[3] These models throw light on the existence of monetary equilibrium as well as the function of money as a substitute for a central transactions authority. However, some economists believe that only in a framework of decentralised exchange can the role of money be understood.[4]

Another group of non-traditionalists introduce imperfect information into their models as a vehicle of studying monetary exchange.[5] However, they disagree about what kind of information should be considered imperfect.

In order to introduce explicitly transactions costs into the classical model, we have constructed elsewhere[6] a class of transactions cost functions for exchanges (each containing the sale of one item and the *quid pro quo* purchase of another) carried out by an individual. This class is based upon several postulates related to the costliness of information.

The first postulate is that the information available to each individual about a particular exchange can be represented by a price quotation. The second postulate is that the distribution of such prices is sufficiently well-behaved to be adequately presented by a standard deviation. The two postulates imply a *price conjecturing process* which takes place as a part of the exchange process.

The distribution of conjectured prices represents the "true" opinion of all traders; its standard deviation represents the true variability of information, or TVI for short. The perception of any individual of those prices represents a different distribution whose standard deviation is called the reflected variability of information; or RVI for short.

The third postulate is that transactors are not equally informed about prices, i.e., their RVIs are different. In other words, information differentials exist between people about each exchange. The fourth postulate is that each individual is not equally informed about different goods, i.e., he has a different RVI for each exchange.

As price searching takes place, the fifth postulate says that sampling traders for this purpose is costly.

Let $t^{\nu}_{i,j}$ refer to the transactions costs of an exchange carried out by an individual ν and involving the sale of the quantity x_1 for the quantity x_j, where $i \neq j$. We can, therefore, write the transactions cost function of that exchange as

$$t^{\nu}_{i,j} = t^{\nu}_{i,j}\,(\sigma_{i,j}, \sigma^{\nu}_{i,j}, \varrho^{\nu}_{i,j}, x^{\nu}_{i}, x^{\nu}_{j});\ i \neq j \tag{1}$$

where $\sigma_{i,j}$ is the TVI and $\sigma^{\nu}_{i,j}$ is the RVI, and

$$\varrho^{\nu}_{i,j} = 1/(\sigma^{\nu}_{i,j} - \sigma^{\nu}_{i,j}) \tag{2}$$

The behaviour of $t^{\nu}_{i,j}$ is determined by:

$$(\delta t^{\nu}_{i,j}/\delta\sigma_{i,j}) < 0 \tag{3}$$

$$(\delta t^{\nu}_{i,j}/\delta\sigma^{\nu}_{i,j}) < 0 \tag{4}$$

$$(\delta t^{\nu}_{i,j}/\delta\varrho^{\nu}_{i,j}) > 0 \tag{5}$$

$$(\delta t^{\nu}_{i,j}/\delta x^{\nu}_{i}) > 0 \text{ and } (\delta^2 t^{\nu}_{i,j}/\delta x^{\nu_2}_{i}) > 0 \tag{6}$$

$$(\delta t^{\nu}_{i,j}/\delta x^{\nu}_{j}) > 0 \text{ and } (\delta^2 t^{\nu}_{i,j}/\delta x^{\nu_2}_{j}) > 0 \tag{7}$$

The above class of transactions cost functions is suited to exchanges involving real goods. This implies that they must also be suited for describing exchanges involving commodity means of exchange, or CME.

III. THE NATURE AND CREATION OF FIAT MEANS OF EXCHANGE

1. The Nature of Fiat Means of Exchange

Fiat assets are defined to be those assets whose holding draws no real rate of return of their own. They are used either for transactions services, or for the (interest) payments their seller may provide. They could be fully or partly convertible into another class of fiat assets. But, they may not be convertible at all into any other kind of assets while the transactions services they render qualify them to be treated as net wealth.

The fiat nature of FME calls for certain measures to entice traders to use them. Because these assets have no real services of their own, their owner, barring other payments, must use them for exchange in order to get any transactions yield. In order to do so, he must himself persuade prospective buyers of the usefulness of FME in transactions. The producer of FME will therefore find it insufficient for his assets to yield transactions services in order that they may be accepted by households as a means of exchange. He must use additional incentives.

One possible incentive is to stand ready to convert these assets, fully or partially, into other, already generally acceptable, FME. Convertibility then would cause people to consider the use of FME in the light of the quality and value of the assets into which they can be converted. When the producer of FME is the government, and when such an institution has a sufficiently high volume of transactions, the mere acceptance of the producer of his own FME as a payment for government services can be sufficient to provide for their general acceptance. Otherwise, when the volume of government transactions is insufficient, coercion should work, when its FME are declared legal tender. One last alternative is to pay the holders of FME a rate of return compensating them for whatever they would earn on alternative assets.

One thing we must stress is that it is possible to do away with the above incentives after the particular FME has been in use for a while. Once FME are used on a large scale in exchange, traders will accumulate sufficient information about their transactions services, and will continue to use them as before. Another thing we must stress, and which will become clear below, is the relationship between those incentives and the process of creating FME.

2. Transactions Cost Functions and Fiat Means of Exchange

The class of transactions cost functions introduced above was designed for exchanges involving real goods. In order to make this class applicable to exchanges involving fiat assets, one variable must be added: the price level in terms of the respective fiat asset. Since such an addition implies some relationship between that variable and the transactions costs of related exchanges, an additional postulate must be provided.

Let us assume that a certain fiat means of exchange, ${}_f\Phi_i$, is already in circulation. Let us also assume the relative prices of all goods in the economy can be calculated in terms of ${}_f\Phi_i$. With the assignment of the proper weights, a price level can be calculated from those prices, which we will call the asset-price level of ${}_f\Phi_i$ and referred to symbolically as ${}_f\Gamma_i$. Naturally, when an individual v makes an exchange involving ${}_f\Phi_i$, he must have some conception about its asset-price level. His conception will be termed ${}_f\Gamma_i^v$.

Given any relative price for a certain exchange involving ${}_f\Phi_i$, the higher the asset-price level as perceived by v, ${}_f\Gamma_i^v$, the lower is his perception of the real value of the quantity of ${}_f\Phi_i$ involved. Since this real value represents his total expenditures, if he is a seller of ${}_f\Phi_i$, or receipts, if he is buying it, the lower his perception of this real value, the less he will search and the less vigorously he will negotiate. Conversely, the lower ${}_f\Gamma_i^v$, the higher will be his perception of the real value of his expenditures or receipts of ${}_f\Phi_i$ from that particular exchange, given any relative price involved. The higher his perception of that real value, the more he will search and the more vigorously he will negotiate.

Therefore, an additional postulate, which is applicable only in the case of exchanges involving fiat assets, can be made. The transactions costs of an exchange involving a fiat asset varies inversely with an individual's perception of its asset-price level.

3. The Creation of Fiat Means of Exchange

A FME is primarily a source of transactions services. Hence, its ability to produce such services, and to qualify as a means of exchange must depend on the nature of its transactions cost functions of the different exchanges in which it may be involved. The production of a certain FME asset is therefore tantamount to the creation of a set of transactions cost functions with certain characteristics. Keeping in mind the postulates provided about the relationships between the total and the marginal transactions cost of an exchange and the different arguments entering its transactions cost function, those characteristics must produce a state of transactions cost differentials that would justify the use of the fiat asset in question as a means of exchange. In other words, the *quality* of a FME asset must depend on the characteristics of the set of the transactions cost functions of the exchanges it enters; such a quality represents the effectiveness of that asset as a means of exchange.

The quality of a FME depends upon the size of its exchange fields as well as the range of quantities at which it can be traded. Both factors are influential in determining the transactions cost saving from the use of such an asset as a means of exchange. This implies that, when two FME assets are compared, the one with the larger exchange field or wider range of traded quantities, or both, has a superior quality to the other.

An important question is what can the producer do in order to *create* a fiat means of exchange? The answer to that is *not* to provide the buyers of such an asset the *actual* relative prices of that asset in its different exchanges. Such a method is impossible to use because the producer, whether a private concern or government, is subject to imperfect information like anyone else. The only difference in this respect is that the money producer is an information specialist, which makes his perception of the exchange ratios of the FME he produces closer to reality than that of non-specialists.[7]

The producer can, instead of providing exchange ratios, manipulate the asset-price level of the FME he produces. This manipulation can be done through the control of the quantity sold. This should be, in our world of imperfect information in which producers are price searchers, available to all producers.

In addition to regulating output, the producer sometimes will have to trade his asset in order to align its current stock with the current (stock) demand. Yet, the producer cannot guarantee the real value of his asset in terms of real goods. This prohibition is made out of theoretical necessity, for such an action would bring about commodity bonds. In addition, there are some peculiarities which depend on whether the producer is a private concern or a government, which are discussed below.

All such activities that the producer undertakes to make the characteristics of his FME prominent will be called the *information characterization* of an asset or, in short, asset characterization.

(a) Production of Government Fiat Means of Exchange, GFME

Starting with a pure CME economy, government production of fiat means of exchange, GFME, even when accompanied by the process of asset characterization, may not earn exchange circulation of an intensity equal to that of CME. In the absence of coercion, GFME will be capable of gaining the trust of traders as a source of transactions services only after a period (perhaps extended) of initially cautious and hesitant use. It might appear paradoxical that "general acceptability" of money is self-generating, for the more people use and accept GFME, the more other individuals will join the bandwagon. However, once the information-generating aspect of exchange is recognised, the paradox disappears. The more often a FME is exchanged, and the wider the participation in that exchange, the more information is generated about its characteristics as a means of exchange. To overcome initial mistrust and hesitation, and to avoid costly and more intensive asset characterization, the government may use a mixture of enticement and coercion to establish general acceptability for its own GFME.

In a multiple CME economy the government cannot circulate GFME whose quality is lower than that of the existing CME without either paying holders for the difference in quality to compensate them for the loss in transactions services resulting from the substitution of CME with inferior GFME, or using coercion. Such action on the part of the government will be ruled out, for it would cause the whole society a dead-weight loss. The government will thus be left with two choices. The first is to produce GFME each of which has quality equal to that of a corresponding CME in circulation. The second is to produce GFME of superior quality to some or all CME. The first action will have effects similar to those of issuing bonds against CME, and such effects have already been discussed elsewhere. The second option is to replace those CME whose transactions services are dominated by GFME, and if all CME were replaced, the economy would become a pure fiat money economy. Examples of such an economy are considered below.

(b) Production of Private (Secondary) Fiat Means of Exchange, SFME

Private production of FME is, in contrast with public production, hindered by two obstacles. On the one hand, private producers do not have sufficient resources to enable them to carry out the asset characterization process on a scale wide enough to bring about general acceptability. On the other hand, private producers do not have the coercive power available to the government which would allow them to gain acceptability for their own FME. Private producers can attempt to enforce their asset characterization effort by offering to pay rates of return on their fiat asset comparable to those on CME. Such offers would make privately issued assets equivalent to commodity bonds, for each asset would be a claim to a stream of returns equal to that of some CME. In such a case, they would not be *fiat* assets.

The only way to overcome their resource and coercive power limitations is for private producers to make their assets convertible into GFME. A scheme of this sort allows them to benefit from the government asset characterization efforts while giving them the liberty of differentiating their own products. Therefore, privately produced FME cannot exist without the existence of GFME; the latter will thus be considered as *primary* or *base* assets while the former will be termed *secondary* fiat means of exchange, or SFME. A pure inside (privately produced) money economy can therefore exist only in a commodity-money world, where such assets would be claims against the future delivery of CME.

IV. PURE GOVERNMENT FIAT MEANS OF EXCHANGE ECONOMY

In this section we consider an economy in which the government issues a collection of GFME whose quality dominates that of the existing CME, so that they effectively replace all the existing commodity money. Under such an arrangement, the government can give away its own GFME, it can sell them, or it can rent them; all three possibilities will be investigated. Then, the questions of the optimality of the stock of GFME and of government policy will be examined.

1. Some Basic Concepts

Now let us introduce a vector of GFME containing elements each of which is a fiat asset whose transactions cost function is superior to a corresponding CME asset, such a vector is

$$_f\Phi = ({}_f\Phi_1, \ldots, {}_f\Phi_h), \text{ and} \tag{8}$$

$$_f\pi = (\pi_1, \ldots, \pi_h) \tag{9}$$

are their corresponding accounting prices.

It is now possible to calculate, in terms of each one of these GFME, a set of relative prices of all goods, and to construct some weighted average of them that represents the price level in terms of a particular GFME. In other words, there will be as many price levels calculatable as there are GFME assets. Let us define such a set of *asset-price levels* as:

$$_f\Gamma = (_f\Gamma_1, \ldots, {}_f\Gamma_h) \qquad (10)$$

It is clear from above that the production of GFME is not costless, because of the needed process of asset characterization. When a particular GFME is issued and used in exchange, it will cause a change in its corresponding price level. Such a price level must be considered at this stage to be one of the information characteristics, which is one of the arguments in the price-conjecturing function of that asset. A change in that argument would necessitate a revision of the price conjecturing process. To counteract this revision, the government will have to incur extra asset characterization costs. In other words, the marginal cost of asset characterization, mcac, of any GFME must be rising with the rate of issuing such an asset.

2. The Supply of Real GFME

Given that the government will issue a set of GFME with transactions cost functions producing superior qualities to those of the initially existing CME, the sale of GFME, if and when it is done at the proper price, will cause CME to fall into disuse as it is replaced by GFME.[8] How much should be produced and at what price will depend on the demand for, as well as the marginal cost of producing, GFME.

The cost of producing one extra real unit of a fiat asset through changing its nominal size depends on two elements: the marginal cost of asset characterization, and the change in the price level in terms of that asset due to a change in the number of its nominal units. As pointed out above, the creation of one real unit of GFME, through a change in the supply of its nominal units, must be accompanied by utilizing resources. Those resources are expended in providing information about the asset-price level of the GFME in question as well as the amount of trading necessary to bring such information as close as possible to reality. The real value of those resources may be less than, equal to, or greater than the value of the extra real unit created, depending, in part, on the change in the asset-price level which may result from such an action.

In addition, the resulting change in the price level in terms of that asset, or equivalently the change in the relative price of the fiat asset, will have to be compensated for in order to effectively increase its *real* stock by one unit. This implies that the creation of one real unit of GFME could be accomplished by utilizing resources which might cost up to, or more than, the value of that unit, depending on the resulting change in the corresponding price level as well as the extra asset characterization costs caused by that change.

It is therefore possible, as in figure 1, to plot the marginal cost of creating an extra unit of a real GFME asset as a proportion of the real value of that unit; this proportion would rise with the real value created of that asset until the rise in the corresponding price level reaches a certain limit, and becomes unity. At that limit, no real fiat units can be added by increasing the nominal quantity. It is quite possible that further increases in the nominal quantity could lead to an erosion of the real stock, which would cause the MC_i curve to bend backwards; such a possibility, however, is not shown on the graph.

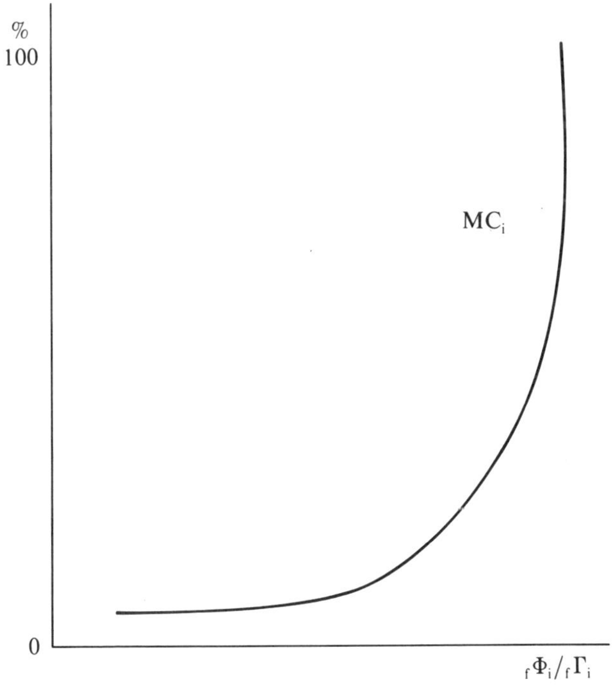

Figure 1

Another aspect of the above supply relationship is how it is influenced by the change in the flow of information available to the traders of the GFME asset in question. An increase in this flow resulting, e.g., from a greater incentive for traders to trade the asset, reduces the marginal cost of asset characterisation. Consequently, the MC_i curve shifts to the right. The opposite is also true.

3. The Demand for Real GFME

Given the information characteristics of the GFME ${}_f\Phi_i$, traders will hold real quantities of that asset until its rate of transactions services, at the margin, deflated by its asset-price level is equal to its net rate of return.[9] Due to the postulate advanced about increasing marginal transactions costs of exchanges, the rate of transactions services will decline with the quantities of the real FME held. Therefore, we obtain a negatively sloped demand curve for real GFME, depicted in figure 2 as ${}_f\rho_i({}_f\Phi_i/{}_f\Gamma_i)$. However, as the quantity of real GFME increases, more transactions services become available. This increase in transactions services reduces the aggregate transactions of the

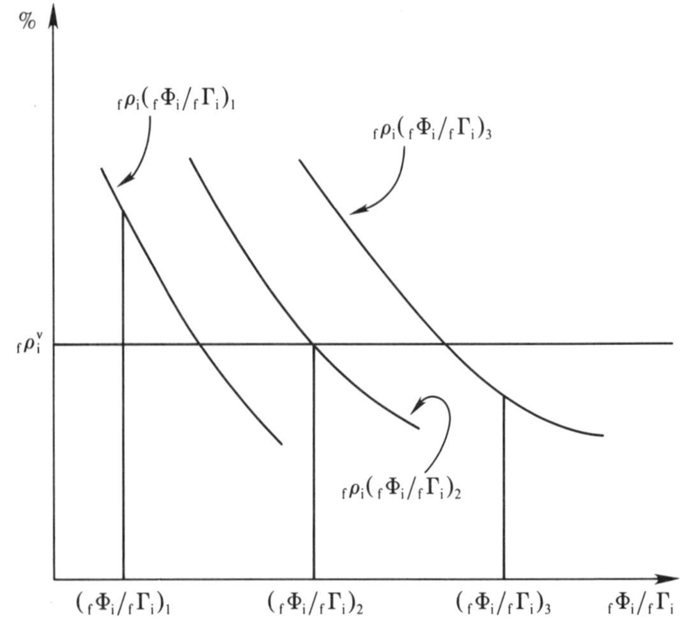

Figure 2

whole community, and increases real income, which in turn increases the demand for real GFME and shifts the ${}_f\rho_i$ curve upward.

An increase in real income, resulting from a decrease in real transactions outlays, increases the demand for real GFME. This implies that when more real GFME is created, people's wealth rises by the present value of the transactions services stream created by that increase, which in turn, given the proper rate of discount, is reflected as an increase in real income. That latter increase leads to a rise in the demand for real GFME by an amount that depends upon the wealth elasticity of demand for real money. Therefore, we can postulate that for each level of real GFME there corresponds a level of income, and consequently, a level of demand for real GFME. Figure 2 shows this relationship by depicting three demand curves for the real balances associated with ${}_f\Phi_i$, each associated with a certain level of real balances. Given any net rate of return, say ${}_f\rho_i^v$, the increase in demand for real balances measured at this rate must be smaller than the increase in real GFME, measured on the horizontal axis, which caused such an increase in demand.

4. Providing GFME for a Price

Using the demand and supply functions introduced above can provide us with some guidelines in the case of the government wishing to produce the market clearing quantity of a certain GFME asset, while charging a price equalling marginal cost. Figure 3 shows one of the family of the demand curves introduced above and the supply curve MC_i. Remembering that each demand curve is associated with a certain level of real money, there is only one demand curve which would intersect MC_i at a point indicating exactly its related level of real balances. Such a point is Q, where the equilibrium level of the real GFME asset produced is $0a$.

The government can sell its real GFME at a payment equal to ${}_f\rho_i$ per fatrah, as *rent*. Alternatively, it can charge the equivalent relative price per unit of real GFME. This affords it some net earning. Assuming such earnings are given back to the consumers as lump-sum subsidies, the total social welfare gained from the production of real money associated with ${}_f\Phi_i$ is equal to the area bQc.

5. Free Provisions of GFME

In order to distribute GFME free, a mechanism must be developed to do so without causing any redistribution effects.[10] Some may sug-

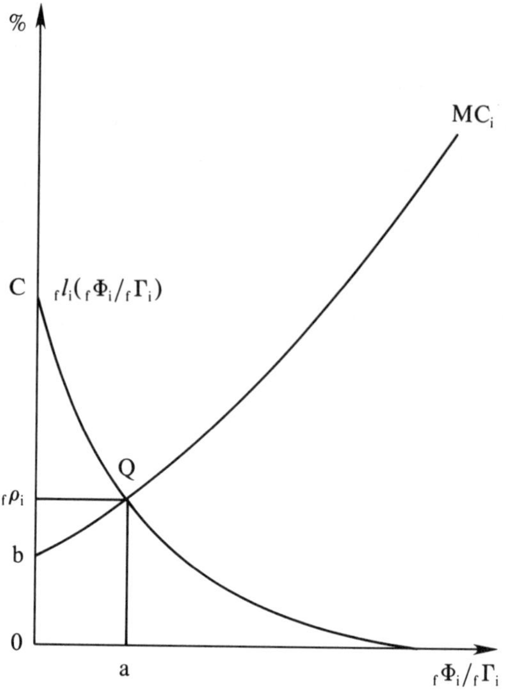

Figure 3

gest, as a means of doing so, that such a distribution should be done in proportion to one's wealth. This method, however, has redistribution effects of its own. An individual's benefit from GFME will be the transactions services he can derive from them, which depends on the difference between his current portfolio and that which enables him to reach his optimal consumption. This difference determines the volume of exchanges a person desires to undertake. When one gets an amount of GFME, while it stands at the same proportion to his wealth as that of any other individual, it may exceed or fall short of his optimal exchange requirements; this causes him to gain transactions services at a proportion to his income which is rarely equal to that of others. It is therefore better to distribute GFME at the same ratio to the absolute value of the difference between the individual's current and desirable portfolio, in order to eliminate such redistributive effects.

Referring back to figure 3, the government can provide the amount $0a$ free of charge, or provide the satiation level of real GFME free of charge. In both cases we will assume it continues financing the costs of production through lump-sum taxation and distributing its net earnings in lump-sum subsidies.

(a) Limited Free Provision

Suppose that the government distributes the quantity 0*a*, shown in figure 4, for free. The reduction in the price of GFME leads to an excess demand, which can be satisfied only through purchases of the same asset, either from the government or from other individuals. As real balances increase, due to the resulting decrease in the asset-price level, the demand curve shifts outward. Meanwhile, the larger volume of trading in the same GFME provides a greater flow of information to traders, decreasing the marginal cost of asset characterization, and thus shifting the MC_i curve to the right.

A new equilibrium point will be established at *Q′* where, in addition

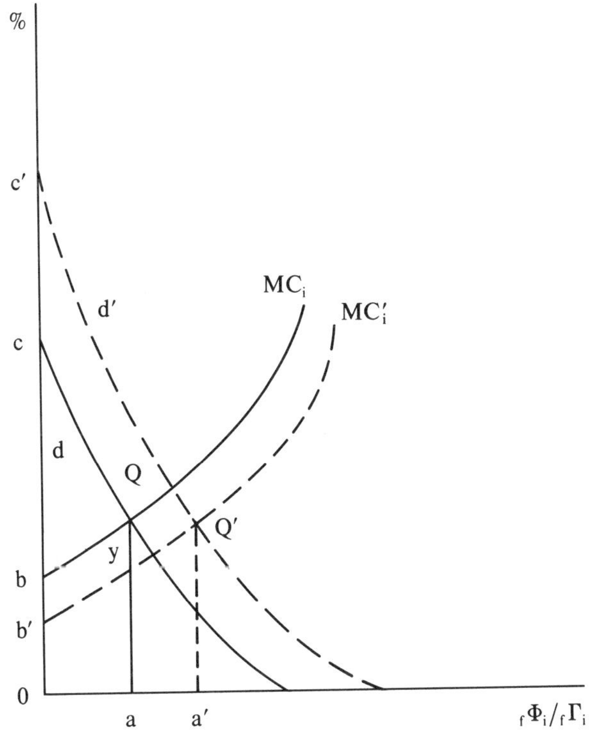

Figure 4

to the free provision of 0*a*, traders will buy *aa*′. The increase in social welfare is equal to the difference between the area *b*′*Q*′*c*′ and the area *bQc*. The increase in social costs is equal to the area *aa*′*Q*′*g*. Obviously, the net benefit to society from this policy is positive. This policy is thus superior to the provision of 0*a* at a price.

where

$$d = {}_f\rho_i({}_f\Phi_i/{}_f\Gamma_i)$$
$$d' = {}_f\rho_i({}_f\Gamma_i/{}_f\Gamma_i)'$$

(b) Unlimited Free Provision

(i) *Providing the Satiation Level of GFME.* Suppose the government distributes sufficient amounts of GFME in order to effectively keep its price at zero, that is, to give away the quantity 0*e* in figure 5. The initial increase in real balances by the amount of *ae* will increase

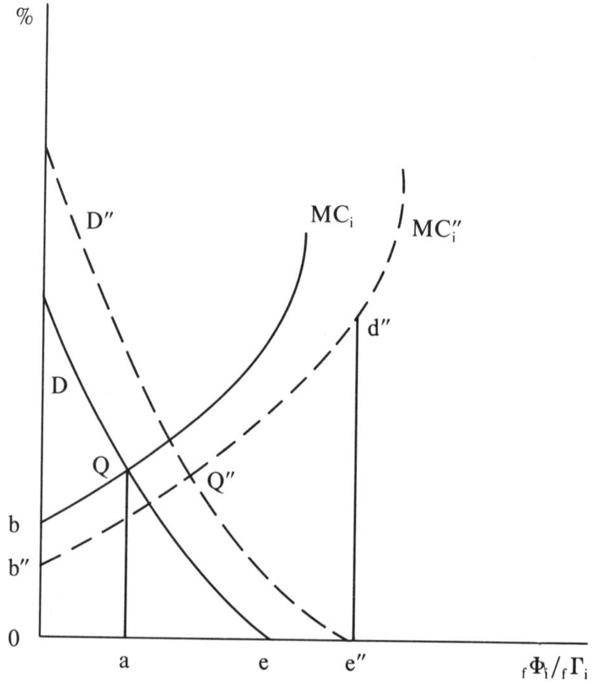

Figure 5

traders' wealth, shifting the demand curve outward. More exchanges using ${}_f\Phi_i$ will result, increasing the flow of information about its asset-price level and thereby shifting the supply curve to the right. To fulfill its policy, the government must finally provide $0e''$. While the level of social welfare increases, there is a dead-weight-loss to society equal to the area $e''Q''d''$.

The social loss resulting from such a policy makes it inferior to the policy of providing a limited free provision of GFME.

where

$$D = {}_f\rho_i({}_f\Phi_i/{}_f\Gamma_i)$$
$$D'' = {}_f\rho_i({}_f\Phi_i/{}_f\Gamma_i)''$$

(ii) *Tracing Equilibrium Levels.* In this case, the government uses the policy of "limited free provision" repeatedly for the purpose of expanding the existing stock of real GFME to its maximum, while increasing social welfare and costing the community no deadweight loss. First, as shown in figure 6, the government distributes the quantity $0a$ free which, as shown in figure 4 will cause the stock of real GFME to expand to $0a'$. Then the government offers an amount equal to aa' for free. This creates a wealth effect which pushes the demand curve to the right by an amount which is less than that caused by the initial gift of $0a$. This is because, given the wealth elasticity of demand for real GFME, aa' is smaller than $0a$.

The latter gift aa'' causes the exchange in the GFME to increase by an amount which is less than that caused by the gift $0a$, leading to a new flow of information about the asset-price level and shifting the supply curve to the right. The economy finally settles at the level $0a'''$ of real GFME. The government can then proceed to distribute a further gift of $a'a'''$, expanding the volume of real balances further.

The repetition of such a policy expands the total supply of real balances by decreasing amounts. This is because the amounts of gifts are decreasing, which causes their effects on the supply and the demand schedules to get successively weaker. The total supply of real balances will ultimately reach a level, say $0a''''$, beyond which no further expansion is possible.

This policy expands the total supply of real GFME beyond what the other policies mentioned above can. Moreover, despite the fact that the government has provided all the existing stock of real GFME

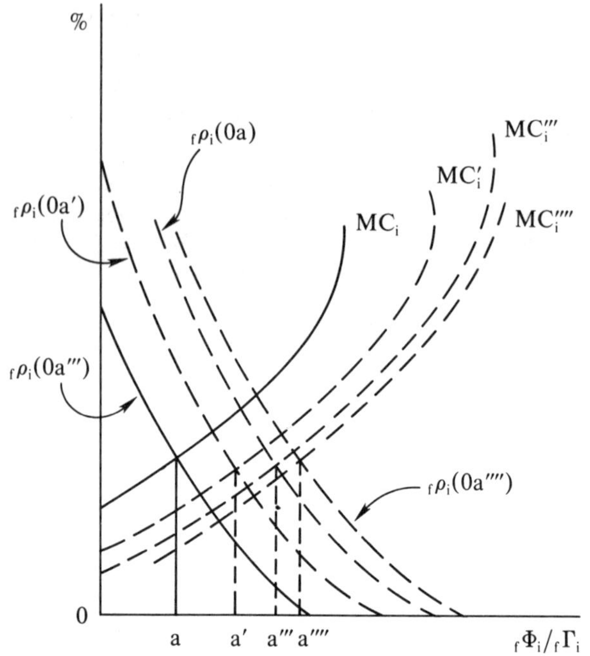

Figure 6

for free, the marginal unit of that stock brings forth a positive net rate of return.

The sale or rent policy reaches an equilibrium where the marginal return from an extra unit of real balances is equated with its marginal cost. The equilibrium quantity of each nominal GFME asset will be associated with an equilibrium price level and an equilibrium rate of return. Under such circumstances, social and private costs are equated with no trace of Friedman-type inefficiency. Non-convexity inefficiencies do not exist either.

Such is also the case with the policy of free provision. Nevertheless, there are two basic and important differences between them. The free provision policy produces a larger quantity of real balances, and in addition, it is associated with a higher level of real income. The rules of Pareto optimality suggest that such a policy would be optimal because of its capability of placing the whole community on a higher level of social welfare.

V. MIXED GFME AND SFME ECONOMIES

1. Secondary Fiat Means of Exchange

It may be recalled from above that the private producer of SFME must incorporate in his contract some provision for convertibility into GFME in order to be able to sell his assets. Yet, even if the private producer could persuade his customers that his SFME provides services identical to those of some GFME, they would not buy it without some additional enticement. The reason is that since the private producer's portfolio is one of the information characteristics considered in the formation of the transactions cost function of his SFME, the GFME asset will always be better because its producer is always solvent. Such enticement may include product differentiation and cheaper prices.[11]

The first kind of enticement is perhaps the most important, for it provides the SFME producer with a chance to improve upon the quality of the aggregate stock of means of exchange. As our economy initially, in a pure GFME world, contains exchange fields each of which is dominated by a GFME asset, the SFME producer can manipulate the quality of his asset in order to have an exchange field of its own. Within such an exchange field, the SFME asset can afford its user services which he cannot derive from any other GFME asset except at higher transactions costs. In order to do so, the transactions cost function of the SFME asset need not be superior to that of any GFME asset; it need just be sufficiently different.

The second kind of enticement, namely lower prices, is related to the question of convertibility. In order that the private producer can save himself a good part of the asset characterization costs, he issues his SFME promising the instant delivery on demand of some GFME asset. Keeping reserves on hand is therefore necessary for the producer to meet his obligation, when encashment is demanded. However, depending on the relative desirability of holding SFME to that of holding the GFME they promise to deliver, the instant encashment clause will not always be fully exercised, which necessitates the holding of only fractional reserves. This means that for every quantity of a GFME asset used as a *base asset,* a multiple of its value of SFME assets can be created. It also means that the SFME producer can offer prices for his SFME assets which are lower than the corresponding GFME assets they promise to deliver. It must be noted though that this is possible only when the government does not require 100 per cent reserves.

The private producer will find that his marginal cost of asset characterization (mcac) rises with his rate of output, for changing that rate will change the relative price of his SFME asset and will require the supply of additional information to its holders. For instance, when the supply of a SFME asset increases and its relative price goes down, its holders may suffer a wealth loss which can be avoided by either resorting to instant encashment into the GFME base asset or by the producer compensating them for that loss. The higher the rate of SFME output, the greater will be the tendency to resort to instant encashment and the consequent necessity to compensate holders, and then reassure them that the current value of the asset still warrants its continued use. All these costs are parts of the mcac, and thus it should rise with the rate of output.

The marginal cost of acquiring reserves, mcar, depends on the cost of changing the producer's portfolio in order to contain higher proportions of base assets. The latter cost is basically the transactions cost of exchanging assets currently held for reserves. The higher the rate of output, the more reserves are needed, and the more reserves a portfolio contains, the greater the difficulty of adjusting it to include even more reserves. Therefore, the mcar must rise with the rate of output.

The marginal cost of producing SFME must therefore rise with the volume produced, because of the similar behaviour of its components: mcar and mcac. Moreover, the production of SFME must be related to that of GFME because of the fact that the former requires the use of the latter as reserves. When SFME producers are left on their own, they will choose some reserve ratio between the base asset they hold and the SFME asset they produce. However, the government may interfere, forcing them to hold reserves at a proportion to their SFME production that is higher than the one they desire to hold. Of particular interest is the case when the government forces a 100 per cent reserve ratio.

In order to account for different conditions of GFME and SFME production, we will consider the economy on hand under conditions of free as well as non-free GFME assets. Each of those cases will be considered when reserves are fractional and when they are 100 per cent. To do so, we will assume that private producers will attempt to produce SFME each of which promises the instantaneous delivery of one of the GFME assets listed in (6.1). The corresponding vector of SFME assets and their asset-price levels will be:

$$_f\varphi = ({_f\varphi_1}, {_f\varphi_2}, \ldots, {_f\varphi_h}), \text{ and} \tag{13}$$

$$_f\gamma = ({_f\gamma_1}, {_f\gamma_2}, \ldots, {_f\gamma_h}) \tag{14}$$

Before dealing with each of those cases, we must outline the relationships between the demand and supply schedules of each SFME and the same schedules of each corresponding GFME. First, taking $_f\varphi_i$ and $_f\Phi_i$ as examples, since they are not the same assets, they must have different demand schedules. However, since there are no *a priori* reasons for one schedule to be higher than the other, we will treat them as if they had the same schedule. Such a simplification will make the diagrammatic treatment below easier to manage. Second, because of the higher mcac to the private producer, the supply curve of the real balances resulting from the issue of $_f\varphi_i$ will always be higher than that of $_f\Phi_i$. However, since the creation of the real money associated with $_f\varphi_i$ involves the issue of more of its nominal units, its asset-price level as well as the asset-price level of $_f\Phi_i$ will be affected. The increase in the real amount of the SFME asset will thus cause a spillover on the real value of the GFME asset. Such a spillover increases the cost of producing the real GFME and shifts its supply curve to the left. Needless to say, the extent of the shift depends upon the amount of the nominal SFME issued.

2. The Case of Government Sale of GFME

(a) 100 Per Cent Reserve Ratio

Starting with the equilibrium in figure 3, the supply curve of real SFME can be drawn as mc_i which lies above MC_i. The introduction of SFME causes MC_i to shift to the left. Such a shift, however, will not be large because of the institutional restraint imposed upon the issue of nominal SFME by the imposition of a 100 per cent required reserve ratio. The final equilibrium as shown in figure 7a, includes the amount $0a_1$ of real GFME which is smaller than that appearing in figure 3.

The producer of real SFME, behaving as a price searcher,[12] will, by consulting his marginal revenue schedule, produce the amount $0b_1$ of real SFME. If the government forces marginal cost pricing upon the producer, the real SFME produced will increase to $0b_2$. In either case,

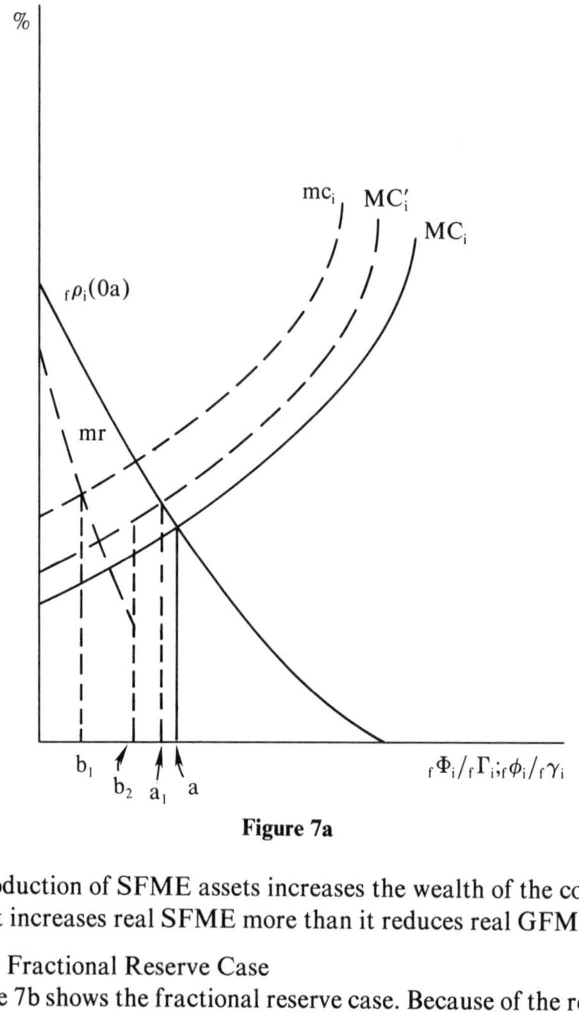

Figure 7a

the introduction of SFME assets increases the wealth of the community as it increases real SFME more than it reduces real GFME.

(b) The Fractional Reserve Case

Figure 7b shows the fractional reserve case. Because of the relative ease with which the nominal units of $_f\varphi_i$ are produced, two differences distinguish this case from the previous one. First, the cost of asset characterization of the real units of $_f\varphi_i$ is higher. Second, the amount of spillover on the marginal cost of the real GFME asset is also greater. This causes the equilibrium quantity of real GFMA, $0a_2$, and the equilibrium quantity of real SFME, $0b_3$, to be smaller than $0a_1$ and $0b_1$ respectively. Even with marginal cost pricing enforced, we get $0b_4$ of real SFME, which is less than $0b_2$. Therefore, under the

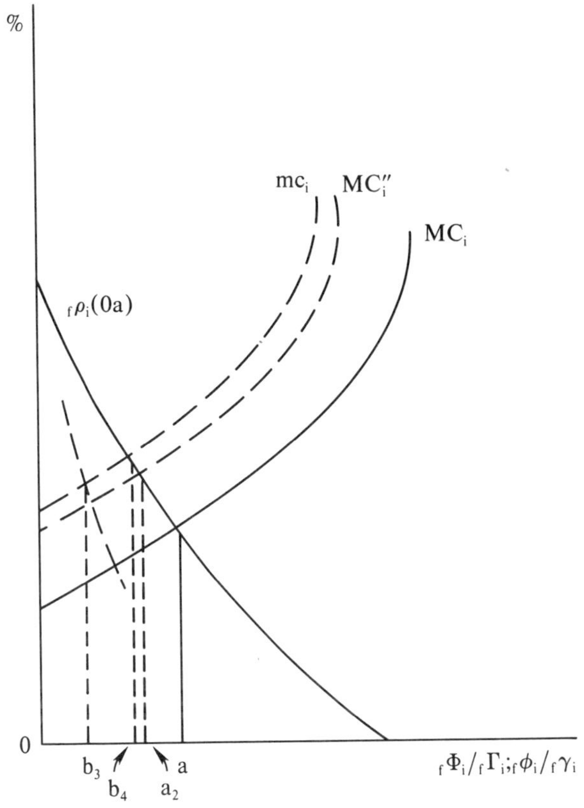

Figure 7b

assumption of the government sale of its FME, the case of 100 per cent reserve ratio is superior to the case of fractional reserves.

3. The Case of Free GFME

When we discussed the pure GFME economy, it was found that the policy of providing free GFME through the tracing of equilibrium levels was the optimal policy. Since our discussion is motivated here by the objective of finding the optimal monetary policy within this new institutional arrangement, we will assume that the government has already reached the objective of free GFME provision through the tracing of equilibrium levels. Given the optimal supply of real GFME produced by such a policy, we will compare the cases of 100 per cent reserve ratio and of fractional reserves to see which provides a higher level of real balances.

(a) 100 Per Cent Reserve Ratio

Figure 8a duplicates the final equilibrium resulting from a free GFME distribution through the tracing of equilibrium levels, from figure 6. The introduction of SFME causes MC_i to shift to MC_i' because of the accompanying spillover. Besides, the supply curve of real SFME, mc_i will lie to the left of MC_i'. The final equilibrium brings forth the quantity $0a_5$ of real GFME and either $0b_5$ or $0b_6$ of real SFME, depending on whether marginal cost pricing will or will not be enforced.

(b) The Fractional Reserve Case

Starting from the same final equilibrium plotted in figure 6, the introduction of SFME will cause a greater amount of spillover on the cost of producing real GFME because of the relative ease of creating nominal units under fractional reserve rules. The shift in MC_i is thus

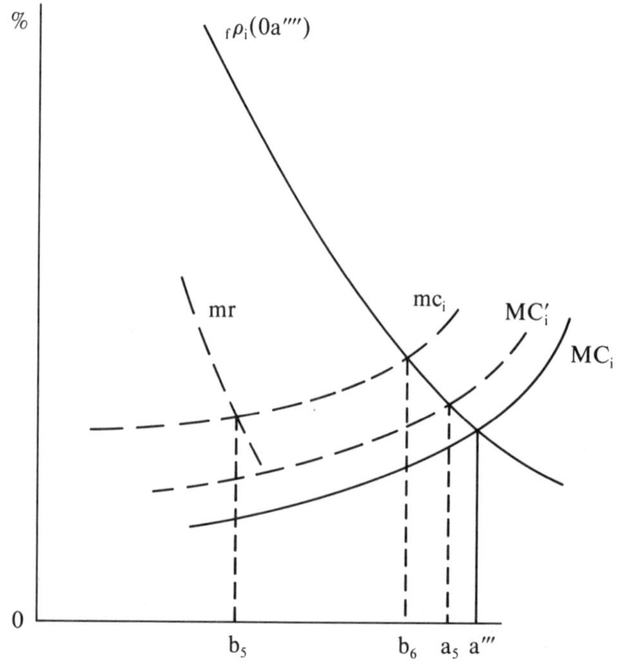

Figure 8a

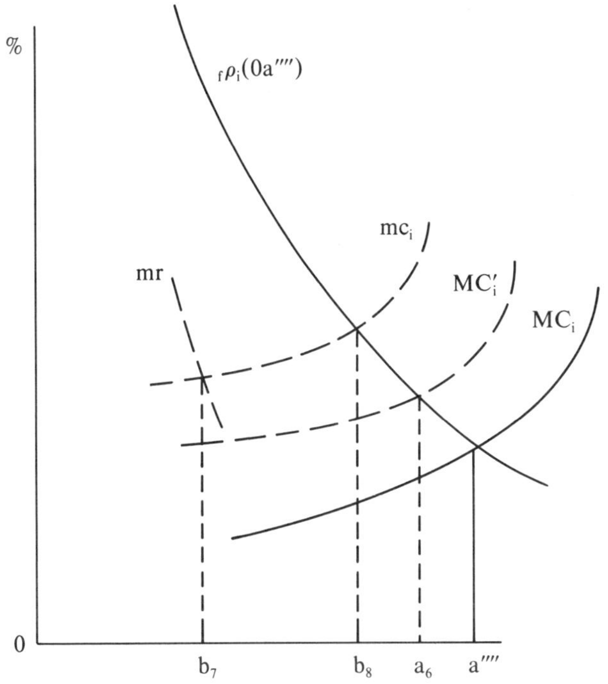

Figure 8b

greater than in the case of 100 per cent reserves. The same relative ease of producing nominal units of SFME causes its supply curve to lie further to the left from the supply curve of GFME than in the 100 per cent reserve ratio case. Therefore, while the total amount of real balances produced increases by the introduction of the SFME asset, the net gain in the case of fractional reserves is smaller than in the case of 100 per cent reserve ratio.

VI. FINANCIAL INTERMEDIATION

Elsewhere, we presented a model in which borrowing was done in a CME economy by issuing private bonds promising the future delivery of CME.[13] That process of borrowing was found to have been enhanced in efficiency when the process of financial intermediation was introduced. In this section, we attempt to consider how borrowing and intermediation will evolve in a fiat-means-of-exchange world.

Two new classes of fiat assets will be introduced: household fiat assets, HFA, and intermediate fiat assets, IFA. Then, the economic effects of intermediation will be considered.

1. Household Fiat Assets

When a trader intends to conduct some exchange involving the purchase of some item, it is generally true in this economy that this can be done with lower transactions costs when the purchase of a certain FME asset is involved than when that of any other item is. Nonetheless, the trader may not have on hand sufficient balances of that means of exchange, in which case he can offer instead a bond promising the future delivery of that asset. The use of this bond will sometimes cause him to incur less transactions costs than the spot or the future trading of any other item.

The borrowing process will therefore be conducted within a FME economy and through the exchange of household fiat assets, which promise the future delivery of some GFME or SFME. Let us consider, as an example, the issue of an HFA by a particular household, ν, promising the delivery of some quantity of ${}_f\Phi_i^\nu$ in the beginning of the next *fatrah*. The bond units of such issue will be denoted by ${}_f\bar{b}_i^\nu$ whose present value is equal to ${}_f\Gamma_i\,{}_f\Phi_i/(1 + {}_f\rho_i^\nu)$, where the ν superscript used on ${}_f\rho_i^\nu$ is used to distinguish it from the rate of return on ${}_f\Phi_i$ itself. Such present value is equal to ${}_f\bar{a}_i^\nu\,{}_f\bar{b}_i^\nu$ where the first term is the price per unit of the bond.

In order to be able to sell his bonds, the individual will have to pay to the buyer (the lender) the rate of return of the FME promised as well as the cost of information the latter must incur in order to make sure that the borrower is within his budget constraint and his portfolio assets of value are sufficient to pay back the debt. This extra cost of information, which we will call *lending costs,* increases at the margin with the size of the debt issue, for the larger the amount of borrowing, the harder it becomes to persuade a lender that the borrower is still within his budget constraint, i.e., that his asset holdings are sufficient to repay his lenders. This must be added to the fact that the demand curve for such a bond issue must be upward sloped, for more borrowing can be done only at higher rates of return.

On the other side of the picture, the bond issuer (the borrower) would be willing to sell more of his bonds as the rate of return that he must pay decreases, so that he moves along a negatively sloped supply curve. Yet, the more he borrows, the more adjustment is needed in his portfolio in order to increase its contents of those assets which can be transformed into the borrowed FME with the least possible transactions costs. Most probably, those assets will be some other FME. The cost of such an adjustment is similar to the cost of acquiring reserves which the producer of SFME has to incur. Such a cost, when accounted for, shifts his supply curve to the left.

Since borrowing a certain FME depends upon the current supply of that asset as well as its rate of return, it will make a difference whether it is presently sold by its producer or provided free up to the satiation point by the government.

(a) Household Borrowing with Costly FME

When the FME borrowed is already being sold at the market rate ${}_f\rho_i$, shown in figure 9, lenders will buy the individual's FME bonds only at rates higher than ${}_f\rho_i$. The demand curve of those bonds will thus take the shape of $D({}_f\bar{b}^v_i)$, when the marginal lending costs, mlc, are not included. At some level of borrowing, beyond which the individual will be exceeding his budget constraint, he can borrow only at infinite rates, which causes the demand curve for his debt to become

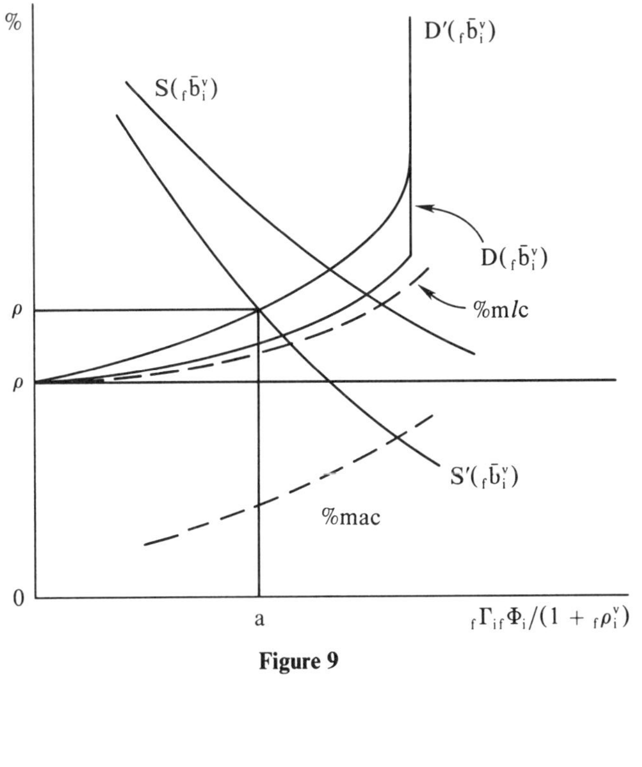

Figure 9

vertical. The addition of the rising marginal lending costs, mlc, as a proportion of the present value of the marginal debt unit, causes the demand curve to take the position $D'({}_f\bar{b}_i^v)$.

The individual's supply curve for his own debt, not considering the cost of adjusting his portfolio, $S({}_f\bar{b}_i^v)$, slopes downward to show his willingness to borrow at lower rates. However, when the increasing marginal cost of adjusting his portfolio, mac, as a proportion of the present value of the marginal debt unit is considered, the supply curve takes the position $S'({}_f\bar{b}_i^v)$, which stands at an increasing distance from the former curve because of the increasing mac.

The equilibrium amount borrowed by v of the asset ${}_f\Phi_i$ is $0a$ and the rate paid is ${}_f\rho_i^v$. This rate is higher than the rate paid for spot trading of the borrowed FME because of the additional costs of borrowing incurred by both the borrower and the lenders.

(b) Household Borrowing and Free GFME

In this section we will discuss the effects of two government monetary policies on private borrowing. First, the discussion of the policy of giving free GFME through the tracing of equilibrium points will enable us to see the effects of an increase in the quantity of real GFME on the volume as well as the social costs of borrowing. Second, we will discuss the effects of providing a satiation level of real GFME on the same variables.

(i) *Tracing Equilibrium Levels.* Figure 10a shows the initial equilibrium level of real GFME $0a$ and the corresponding level of borrowing $0\bar{a}$ in figure 10b. When government policy of free distribution of GFME through the tracing of equilibrium levels produces the greater volume of real GFME $0a''$ ', the demand and supply schedules must change.[14] The demand for bonds will go down, signifying that, because of the relative abundance of real GFME, lenders are willing to lend greater amounts at the same rate of return. Meanwhile, the supply curve will shift down, showing that the borrower will borrow less at each rate of return. This causes the amount of borrowing to go down from $0\bar{a}$ to $0\bar{a}'$. Figures 10c and 10d show the marginal costs of adjusting portfolios and the marginal lending costs respectively. The sum of the areas under the two curves, up to the amount of borrowing, represents the resources expended in the process of borrowing. The reduction of the amount of borrowing, because of free GFME, reduces this social cost by the sum of the two shaded areas in the latter diagrams.

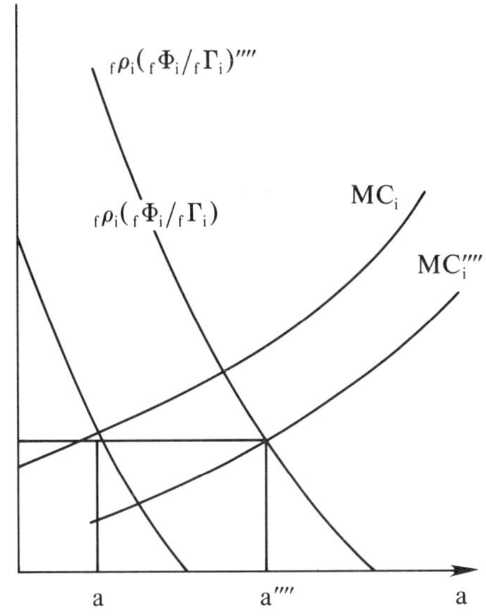

Figure 10a

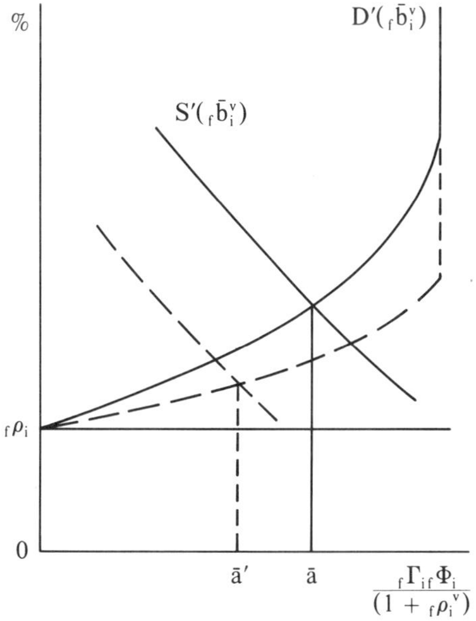

Figure 10b

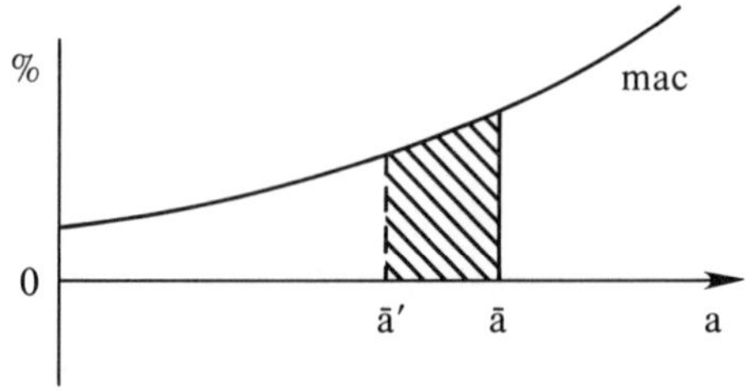

Figure 10c

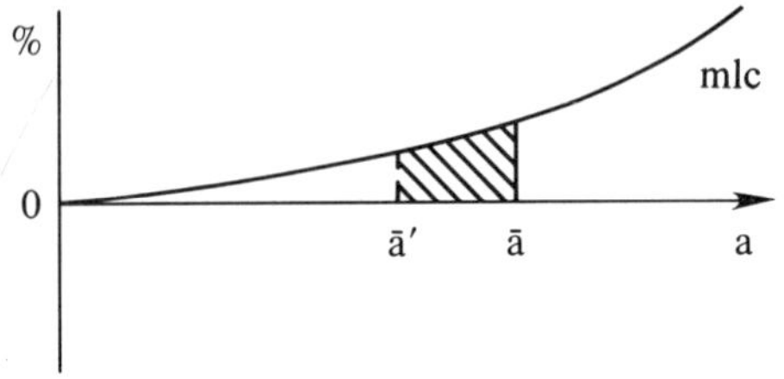

where
$a = {}_f\Gamma_i\, {}_f\Phi_i/(1 + {}_f\rho_i^v)$

Figure 10d

(ii) *Providing the Satiation Level of GFME.* Figure 11a reproduces the case of free government provision of GFME up to satiation level plotted in figure 5 above. The production of $0e''$ of real GFME costs the society a deadweight loss equal to the striped area $Q''e''d''$, and brings the rate of return on the marginal unit of real GFME down to zero. Since real GFME is freely available, lenders are willing to buy bonds at any rate above zero, but high enough to cover the marginal lending costs. This brings the demand curve to $D''({}_f\bar{b}_i^v$ in figure 11b, which exactly traces the mlc curve. Moreover, the demand for borrowing at rates of return higher than zero disappears. Because people can satisfy their demands for means of exchange without cost, and because borrowing itself causes borrowers to incur portfolio adjustment costs, borrowers would sell their bonds only at negative rates of return. This means that they would demand compensation for the cost of borrowing in order to do so. This causes the supply curve for bonds to appear in the fourth quadrant, where it indicates at each quantity lent the corresponding (negative) values on the mac curve.

The sum of the shaded areas under the mac and mlc curves in figures 11c and 11d respectively measure the social costs associated with

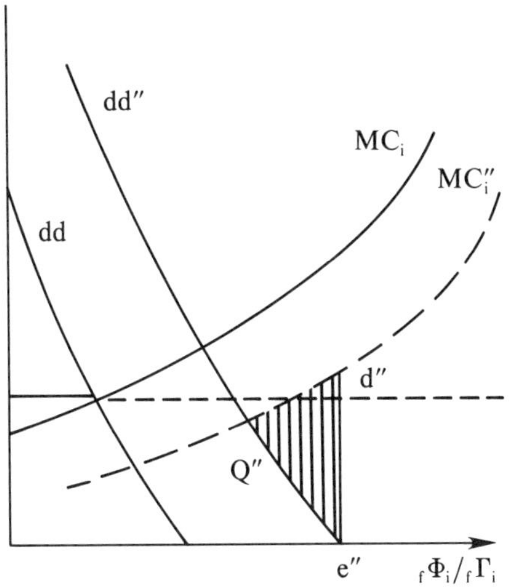

Figure 11a

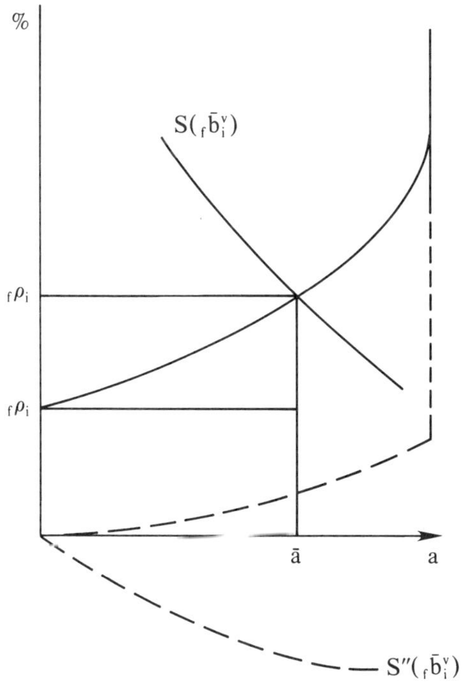

Figure 11b

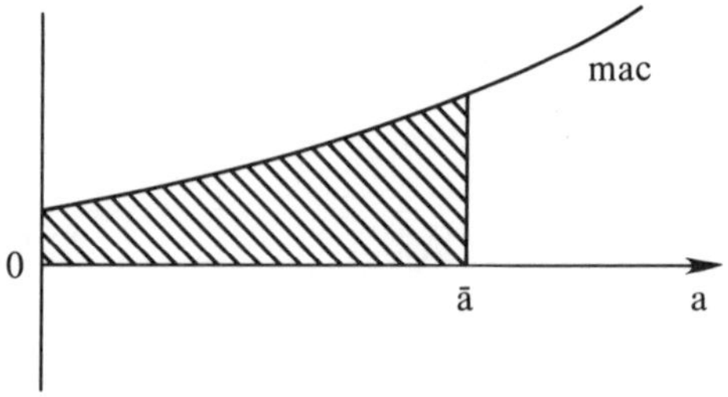

Figure 11c

where

$$dd = {}_f\rho_i({}_f\Phi_i/{}_f\Gamma_i)$$
$$dd'' = {}_f\rho_i({}_f\Phi_i/{}_f\Gamma_i)''$$
$$a = {}_f\Gamma_{if}\Phi_i/(1 + {}_f\rho_i^v)$$

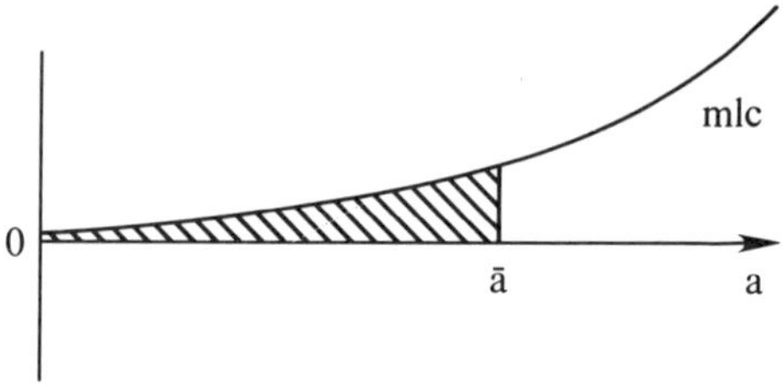

Figure 11d

the volume $0\bar{a}$ of private lending. When that lending disappears because of free GFME provision, that cost disappears too. However, such a saving in resources is associated with a welfare cost measured by the area of $Q''e''d''$. The merit of the policy of free GFME up to satiation levels must therefore be judged through the comparison of the saving on lending costs and the welfare costs indicated in figure 11a. This, at the moment, is an empirical question.

2. Intermediate Fiat Assets

(a) Financial Intermediation

The reason for the existence of financial intermediation in this theoretical framework is information imperfection coupled with the ability to gain from specialising in the collection of information. No individual in this model can perceive the vector of prevailing prices perfectly. The set of each individual's conjectured prices, which determines the composition of his portfolio, will always fail to be the same as his vector of trading prices. Therefore, such a composition will always fail to minimise the transactions costs of fulfilling his obligations, when the bonds he has issued come to maturity. He must therefore continue to adjust the composition of his portfolio, which causes him to incur the portfolio adjustment costs mentioned above.

As a borrower, when the individual specialises in the information about the optimal portfolio composition, i.e., that which minimises his transactions costs at the time of the maturity of his debt, he can reduce his mac below the level reached by non-specialists. Such an intermediary can thus issue intermediate fiat assets, IFA, of quality superior to the household fiat assets, HFA, issued by non-specialists. The IFA are superior in the sense that they are issued at a lower mac than the HFA. The supply of IFA, at the same rates of return, is thus higher than that of HFA.

As a lender, the individual must collect information about the com-

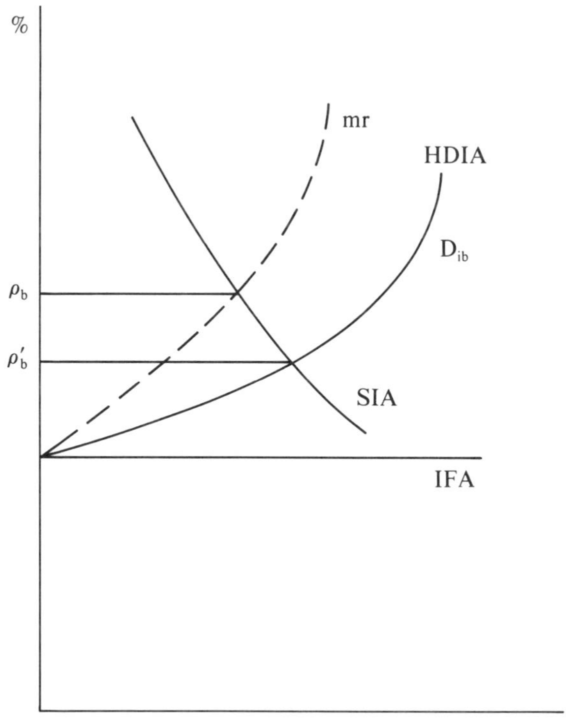

Figure 12a

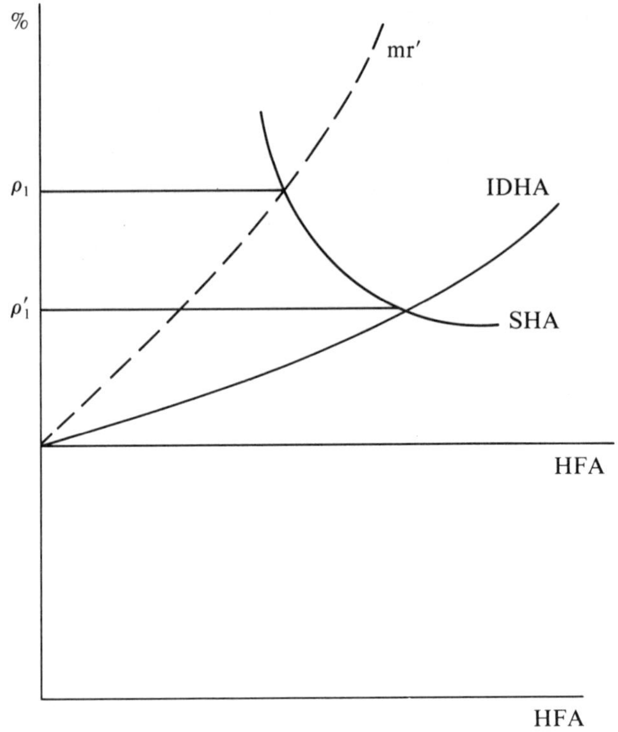

Figure 12b

position of the portfolios of his borrowers. Doing so costs him the mlc. If he is an information specialist, his mlc will be below that of a non-specialist. Being able to lend more cheaply causes the intermediary's demand for HFA to be higher than that of non-specialists for the same assets, at the same rates of return.

Figures 12a and 12b plot the markets of IFA and HFA, respectively. In the first diagram, the SIA schedule represents the supply of IFA. In the second diagram, the SHA schedule represents the supply of HFA. Their relative positions are such that, if they were on the same diagram, the former would be closer to the ordinate than the latter, reflecting the lower level of mac associated with intermediate borrowing. Similarly, the schedule of households' demand for IFA, appearing in figure 12a, would be to the left of the schedule of intermediaries' demand for HFA, appearing in 12b, were they drawn on the same graph. This reflects the lower mlc associated with the latter.

In our model of imperfect information, all sellers behave as price searchers. The consideration of the marginal revenue curve associated with each demand curve in the above diagrams yields ρ_b and $\rho\ell$ as the borrowing and lending rates, respectively paid and received by intermediaries. The difference between both rates represents the margin of profit.

(b) Intermediation and Pricing Control

The government can undertake a policy of forcing non-monopolistic pricing in both the IFA and HFA markets. This reduces the borrowing and the lending rates to ρ_b' and $\rho\ell'$ respectively, but still keeps a profit margin for intermediaries to operate with. Moreover, the volume of lending through intermediaries expands. However, while the enforcement of marginal cost pricing on intermediaries may be easy, for they would be small in number, its enforcement on issuers of household fiat assets may be very costly, for they would be rather numerous. An enforcement of marginal cost pricing on intermediaries only will force them out of business, because it reduces their borrowing rate.

(c) Intermediation and Free GFME

While intermediaries reduce the costs of borrowing and lending, they must borrow and lend at rates equal to or below the rates which are available to households directly. The reasons are that the intermediary lending rate must be no greater than the household's rate, and that the intermediary borrowing rate must be below their lending rate.

The government's successive offers of free GFME through the tracing of equilibrium points will greatly reduce the cost of borrowing to households, but will not eliminate them. The resulting reduction of the household lending rate will necessarily reduce the margin of profit obtained by intermediaries, and, consequently, curtail their operations.

The provision of free GFME up to the satiation level reduces the costs of household borrowing to zero. This totally eliminates all intermediation.

VII. THE OPTIMAL SUPPLY OF FIAT MEANS OF EXCHANGE AND GOVERNMENT POLICY

In a world of only GFME, it was found that the optimal monetary policy would be to expand the stock of real balances through successively decreasing gifts of means of exchange, always keeping the rate of return on the marginal unit of real GFME equal to its marginal cost of production. The advantage of this policy is that it allows the stock of real balances to expand to the maximum possible amount without violating the efficiency rules.

In a world containing both GFME and SFME, the conditions under which SFME are produced become important. While the policy of successively tracing equilibrium points in the market of GFME remained optimal, it must be coupled with a 100 per cent reserve ratio and an enforcement of marginal cost pricing in the SFME market.

The policy of providing GFME free of charge up to the satiation level was initially discarded because of a deadweight loss associated with its inefficiency. Nonetheless, when private borrowing was considered, the merits of discarding such a policy became less apparent. The reason is that such a policy would completely eliminate any need for private borrowing, thus saving the community the resources expended in marketing household fiat assets. The possibility that the real value of those resources could offset, and might exceed, the deadweight loss associated with the satiation level of GFME must therefore be considered. We could not, however, provide a theoretical support that the former gain will outweigh the latter loss. Such support can only come from an empirical evaluation.

While efficiency in the debt market requires the imposition of marginal cost pricing on household as well as intermediate issuers of fiat assets, there are reasons to believe that costs of this imposition on households could exceed the benefits. The imposition of pricing regulations on intermediaries alone will force them out of the debt market, causing the community to lose their services.

This dilemma can be solved by the policy of free GFME up to the satiation level. The abundance of GFME in this case eliminates the need for a debt market, and the existence of intermediation will therefore be unnecessary. This must be considered as an extra advantage of the GFME satiation policy.

Notes

1. Friedman (1959), Johnson (1967), Levhari and Patinkin (1968), Marty (1961), Patinkin (1965), Samuelson (1969), Sidrauski (1967), Stein (1969), Tobin (1958), Tobin (1968), Tolly (1957), Tsiang (1969). (See Bibliography.)

2. Akerlof (1973), Arrow (1952), Clower (1970), Johnson (1970), Tobin (1958).

3. Hahn (1971), Kurz (1974), Niehans (1969), Niehans (1971), Sontheimer (1972), Starr (1970), Wallace (1972).

4. Clower (1971), Ostrey (1971).

5. Arrow (1964), Brunner and Meltzer (1964), Brunner and Meltzer (1971), Debreu (1959), Howitt (1973), Howitt (1974), Ostrey (1971), Ostrey (1973), Radner (1968), Radner (1970).

6. Mabid A. M. M. Al-Jarhi, "The Optimal Supply of Money and Optimal Monetary Policies," Ph.D. Dissertation, University of Southern California, 1975, Ch. III.

7. A producer with a profit motive will find it hard to sell such information because of the characteristics of information which make it resemble public goods.

8. This should not be construed as "good" money driving "bad" money out of circulation in violation of *Gresham's Law*. To do so would be to confuse the "superiority" of an asset in the sense of costing its user less transactions costs with its "superiority" as a store of value.

9. The net rate of return of an asset, η_i, when multiplied by the nominal value of the asset Φ_i, gives the net value of services $\eta_i\Phi_i$. That net value must be generally equal to the value of real services which is, for fiat assets, equal to zero plus the value of transactions services. If the rate of transactions services obtained from Φ_i is equal to I_i, then:

$${}_f\ell_{if}\Phi_i/{}_f\Gamma_i = {}_f\ell_{i\,f}\Phi_i, \tag{11}$$

which implies that

$${}_f\ell_i/{}_f\Gamma_i = {}_f\ell_i' \tag{12}$$

where ${}_f$ refers to the *fatrah* during which the exchanges are made.

10. The attempt to exclude such effects is not due to their undesirability, but rather to the analytical problems their existence may cause. For a free doubling of initial GFME, see, for example, D. Patinkin, *Money, Interest, and Prices,* 2nd ed. (New York: Harper and Row, 1965), ch. II. Another case is the famous Friedman's helicopter which, with an Arabian-Night magic, doubles the initial money holdings of everyone; see M. Friedman, "The Optimum Quantity of Money," in *The Optimum Quantity of Money and Other Essays* (Chicago: Aldine, 1969), pp. 4–7. Doubling initial holdings of GFME cannot be done here, for we are introducing them into an initially CME economy where such holdings are zero at the outset.

11. For a parallel treatment of this point see B. P. Pesek and T. R. Saving, *The Foundations of Money and Banking* (New York: Macmillan & Co., 1968).

12. It would be inconceivable, under the present assumption of information costs, and with costly transactions, to have a perfectly competitive market anywhere in the economy.

13. Mabid Ali Al-Jarhi, "The Optimal Supply of Money."

14. Although this policy may change the rate of return at equilibrium in any direction, we have, for diagrammatic simplicity, assumed it unchanged.

4

*Towards an Interest Free Islamic Economic System**

Waqar Masood Khan

Waqar Masood Khan is Chief Economist and Vice President, Bankers Equity Limited, Pakistan. This work is part of his Ph.D. dissertation, presented at Boston University.

INTRODUCTION

Elimination of 'Ribā' is central to reorganizing a financial system on the basis of Islamic principles. Although adoption of an Islamic code can never be conditional on the result of an economic benefit cost exercise, such an exercise is nevertheless useful in determining the steps policy makers should take to minimize associated costs. The institution of '*Ribā*' is deeply embedded in the modern financial system. Accordingly, the job of Islamic scholars to devise a system which can smoothly replace the modern system is formidable.

In this paper we have rigorously investigated the implications of prohibiting the charging of interest in the economy. The main contribution of this paper is that the prohibition problem is discussed in the mainstream economics frame work. The problem essentially lies in the domain of the 'theory of contracts' and 'economics of information'. Accordingly, our framework relates to these two areas of economics.

The paper is divided in two parts. In Part I we discuss implications of moving towards the new system, and in Part II we discuss how the results of Part I change due to a major change in the environment of Part I. All proofs are contained in the appendix.

PART I
IMPLICATIONS OF PROHIBITING DEBT FINANCING

The objective of this part is to develop a framework that with allow us to compare the Islamic financial scheme with the traditional one. This will then be applied to issues connected with the prohibition of interest from the economy.

A financial system is simply a collection of contracts. The nature and characteristics of these contracts define a given financial system. Accordingly, we identify a given system by the type of contract it offers to the market. In our view, which we also believe is the orthodox view, an Islamic financial contract does not allow for a fixed return over and above the principal amount loaned. Thus we identify a non-Islamic contract as one which requires from the borrower a fixed return over and above the principal amount. A debt contract is one example of such a contract and we use this as the prime representative of the non-Islamic set of contracts. On the other hand, a contract which stipulates the sharing of the return from the enterprise created by the use of loaned money is taken to be an Islamic financial contract. The well known *muḍārabah* contract is the prime representative of the Islamic set of contracts. These definitions are made more precise in section II.

In Section II we begin with a careful description of the environment under which our analyses are undertaken. This is done by specifying the assumptions of the model.

Under this given set of assumptions, we show that the Islamic scheme is superior to the traditional scheme. This is one of the fundamental results in this paper. Given the significance of this result, it is imperative that one should be very clear about the underlying conditions. Thus, Section III is fully devoted to a critical examination of the assumptions of our model.

We conclude that the result is fairly robust and can only be reversed through significant changes in the environment of the model.

Assumptions, Basic Model and Results

For any theory, a careful specification of the environment in which the theory is applicable is an essential prerequisite. Like any other theoretical work, we have simplified the economic scenario by abstracting from real world complications.

Let us first outline the assumptions governing the environment of our model. These are:

i) There is one financial institution called a lender.
ii) The supply of loanable funds is fixed.
iii) There are investors in the economy demanding identical loans.
iv) The credit market clears.
v) A project's performance is independent of the financing decision.
vi) The projects of different investors are uncorrelated.
vii) Investors are risk averse.
viii) Both the lender and a typical investor have identical beliefs about the probability distribution of the project return and both can observe it costlessly.

Basic Model

Let L be the fixed supply of loanable funds; then iv) implies that:

$$zn = L \tag{1}$$

where n is the number of investors and z is the size of the loan.

Let zR_i be the return to the ith investor when he invests z. We assume that R_i is a random variable which is identically and independently distributed across different projects with the density $f(r)$. For simplicity we restrict R to take only the positive real values. Finally, R has a finite first two moments, namely its mean, $E(R)$ and variance $\text{VAR}(R)$.

Note that the above formulation implies constant returns relative to the loan size. This is dictated by the simplicity achieved in modelling. There could be increasing returns relative to the loan size, but we ignore it in order to keep our analysis manageable.

Before we define the two schemes formally let us make a few remarks. The traditional financial scheme we have in mind roughly works as follows: the lender transfers a certain amount of money, called principal, to the borrower on the condition that the principal and a fixed percentage return on the principal is payable on a future date. Although these payments are stipulated as fixed amounts, it is understood in many cases by both parties that if the earnings fall below the required payments then a lesser amount will be paid. In the present framework we have lumped all types of fixed payments into a single fixed payment that can be thought of as the principal plus the interest. Let D denote this fixed payment. Then, if R is greater than D, the lender will receive D; otherwise, it is understood that lender will receive everything, i.e., the entire R.

On the other hand, the Islamic scheme is exemplified by the well-known *muḍārabah* arrangement, in which the lender receives an agreed-upon share in the return from the project he helps to fund. When the return is zero, no party gets anything. Our analysis of the Islamic scheme takes as its paradigm the *muḍārabah* contract; however, the analysis is broad enough to accommodate the *mushārakah* (partnership) contract as well. In the latter, part of the capital is brought by the investor himself. Assuming that each investor brings an identical amount of his own capital, say Z_1, and borrows Z_2, and assuming further that both the investor's own capital and the borrowed capital are necessary to undertake the project, one can formulate a return function,

$$R\,(Z_1, Z_2) = Z_1 Z_2\, R_i$$

for each investor. Thus, all results in the paper will carry over to the case of the *mushārakah* contract by letting $Z = Z_1 Z_2$.

It is important to note that at this stage neither of the two schemes we are considering requires collateral from the investor. In other words, the lender accepts the possibility of default by the investor. In practice this is rarely true of the debt scheme since many of these loans are secured against a collateral. We will have more to say about this later.

For the sake of convenience, in our subsequent discussion we shall designate the traditional scheme as the Fixed Return Scheme (FRS) and the Islamic Scheme as the Variable Return Scheme (VRS). We now formally define the two schemes:

DEFINITION: (FRS) A financial contract which specifies the following payoffs for the lender and the investor, respectively, is FRS:

$$P_i^F = z\,(\min\,(R_1, D));\; Y_i^F = z\,(\max\,(R_1 - D, 0)) \qquad (2)$$

Note that P_i^F and Y_i^F are random variables and their distribution is determined by the distribution of R_i. The aggregate payoff to the lender is given by:

$$P^F = \sum_{i=1}^{n} z\,(\min\,(D, R_i)) \qquad (3)$$

DEFINITION: (VRS) A financial contract which specifies the following payoffs to the lender and the borrower, respectively, is VRS:

$$P_i^V = (1 - a)z^R i; \qquad Y_i^V = azR_i \text{ where } 0 < a < 1 \qquad (4)$$

The aggregate return to the lender is given by:

$$P^V = z\Sigma\,(1 - a)R_i \qquad (5)$$

Given the above specification of these two types of contracts, our problem is to see which will be preferred to the credit market. We are interested in that scheme which is Pareto optimal. This problem can be attacked in several ways. For instance we might assume that the lender is risk neutral, and accordingly looks only at the expected return from the two types of contracts. But is is possible to choose a and D such that the expected return from the two schemes is identical. Then, the choice of the type of contract depends on the preference of a typical investor.

Another approach would be to find the pair (a, D) so that a typical investor has identical utility across both forms of contract. Then at this point we can see the preference of the lender for the two schemes.

We take the first approach without assuming that the lender is risk neutral; instead, we examine the lender's behavior by utilizing the law of large numbers.

Some Asymptotic Results

In the following two lemmas, we look at the behavior of expected payoff to the lender as he partitions the total supply of loanable funds in the finest possible ways These two lemmas would be essential in determining lender's attitude toward the financial schemes.

The lender's expected payoff under FRS is given by:

$$E(P^F) = z\sum_{i=1}^{n} E\min\,(R_i, D) = L \cdot E\min\,(R_i, D) \qquad (6)$$

while the variance is given by

$$\text{Var}\,(P^F) = \text{Var}\left(\sum_{i=1}^{n} z \min\,(R_i, D)\right)$$

$$= z^2 n \,\text{Var}\,(\min\,(R_i, D))$$

$$E(P^F) = z\, L\, \text{Var}\,(\min\,(R_i, D)) \tag{7}$$

Thus P^F is distributed as:

$$P^F \sim \{L \cdot E \min\,(R_i, D);\, z\, L\, \text{Var} \min\,(R_i, D)\} \tag{8}$$

Now we have the following:

LEMMA-1: Let P^F be a sequence of identically and independently distributed random variables with the moments given in (8) then

$$P^F \longrightarrow LE \min\,(R_i, D), \text{ as } z \longrightarrow 0$$

Proof: In Appendix 2.

This lemma determines the behavior of the lender's payoff as he partitions the available funds into smaller loans. What it says is that, if the lender extends the smallest possible loans, then he can reduce the probability of default from any one investor to an arbitrarily small level. In other words, in the presence of a large number of investors, if one investor defaults, then its effect on the lender's expected payoff is negligible.

Similarly, the lender's expected payoff under the VRS is given by:

$$E(P^V) = L\ (1 - a)E(R_i) \tag{9}$$

and the variance of return is given by:

$$\text{Var}\,(P^V) = z^2 n\,(1 - a)\,\text{Var}\,(R_i)$$

$$= z\, L\,(1 - a)\,\text{Var}\ (R_i)$$

Thus P^V is distributed as:

$$P^V \sim \{L(1 - a)E(R);\, zL(1 - a)\ \text{Var}\,(R)\} \tag{10}$$

Thus, we have a result similar to that in lemma-1 for the sequence of random returns P^V under VRS.

Since the lender is not assumed to be risk neutral, we need to look at his expected utility in order to determine his preference for any contract. Let U_b be the utility function of the lender. We assume that U_b is continuous. The following lemma determines the lender's utility level under both FRS and VRS:

LEMMA-2: Let P^F and P^V be the two sequences of independent and identically distributed random variables converging in probability to $E(P^F)$ and $E(P^V)$ respectively. If U_b is a continuous function then:

$$U_b(P^F) \rightarrow U_b(E(P^F) \text{ as } z \rightarrow 0$$
$$U_b(P^V) \rightarrow U_b(E(P^V) \text{ as } z \rightarrow 0$$

Proof: In Appendix 2.

This is a very important and useful lemma. It establishes the fact that if the lender has a continuous utility function then he would look only at the expected payoff from the two schemes. Notice that the assumptions underlying the two lemmas are much less restrictive than assuming risk neutrality on the part of the lender. The crucial requirements for the lemmas are uncorrelated investment projects and a continuous utility function for the lender. There is one further important requirement for these lemmas to hold: the lender's ability to partition the total supply in the finest way. This essentially requires that the lender be able to extend arbitrarily small loans. One can easily make a case for a critical loan size determined by the associated cost of making the loan.

There are two things to be noted. First though we require a fine partition of the available funds, it doesn't mean a very small loan. Indeed we can easily show that for each positive e there is a z' such that for all $z < z'$ the probability of realizing the expected return is greater than $(1 - e)$. Second, if this procedure fails we can expect, with only one lender, that the relative loan size z/L will still be very small.

As we have seen, the preference of the lender across two contracts is determined by looking only at the expected payoff. Consequently the lender will be indifferent across both schemes if they offer the same expected payoff. Indeed if the bargaining process for choosing a financial contract is continuous, in the sense to be made precise below, there will always exist a situation such that the lender is indifferent between two schemes. The following lemma formally illustrates this fact:

LEMMA-3: Fix D and let $0 < a < 1$, then there exists an a^* such that:

$$E(P^F) = E(P^V)$$

Proof: In Appendix 2.

There is an important corollary to lemma-3. This shows that the lender will strictly prefer a scheme which offers a higher expected payoff:

COROLLARY-1: For all $a < a^*$ lender strictly prefers VRS

Proof: In Appendix 2.

From lemmas 1–3 it is clear that the choice between these types of financial contracts hinges upon the preference of the typical investor. We will now show that the investor's preference for the contract is determined by his attitude toward risk. If we suppose the typical investor to be risk neutral then we have the famous result:

PROPOSITION-1: (MILLER-MODIGLIANI) Suppose that lemmas 1–3 are true. If a typical investor is risk neutral, then the choice of a financial contract is irrelevant.

Proof: In Appendix 2.

This is a simple version of the well known and controversial Miller-Modigliani Theorem in the theory of finance, which asserts that the value of a firm in a given risk class is independent of its capital structure (Debt-Equity Ratio). Here it implies that if a firm is risk neutral, then given the indifference of the financer, the firm should be indifferent between the FRS or VRS financing of its project.

However, since we have assumed that a typical investor is not risk neutral, but risk averse, it is not easy to determine the choice of contract where, as in the case we are considering, the expected payoff to the investors is identical across both schemes. In order to see which of the two types of contracts is to be preferred by a typical investor, we need to examine the expected utility of the payoff at the point where the expected payoff is identical under two schemes. It is obvious that a risk averse person would prefer the least risky income stream among all those income streams having an identical expected payoff. Thus our problem essentially reduces to the task of determining the riskiness associated with payoffs across these two schemes. This is formally set forth in the following reasoning.

From (2) and (3) we have:

$$Y_i^F = z \max (R_i - D, 0) \text{ and } Y_i^V = a\,(zR_i)$$

At a^* we also have:

$$E(Y^F) = E(Y^V) \qquad (11)$$

Let U_i be the utility function of the it h investor. We assume that U_i is a concave and bounded function. Given (11) an investor prefers VRS if:

$$E \cdot U(Y_i^V) > E \cdot U(Y^F) \qquad (12)$$

Fundamental Result

To establish the typical investor's preference for VRS financing, it is necessary only to show that for a risk averse investor (12) is true. Our argument, however, proceeds at a higher level of generality, and the conclusion we seek then follows as a corollary of the more general result. In the next Proposition we will make use of the following definition:

DEFINITION: For $0 < a < 1$, an a-sharing rule is a function

S:I---- IR

where IR is the real line, and such that

$$\text{i)}\quad 0 \leq S(R) \leq R \qquad (13)$$

$$\text{ii)}\quad ES(R) = aE(R)$$

PROPOSITION-2: Let

$$S^*(R) = \min (R, D)$$

and

$$S^*(R) = \max (R, D')$$

Fix D and D' and choose a so that $S^*(R)$ and $S^*(R)$ are a-sharing rules. Then, for any bounded and concave utility function U and any a-sharing rule $S(R)$,

$$E\,U[S^*(R)] \geq E\,U[S(R)] \geq E\,U[S^*(R)]$$

Proof: In Appendix 2.

Proposition-2 identifies the most preferred and the least preferred a-sharing rules for a risk averse investor. But this also allows us to compare the VRS and FRS schemes, showing that FRS is the least preferred scheme and therefore VRS strictly dominates it. The following corollary establishes this fact:

COROLLARY-2: A risk averse investor strictly prefers VRS over FRS.

Proof: In Appendix 2.

Now we are in a position to state the most important result of this paper.

THEOREM-1: Corresponding to each FRS there is a VRS which improves everyone's welfare.

Proof: In Appendix 2.

We find figures 1 and 2 very helpful in understanding this theorem. In figure 1 we have shown the payoffs to the investor under VRS and

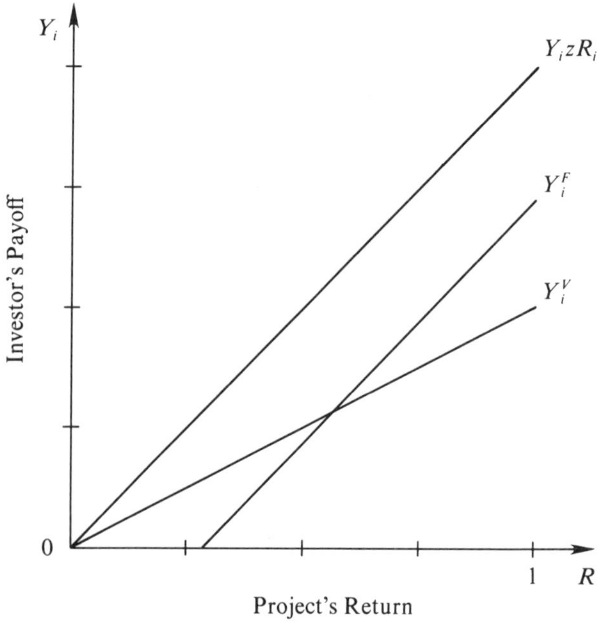

Figure 1

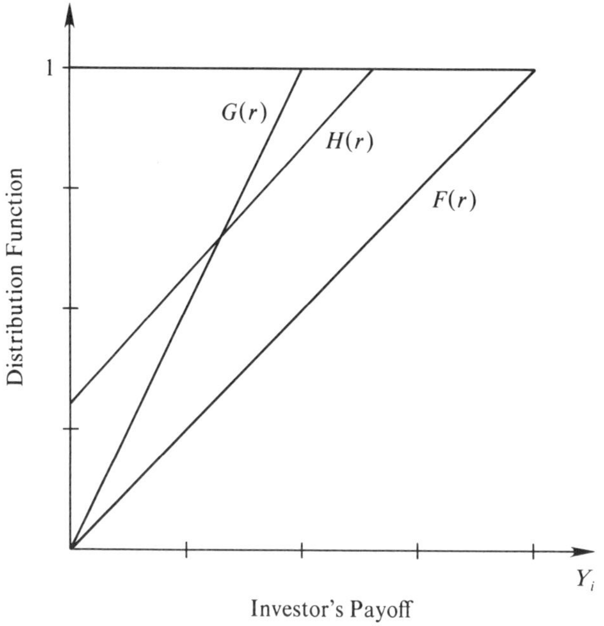

Figure 2

FRS. The line Y_i^V shows his payoff under VRS and the line Y_i^F shows his payoff under FRS. Assume that the random project return is uniformly distributed between 0 & 1. Then we can derive the distribution function for both Y_i^V and Y_i^F. This is done in figure 2. The lines $F(r)$, $G(r)$ and $H(r)$ give the distribution functions of r, Y_i^V and Y_i^F respectively. Note that $G(r)$ and $H(r)$ cross at some point, so we can fix the corresponding means at some values of a and D. Thus $G(r)$ and $H(r)$ are the distribution functions with identical expected value. Now a risk averse individual will prefer that distribution which is less risky. It is clear from figure 2 that $G(r)$ is less risky since it is uniformly smooth whereas $H(r)$ takes jumps at the extreme values. The reason for the riskiness of $H(r)$ lies in the fact that it has a positive probability mass at zero, an extreme value.

This theorem is the most significant and fundamental result of our research, for it suggests that, under assumptions i–viii, the type of contract which is Pareto optimal is VRS. The intuitive reasoning behind the theorem involves a recognition of the crucially different ways in which risk is distributed in each of the two schemes. Given the fact that the choice of the type of contract depends on the preference of a typical investor, where the lender is indifferent the investor prefers the one that is less risky. VRS has the characteristic of spreading risk more evenly than FRS; consequently, given risk averse investors, VRS dominates FRS. This is the single most important gain of VRS and it has far-reaching implications for the stability of a financial system based on VRS.

Disregarding the transaction costs involved in the process of moving towards VRS arrangements, it seems that the move is likely to be Pareto optimal.

This is a somewhat paradoxical result since it demonstrates inferiority of debt, the predominant form of financial contract. Note also that in this model full equity is the optimal choice, for a combination of debt and equity is also dominated by an equity contract.

Since the above conclusion is central to our analysis in this paper, it is essential that we look very carefully at the underlying assumptions. In the next section we critically examine each of the assumptions to discover how sensitive to model specification our basic result is.

A Critical Examination of the Assumptions

The art of theorizing requires certain simplifying assumptions which might not be true. If they are not true and are made for mere simplification, then the essential results of a theory should not be sensitive to the assumptions. If, however, a prediction of the theory crucially depends on a particular assumption, then that assumption must be realistic or else justified on some other grounds.

The assumptions i, ii, iv, and identical distribution of a project's return are made for convenience. So long as the law of large numbers holds for each of the several lenders we will get the dominance of the equity contract.

Given a fixed supply of loanable funds, our model is basically a demand side model. We have not explained where this supply of funds comes from. We may interpret this as reflecting *given* savings decisions. But then one might well argue that these decisions would depend in the first place upon the type of contracts being offered by the financial institution. This is essentially the problem of determining the effect of introducing the system of profit-sharing on the savings behavior of individuals.

If the financial institutions offered only the equity financing, i.e., only the risky contracts, then one might suggest that total supply of loanable funds would be smaller than otherwise. This suspicion might arise from the idea that savings incentives would be diluted if only the risky assets were offered. Therefore it might be thought that results based on the assumption of a fixed supply of loanable funds cannot be relied upon.

There are two reasons for making such an assumption besides the argument that it is just the beginning effort of formally modelling the interest-free economy. First, though it may be true that the availability of risk-free assets at the individual level induces more savings, it is not clear that aggregate savings in the economy are also affected by the non-availability of such assets. That is, the aggregate savings function does not depend on the interest rate. Second, in many of the countries that we have in mind, the interest rate is controlled by the government and hence it plays little if any role in determining the level of savings. In fact, savings decisions are strictly based on the level of income. Most of the savings are either in the corporate sector or the public sector. Individual savings constitute a negligible part of the total savings. Therefore it seems natural to start off with the assumption of a fixed supply of loanable funds.

But there is the further question of whether in the model where we do have a variable supply of loanable funds, the Pareto optimal contract will be different. It is not clear in which direction savings are going to change. This is a dynamic allocational problem. The introduction of Islamic schemes would make future income more risky than what it is currently at any moment of time. Given this increased uncertainty, what changes in the consumption pattern would take place so that the expected utility over time is unchanged? Lyland (1969) has shown that if the utility function were characterized by decreasing risk aversion, savings would increase. The idea is that with increased uncertainty and decreasing risk aversion, in order to maintain the same expected utility over time, an individual has to cut his present level of consumption.

Lyland's model does not answer the above question in sufficient generality; however, it serves as a good counterexample to those who would argue that the introduction of the new system would necessarily lead to a reduction in the supply of loanable funds. Thus we can safely conclude that the nature of the optimal contract would not necessarily change if we allow for the variable supply of loanable funds.

There is no problem in making an assumption like vi), uncorrelated investment projects, in normal economic conditions. The only occasion where one can doubt the validity of such an assumption is in the downswing of the business cycle when there is an economy-wide recession and declining profitability. But this in fact counts in favor of the VRS because losses would be spread thoroughout the credit market. It is ironic that VRS contracts would minimize such losses because there would be bankruptcies as would be triggered otherwise.[1]

We now turn to the assumption regarding the separation of the project's performance and the financing decision. We have assumed that the nature of the contract does not influence the project's performance. More formally, the production function is independent of whether the funds are obtained through equity or debt.

In principle there can be no objection to such an assumption since the marginal product of a dollar of investment, ceteris paribus, should be independent of whether the dollar is raised through debt or equity. But then this assumption has the implication of ruling out incentive effects associated with the ownership structure of the firm. There are two similar ways in which these incentive effects may arise.

Jensen and Meckling (1976) have argued that the behavior of the manager-owner depends crucially on the ownership structure of the firm. They have demonstrated that a manager behaves differently where he is not the sole owner of the firm from the way he behaves when he has full ownership of the firm. The idea is that with the management of any firm the managers derive utility both from pecuniary returns (such as income from the project) and non-pecuniary returns or so-called perquisites (such as an air-conditioned office, attractive secretarial staff, purchases of inputs from friends, etc.). There is always an optimal level of such perquisites consistent with the value maximization objective of the firm. When the firm is not managed by the owners, there is an incentive to carry the level of perquisites to a greater than optimal level, since the managers do not bear the entire cost of increased perquisites. Therefore the value of the firm will decline relative to what it would have been if the firm were owned by the managers.

On the other hand a similar problem exists if the manager raises funds through debt. But here it is less severe since the manager on the margin captures full benefits from the project (except in a state of bankruptcy).

Another way of incorporating the incentive effects would be to allow the investor's actions as an argument in the production function. Actions are the efforts devoted to the project by the investor. If the investor chooses an optimal level of effort, then the supply of effort will be a function of the type of contract offered. Under the assumed conditions and disregarding the problem of monitoring the level of effort, the optimal contract is still VRS since it distributes the risk optimally. But the real problem here is that the level of effort is not observable. Under these circumstances the investor will not bring an optimal level of effort in the case of the VRS since he does not pay the full reduction in the value of the firm from a sub-optimal supply of effort. Thus the loss of utility to the investor resulting from lower value of the firm is smaller than the gain he receives from supplying a sub-optimal level of effort. But a debt contract will not produce similar effects since on the margin the above trade-off will be balanced in this contract if the project is successful.

Stiglitz (1974), Jensen and Meckling (1976) and Grossman and Hart (1982), have argued that there is in fact a trade-off between the benefits of risk-spreading under equity and the incentive effects of debt, and in general there is an optimal level debt-equity ratio corresponding to maximizing behavior of the firm.

The above consideration falls into the general problem of 'moral hazard' which exists in the credit market. In Part II we will discuss this problem in detail. There we shall argue that the major reason for the preference of debt is the existence of the 'moral hazard' problem.

The assumption regarding risk aversion on the part of investors is very important for the main result of this paper. This is not an unrealistic assumption given the wide-spread use of outside equity in the capital structure of many firms. Indeed the very existence of stock markets reflects society's desire of building up institutions for shifting risk to those most suited for this purpose, namely the stockholders.

The assumption of identical beliefs about the distribution of random return is a consequence of rational expectations on each side of the market. If this is not true then it can be shown that debt will be preferred even if the investors are risk averse. If an investor knows that the probability of default is very low, then by getting funds through debt financing he can capture the upper tail of the return distribution, whereas in case of loss he loses nothing. This is also a kind of incentive problem (see Stiglitz and Weiss (1981)). Here, because of the differential information structure, investors have an incentive to undertake more risky projects than those which are in the interest of the financer. The fact that instances of full debt-financing of a firm are rare suggests that the assumption of rational expectation is a reasonable one.

Another important assumption of this paper is the costless observation of the project return by both the lender and borrower. In fact, this assumption and the separation assumption have close links since both avoid the potential problem of 'moral hazard' which would otherwise arise.

Since in practice only the investor can costlessly observe the performance of the project, one should ask what is the implication of relaxing the assumption of costless observation by the lender. Thus one needs to look at the choice of financial contract when there is asymmetrical information in the credit market. Indeed it turns out that the predominant role played by debt in the real world can be explained on the grounds of asymmetrical information in the credit market. Debt has the characteristic of minimizing the informational requirement of a financial contract and, given the costliness of information collection, debt turns out to be the most attractive instrument of finance. We postpone further discussion of this problem until Part II, where this is our main concern.

An assumption which is implicit in our formulation is the absence of any collateral requirement. In practice many debt schemes, especially in the agricultural sector in LDCs, require collateral. On the other hand, as we saw in Part I, the Islamic scheme does not have any collateral requirement. Our results will be reinforced if we introduce it in the model.

Furthermore, it is clear that the requirement of collateral restricts the entry of potential investors into the credit market. This is especially true of the agricultural sector, where small farmers have virtually no access to the organized credit market because they can not bring the required collateral, (see Agarwal (1982)). The introduction of the Islamic scheme would help to overcome this problem and consequently there would likely be a lot more investment activity in the economy.

Another important characteristic of the Islamic financial scheme, not captured by our model, is that such a financial system allows more risk taking in the economy. To see this, assume that bankruptcy is costly. Now many of the investors who plan to undertake risky projects will be denied financing under a debt scheme, because in practice financial institutions operating with fixed liabilities are not allowed to choose a portfolio beyond a specified level of associated risk (e.g., restrictions imposed by the FDIC in USA). But under an Islamic financial system no such restrictions are needed, since under such a system financial institutions will not issue fixed liabilities to their depositors. Accordingly, these institutions can finance more risky investment and thus assure a higher expected return in the economy. In fact there is a continuous decline in the volume of risky investment in Western Europe, indicating a greater desire for a financial system based on equity financing (see Albach (1981)).

PART II
INFORMATIONAL ASYMMETRY, MONITORING AND FINANCIAL CONTRACTS

In Part I we have demonstrated the superiority of the Islamic financial scheme over the traditional scheme; moreover, we have shown this result to be fairly robust, in that small deviations from the required conditions do not affect the preferability of the Islamic scheme. Given the internal consistency of our model, we must now account for the predominance, in the real world, of Fixed Return Schemes. The burden of Part II will be to show that this can be explained by the informational asymmetry which is present in the credit market.

Our problem here is the well-known problem of explaining the existence of debt in the capital structure of a firm. Thus we will draw upon the existing theories of optimal capital structure in the theory of finance, but will also offer a new explanation for the preference of debt as an instrument of finance. In the first section we review the existing work in this area and indicate the place of the present effort. Section II formally describes the problem considered and summarizes the results. Section III develops the basic model. In Section IV we again compare the two schemes under the new environment. Some concluding remarks are contained in the last section.

The Role of Debt in the Financial Structure of a Firm: A Survey

In modern business organizations, capital requirements are so immense that a single source of finance is insufficient. Therefore, large corporations in general have a diversified ownership structure. It is not difficult to understand the motivation for such an ownership structure, but it is somewhat more difficult to understand why these organizations use different kinds of financing methods. In particular, why do firms use both debt and equity to finance their capital needs?

The traditional wisdom, until the late fifties, was that the value of a firm could be increased by the judicious employment of debt in the capital structure of a firm. The controversy over the role of debt in the financial structure of a firm started after the Miller-Modigliani theorem, which states that the value of the firm is independent of its financing decisions. This is a paradoxical result, given the fact that most firms have some amount of both debt and equity in their capital structure. Many authors have tried to determine the role of debt in a firm's capital structure by relaxing the assumptions of the M-M theorem. In the beginning, efforts centered on the no-bankruptcy and no-taxes assumptions. If the probability of bankruptcy is positive (and it is costly to go bankrupt), then firms and individual borrowers cannot have equal access to credit markets. Firms can issue debt at a lower rate that individuals, and this raises the value of the firm. On the other hand, if debt payments are tax deductible, then, again, debt would be cheap relative to equity.

A different line of attack is taken by Stiglitz (1974), Jensen and Meckling (1976), and Grossman and Hart (1982). They have relaxed a different assumption of the M-M theorem: that the firm's production function is independent of its financial structure. Stiglitz and Jensen and Meckling consider the situation of an investor who has access to an investment project but does not have sufficient funds to finance it. If the investor raises funds by issuing equity, then, as he will have a less than 100 per cent interest in the project, he will not manage it as carefully as he would had he been a full owner. If on the other hand, the investor issues debt, then his incentive to work will be reduced much less since, except in bankrupt states, he gets full benefits from any increase in profits. Thus, to Stiglitz and Jensen and Meckling, debt is a way of permitting expansion without sacrificing incentives. The trade-off for the investor is between equity, which permits the sharing of risks, and issuing debt, which leads to a higher market value of the project through the incentive effect. Grossman and Hart (1982) have utilized the same idea except for the fact that they assume that the management/investor may have zero shareholding in the firm, so bankruptcy penalties have a significant effect on their model.

Ross (1977, 1978) on the other hand has given a different explanation using the signalling model. For Ross, in a world where there are firms of different quality, debt is a signal of the quality of a firm. In equilibrium the value of the firm is positively correlated with the debt-equity ratio. The idea is that, given costly bankruptcy, it is not in the interest of low quality firms to have more debt in their capital structure.

Our model is different from the above models. Bankruptcy is not costly in our model, nor is there differential tax treatment across different financial instruments. We have assumed that the production function is independent of the financial structure and that there are no quality differences across firms. In other words our model does not rely on (i) imperfections in the capital market, (ii) differential tax treatment, (iii) incentive effects or signalling potential of debt. *Rather we find a role for debt on the ground that it minimizes the information requirement of a financial contract, when the performance of the project is not observable by the financial institution.*

Since our motivation for the present analysis is to examine the implications of prohibiting debt from the economy, we will argue later in this paper that the success of this proposal depends on the availability of information in the economy. The implementation of a profit sharing system as the basis for financial intermediation will force financial institution to invest additional resources in information collecting activities. These information costs are a deadweight loss to the society, and as such the introduction of the new system may lead to a Pareto inferior outcome.

Basic Problem and Results

In this section we informally describe the problem considered in this part and summarize the results.

Assume that there is a financial institution extending loans to an investor. Also, as in Part I the supply of loanable funds is fixed. Moreover, both the lender and the financial institution have identical beliefs about the probability distribution of the return from the project where funds are invested.

The payoffs to the lender and investor are under FRS and VRS are the same as in Part I.

It was demonstrated in Part I that in the absence of any kind of informational problem, the Pareto optimal contract is the VRS. Our objective now is to show that the predominant role played by the fixed return contracts is the result of informational asymmetry.

The basic problem considered in this section of the paper is the following:

When the lender extends a loan to an investor, the investor observes the return of the project without incurring any costs while the lender cannot observe the return. If it is prohibitively expensive for the lender to observe the return then the market for financial loans will not exist. There is, in the case of the lender's inability to observe the project's performance, a strong incentive problem: investors wil tend to under-report the project's performance. Thus the best strategy for the lender is not to extend any loan.

Although the problem of informational asymmetry is a severe one it does not necessarily lead to market failure, for there are safety mechanisms like collateral, auditing, participation in the board of directors of the firm, and other forms of monitoring which to a large extent resolve the problem of informational asymmetry. Furthermore, in a multiperiod framework the fear of losing reputation in the credit market can function as a strong incentive for investors to refrain from misrepresentation. Indeed, the types of contracts offered in the credit market are designed to resolve the incentive problem.[2]

Therefore in the present analysis we allow for the possibility of monitoring the performance of the project by the lender at some expense. Later in this paper we will reflect on the practical feasibility of monitoring investment projects by the financial institutions.

Given the possibility of monitoring, a few questions remain. What types of monitoring technologies are available and what are the characteristics of an optimal monitoring technology? How does the monitoring technology differ across these two types of contract? Given optimal monitoring technologies across these schemes, is there some basis for choosing between them? Similarly we must look at the behavior of an investor to determine his optimal response for under-reporting the project return.

We summarize our results below:

(i) The optimal monitoring technology is a randomized strategy which gives the probability of monitoring a reported return. It allows investors to under-report only to the extent that the gain from monitoring is equal to the cost of monitoring. The probability of monitoring goes down for a given reported return the higher is the cost of monitoring.

(ii) Given a uniform distribution of returns, the expected monitoring costs are lower under the FRS. Since these costs are a deadweight loss to the society, this loss is greater under the VRS. This result in general depends on the density of returns. For the densities having smaller mass below D, the FRS dominates, while for others the result would change.

(iii) The choice of a particular contract crucially depends on the attitude towards risk of the investor. There is no straightforward dominance of either scheme if investors are risk averse. Though FRS minimizes the monitoring costs it does not spread the risk optimally. Thus, for a sufficiently high degree of risk aversion, VRS may dominate FRS.

(iv) The above results can be used to provide an explanation of why the *M-M* theorem does not hold in a world of informational asymmetry. An expanding firm looking for outside sources of finance may find it more attractive to borrow funds on the basis of the FRS rather than to issue equity.

The Model

Suppose both the lender and the investors believe that R is uniformly distributed in $(d, 1)$, where d is some positive constant which is different across two schemes.[3] The assumption of uniform distribution is made for convenience. Though some of the results do depend on this specification, the essential features of the solution are independent.

Let G be the space of all possible ways of under-reporting the return. The investor picks G which translates R into some reported return, i.e.,

$$g: (d, 1) \rightarrow (d, 1) \tag{1}$$

Let H be the space of all possible ways of monitoring the reported return $g(r)$. In general H is a very large space and includes things like collateral, auditing, participation in the management, etc. But we restrict H to include only the ways in which the lender makes a decision whether or not to go for auditing. That is, after looking at the reported return the lender may either decide that it is acceptable, or he may subject it to auditing. In case the lender decides to have it audited, he can look at the accounts of the firm or ask the firm to verify its accounts by independent auditors. We assume that monitoring (auditing) is perfect in the sense that once the lender receives the results from the monitor, he knows for sure what the true return was. Furthermore there is no separate problem of recovery. Thus the lender picks $h \in H$ that describes the monitoring possibilities. Note that $h = 0$ if he decides not to monitor a given reported return, whereas $h = 1$ means he surely monitors. If h takes a value in the interval (0, 1) then we interpret it as giving the probability of monitoring a given reported return. In other words, the lender may choose either a pure strategy ($h = 0$, or $h = 1$) or a randomized strategy. The same is true of the investor relative ot his under-reporting strategies. Thus:

$$h: (d, 1) \rightarrow (0, 1) \tag{2}$$

The optimal h and g will have different characteristics. They will depend on the cost of monitoring and the optimal h, respectively.

Let b be some fixed cost of monitoring. The problem of the investor is to choose $g(r) \in G$ for a given $h(g; b)$ to maximize

$$\max EU(Y) = EU(Y(r, g, h(g, b))) \tag{3}$$

where r is the observed value of R and $Y(.)$ is the payoff to the investor. U is the utility function. The solution of (3) gives the optimal under-reporting strategy of the investor which is the mapping:

$$g^*(r): (d, 1)\, XH \rightarrow (d, 1) \tag{4}$$

On the other hand, the lender's problem is to choose $h \in H$ for a given $g(r)$, to maximize

$$\max EU(P) = EU(P(h(g, b), g(r))) \tag{5}$$

The solution to (5) gives the optimal h, which is the mapping:

$$h^*: (d, 1)\, XG \rightarrow (0,1) \tag{6}$$

Equations (3)–(6) define the game whose solution is what we are looking for. The solution (Nash Equilibrium) of the game is the pair (g^*, h^*) satisfying:

$$EU(Y(g^*, h^*)) \geq EU(Y(g, \mathrm{h}^*)) \text{ for all } g \in G \tag{7}$$

$$EU(P(g^*, h^*)) \geq EU(P(g^*, h)) \text{ for all } g \in H$$

In what follows we will solve the game explicitly across both the contracts.

Solution Under VRS

In this contract the investor, observing r, reports $g(r)$, out of which $(1, a)g(r)$ is given to the lender. If he is monitored then he loses $(1 - a)(r - g(r))$; thus his expected payoff is given as:

$$Y^V = r - (1 - a)g(r) - h(g)(1 - a)(r - g(r)) \tag{8}$$

Although the investor is assumed to be risk averse, for the moment we shall ignore the utility function and maximize (8) over $g(r)$. The solution of (8) is given by:

$$g^*(r) = r + (1 - h(g))/h'(g) \tag{9}$$

where $h'(g(r)) = dh(g(r))/dg(r)$ indicates the change in the probability of monitoring when the investor reports more. Note that we should expect $h'(g) < 0$. If the probability of monitoring is unaffected by how much the investor reports, then the investor will report the minimum possible return. In fact this is the dominant strategy for the investor. Since there is no explicit penalty for under-reporting, an investor loses nothing (in a single period model) by taking a chance and under-reporting to the fullest possible extent.

Therefore a monitoring technology which induces investors to report more should have an inverse relationship with the reported return. As such there will be an implicit penalty for under-reporting in the form of increasing the probability of monitoring. Thus the investor faces a trade-off between the loss from reporting more and a decrease in the chances of being monitored, when he reports more. The first order condition which yields (9) shows the point where the two things are balanced.

The payoff to the lender under the VRS is given by:

$$E(P^V) = \int_d^1 \cdot [(1 - a)g(r) + h(g,b)(1 - a)(r - g(r) - b)]\, mdr \tag{10}$$

where $m = 1/(1 - d)$.

Note that r cannot be an argument in his maximizing problem since he does not observe r. However we can still maximize (10) by maximizing only the integrand for a given $g(r)$.

We have assumed that monitoring is perfect in the sense that whenever the lender monitors he knows for sure what the true value of r was. In particular this assumption has the implication that in equilibrium the lender can figure out the entire $g(r,.)$ mapping. But this requires that $g(r,.)$ should be invertable for r. For if this were not possible then the lender could never determine the feasibility of monitoring. Hence, he would never engage in the contract.

Let C be the costs of monitoring under the VRS; then

$$E(C^V) = \int_{g(r)}^{bh} (g(r))\, dg(r) \tag{11}$$

is the expected monitoring cost under the VRS.

Now we have the following proposition giving the solution pair for the VRS:

PROPOSITON-1: Let (Y^V, p^V, g, h, C^V) be the game defined above. Then the Nash solution is given by the pair

$$(g^*, h^*) = (r - b/1 - a, 1 - \exp - [(1 - a) \cdot (1 - g(r) - b)/b]) \tag{12}$$

and minimizes the expected cost of monitoring.

Proof: In Appendix 3.

The optimal strategy of the investor is a pure one. This makes sense since the lender, after observing r, can report anything in the interval (0, 1), which is a convex and compact set. Given the optimal strategy of the lender, the best he can do is to under-report only to the extent that the lender is indifferent between monitoring and not monitoring. This can be seen by rewriting $G^*(r)$ as:

$$(1 - a)(r - g^*(r)) = b \tag{13}$$

The left hand side is the gain from monitoring to the lender while b is the cost of monitoring.

On the other hand, the lender's optimal strategy is randomized monitoring. To see that this makes sense, assume that the lender is restricted to a pure strategy. His optimal strategy would then be to monitor all the time, for if he did not, the investor would under-report to the fullest extent possible. But even with constant monitoring, the optimal strategy of the investor remains reporting the minimum possible return. Indeed, this is the dominant strategy of the investor. Furthermore, under this equilibrium, full monitoring costs would be incurred. Another problem that arises here is the instability of this equilibrium, because in the presence of a small penalty there is no Nash equilibrium. Moreover, if one investor tells the truth, this would be sufficient to render the lender's strategy sub-optimal.

Thus we have demonstrated that neither constant monitoring nor no monitoring can be optimal. Randomization of the lender's strategy also induces the investor not to under-report outright. Thus as we expected $h < 0$. This, in fact, acts like an implicit penalty which provides investors an incentive to refrain from outright misrepresentation.

Another important characteristic of this monitoring technology is its relation to the cost of monitoring. As one might expect, the technology is an inverse function of the cost of monitoring. For a given level of reported return the probability of monitoring decreases as the cost of monitoring increases. Note that for a sufficiently high value of b no monitoring takes place.

Solution Under FRS

In this contract, the investor observing r, reports $g(r)$ that is given to the lender. Note that here there is no need for reporting $g(r) > D$. At most $g(r) = D$. Thus the investor's payoff is given by:

$$Y^F = r - g(r) - h(g(r))\,(\min\,(r, D) - g(r)) \qquad (16)$$

maximizing (17) over $g(r)$ gives:

$$g^*(r) = \min\,(r, D) + (1 - h(g(r)))/h' \qquad (18)$$

The payoff to the lender on the other hand is given by:

$$E(P^F) = \int_d^1 \cdot\, [g(r) + h(g(r))\,(\min\,(r, D) - g(r) - b)] \cdot mdr \qquad (19)$$

Maximizing along the same line as in case of the VRS we can get the optimal h.

Let C^F be the cost of monitoring under the FRS; then

$$E(C^F) = bh(g(r))dg(r) \qquad (20)$$

gives the expected monitoring cost under the FRS.

We now have the following proposition:

PROPOSITION-2: Let (Y^F, P^F, g, h, C^F) be the game defined above for the FRS. Then the Nash solution is given by the pair:

$$(g^*, h^*) = (\min\,(r, D) - b; 1 - \exp - [(D - b - g(r)]) \qquad (21)$$

and minimizes the expected cost of monitoring.

Proof: In Appendix 3.

The optimal strategies of the lender and the investor are the same except for the parametric differences across the two contracts. Here the extent of under-reporting is b rather than $b/1 - a$ and the lender does not monitor above $D - b$. The optimal payoffs corresponding to (21) and the expected monitoring costs are given in Appendix 2.

In the next section, we develop a criterion which allows us to compare the two schemes and which also helps in the selection of type of contract.

Comparison of Two Schemes

In the preceding section we have demonstrated that in the presence of informational asymmetry monitoring costs exist across both kinds of contract. Thus the choice of scheme should somehow take into account the existence of these costs. In what follows, we will argue that the size of these costs determines the choice of the contract.

Given the fact that there is just one financial institution in the model, it seems natural to assume that it only cares about the expected return across the two schemes. Even if it is risk averse, an appeal to the law of large numbers, as in Part I, would allow the lender to look only at the expected return. Since the VRS is a continuous scheme in the sense that for every D there is an a such that the lender's expected payoff across the two kinds of contract is identical, the choice betweem them again hinges upon the preference of the investor. Thus we first look at the conditions under which the lender is indifferent across both types of contract. This can be accomplished in two different ways:

(i) The lender can equalize the payoffs under the two schemes with the information costs. This means that for every D we need to find an a such that:

$$E(P^F) = E(P^V)$$

Then at this point we look at the behavior of the investor to see which scheme will be chosen.

(ii) The lender can equalize the payoffs under the two schemes as well as across the two situations (with or without information costs). This means that he passes on the monitoring costs to the investor in the form of a lower 'a' and a higher 'D'. Then again at this point we can look at the preference of the investor.

For its computational ease we take the second approach. The following proposition determines the size of the monitoring costs across the two contracts:

PROPOSITION-3: Let R be a uniformly distributed random return. Choose a and D so that

$$E(P^F) = E(P^V)$$

Then the expected monitoring costs under the FRS are smaller than under VRS.

Proof: In Appendix 3.

The second condition in the proposition gives a point of reference by establishing a link between a and D, the parameters of the two contracts.

This is intuitively the most important result of this paper, and it is central to our claim that the predominant role played by the fixed rate transactions in the real world is the result of informational asymmetry in the credit market.

Under the FRS type of transactions, since the lender requires a fixed return, only a reported return below that fixed return is suspicious. As such, monitoring need not take place above this return. On the other hand, under the VRS the upper limit on monitoring is much higher. This makes monitoring more frequent under VRS.

There is another interesting difference across the two schemes. Under FRS, below D whatever is discovered goes to the lender, whereas under the VRS only $(1 - a)$, of this discovery goes to the lender. Thus for small values of return there will be little inclination for monitoring under the VRS. But this last fact is disguised by the assumption of uniform distribution. As such, we get a straightforward dominance of the VRS because of its feature of minimizing expected monitoring costs.

In general the result depends on the probability mass of R below D. For the densities having smaller mass below D the above result holds, while for others it may reverse. Assuming that the lender will behave competitively, he will pass on these costs to the investors in the form of higher D and lower a. This fact is established in the following lemma:

LEMMA-1: Let $(1 - a)$, $(1 - a')$, D, and D' denote the share and the fixed return of the lender without and with information costs respectively. Then if the lender equalizes his return across the two schemes under both situation, then:

$a' < a$

$D' > D$

Proof: In Appendix 3.

Now we are in a position to state the fundamental result of this part.

PROPOSITION-4: The choice of a financial contract depends on investor's attitude toward risk. For a sufficiently low degree of risk aversion the FRS dominates over the VRS.

Proof: In Appendix 3.

Thus we have shown that one of the most important reasons for the preference of the FRS type of financial contracts is the informational asymmetry in the financial markets. A debt contract minimizes the information requirement associated with any financial contract. Given that information collection is costly, this contract appears most attractive.

In the next section we will comment on the feasibility of monitoring under the Islamic financial system.

Monitoring Under the New Financial System

The analysis in the preceding section is based on the assumption that the lender is in a position to monitor the performance of the project at some expense.

The results point to the existence of higher monitoring costs under the Islamic scheme. In fact we have argued that observed dominance of debt schemes is the result of its cost-minimizing characteristics. Debt contracts require the least organizational costs and hence are popular throughout the world. The additional costs under the new system primarily stem from the fact that being a partner in a firm requires more active vigilance of the firm's activities in order to protect one's interests. A creditor of the firm does not have an equivalent stake in the firm.

A natural question that arises is whether the resulting costs are so prohibitive as to cast doubt over the viability of the new system. There are a number of considerations which point to the fact that the additional costs will not be prohibitive.

First, the problem of 'moral-hazard' we have described is not unique to the financial sector. In fact it mainly exists in the insurance business, which has, over a long period of time, evolved efficient methods to combat the problem. The solution has been primarily in the form of designing 'incentive compatible' policies which either eliminate or minimize the incentive for misrepresentation by the insured. The ever increasing coverage provided by the industry is a reflection of the fact that it has steadily found ways to provide insurance in areas where, because of lack of information, it could not have provided it earlier.

Second, the information collection industries are decreasing cost industries, since this activity requires fixed costs of considerable size. Therefore such an activity can be performed efficiently by a single firm in the industry. If there is a large financial institution, as we have assumed in our model, then the resulting costs can be minimized.

Third, in modern corporations a large amount of equity is owned by individual shareholders. Individual holdings are, however, small relative to the total assets of the corporation. This generates an externality: a shareholder acting individually cannot monitor the actions of the managers who thus acquire a great deal of decisionmaking power, which may not be in the best interest of all owners. On the other hand, when these corporations issue debt, especially to banks, the banks closely watch the performance of the managers. Since bank loans are a sizable portion of total capital, in order to attract bank financing, managers agree to refrain from certain actions which they would normally take.[4] Therefore banks to a large extent are able to internalize this externality. The new system can hope to derive one of its most important benefits from such internalization of this externality. When a financial institution holds a large part of a firm's equity, one should expect that the lender would be more energetic in monitoring the firm's activities than when the lender issues debt. Given this increased participation of the financier, one can also hope for a better overall performance by those managers who have little, if any, self interest in the corporation.

Fourth, there are already in place systems which are more complex than the system of profit and loss sharing under examination here, and which have an excellent performance record. For example, all taxation systems in which taxes are directly collected are forms of PLS. In some developed countries, such as the USA, direct tax collections are as high as 80 per cent of total collections. The system of income tax can be thought of as a system of revenue-sharing between government and individuals, because a certain percentage of unknown income is taken as tax. Each year millions of taxpayers report their income and pay taxes. There is a huge monitoring expenditure incurred by the state to correctly assess the incomes of the individuals. The existence of such a system is the required proof of its viability.

Finally, one should also allow for those benefits which the new system will bring about. These are, as we noted earlier, greater risk-spreading and more risk-taking. Also, there is the advantage of greater stability in financial intermediation.[5]

In the light of all these considerations, we conclude that the monitoring costs will not be prohibitive for the new system. Of course there is a painful transitional period which the new system will have to face. Much depends on the ability of financial institutions to develop effective monitoring methods. This cannot be done in a short period of time; consequently, a gradually evolving change would seem the right course of action.

CONCLUSIONS

In this paper, we have sought to provide an analysis of the effects, on the demand side, of prohibiting *ribā* from the economy. We found in Part I that, under a given set of assumptions, the Islamic financial scheme was superior to the traditional scheme because of the risk-spreading character of the former. But when, in Part II, the assumption of asymmetric information between lender and investor was relaxed, the debt contract emerged as the most efficient type of contract because it minimizes the monitoring costs associated with asymmetric information.

The major finding of this paper is that the Islamic financial system is superior to a non-Islamic system if there is no dishonesty. To us, as to many others, this is not a very surprising result. But at the same time, the requirement of honesty for the success of the Islamic system is very stringent. Perhaps the deepest question raised by this research is whether the efforts of Islamization, especially with respect to the implementation of the Islamic economic system, would be successful or not. The answer in the very short run seems to be negative.

But we strongly reject the implication that these efforts should be abandoned. Certainly society will have to pay a very high price for Islamization, and indeed the benefits of Islam, as history shows, come after sacrifices are made. One must also consider the benefits society might be expected to derive from the preservation of spiritual values. Thus, policy makers should weigh carefully the benefit/cost of this policy change.

It is very important that the other institutions based on non-Islamic principles should also be changed. This is a long run menu, and one should not expect a miracle to change everything in the desired direction overnight. But in the short run, costly partial moves can be sustained in the hope of dynamic gains from the changing attitudes in the society over a longer period of time.

The problem of dishonesty is to a large extent overemphasized in our model, which is a single period model. In our opinion dishonesty is a function of the incentive structures afforded by the society, and also, in a value-oriented society, of the fear of God. The second factor is by-and-large exogenous and can only be changed in the very long run. We believe that the short run costs can be minimized by devising incentive structures that ensure the honesty of agents endogenously.

The credit market is the kind of market where agents transact repeatedly. It is possible, therefore, to device financial schemes embodying incentive mechanisms, so that agents reveal the truth even if they are not sufficiently afraid of God. This is the area of research where Islamic economists will have to devote most of their energies if successful replacement of the present financial system is to occur.

NOTES

*I am thankful to the member of my committee, profs. Michael Manove, Asad Zaman (Columbia University), Oldrich Kyn and Ingo Vogalsang. I assume the responsibility of all errors and omissions and the views expressed here.

1. For a detailed analysis of this claim see Khan, W. (1983), Chapter 4.
2. See the literature on the principal/agent problem, Albach, M. (1981), Khan, W. (1983), Ross, S. (1977), Rothschild, M. & Stiglitz, J. (1979). The primary problem is to resolve the conflicting interests of the principal/agent through the nature of the contract.
3. This assumption is made to address a technical problem that arises in the inversion of the investor under-reporting function.
4. See Jensen and Meckling (1976).
5. For detailed discussion see Waqar M. Khan (1983).

5

An Economic Analysis of a PLS Model for the Financial Sector

Shahrukh Rafi Khan

Reprinted from *The Pakistan Journal of Applied Economics,* Vol. III, No. 2, (1984). Shahrukh Rafi Khan is at the Pakistan Institute of Development Economics, Pakistan.

I. INTRODUCTION

Two related issues are central to this paper. The first issue is the substitution of profit and loss sharing (PLS) for interest as a basis for conducting financial transactions in the market for loanable funds. PLS is a financial mechanism linking finance capital to industry and commerce without the use of interest. Essentially it is a form of equity capital where lenders have a share in the profits of the borrowers, if there are any, and are also liable to share in the losses which are incurred during normal business practice. The share in the profits rather than a specific rate of return are prespecified in the contract. How the market may be relied upon to determine shares is discussed later.

The second issue is the abolition of the banking system in its present form in the market oriented economies, and the substitution in its stead of institutions that are solely intermediaries between lenders and borrowers.

Both these issues are related to the functioning of an economy with *ribā.* This concept has been defined broadly as any kind of gain for which a corresponding socially productive countervalue was not forthcoming.[1] As it turns out, this definition prohibits the earning of income from interest, speculative activity, absentee land ownership, and profits accruing due to a monopoly position. Given such a definition, one set of policies related to an institutional change of the financial sector—to make it *ribā*-free—include the substitution of PLS for interest and the conversion of banks into pure intermediaries in a monetary sense. It is important to bear in mind that PLS is only one element—albeit a pivotal alone—in a package which is geared towards establishing a *ribā*-free economy.

This paper is subdivided into seven sections. In the second section, profits are briefly defined using sources that also set the context for the PLS contract. In section three, the basic PLS model is outlined formally. In section four, PLS is compared with conventional banking methods to show how returns to lenders and borrowers fare under these alternative arrangements. A simple portfolio model is presented in which the "Islamic case" of allowing only PLS is contrasted with a "capitalist case" that allows first only fixed interest, and then both fixed interest and PLS. The results of these comparisons with respect to the supply of loanable funds are utilized in the next section.

Section five is concerned with the mechanics of the PLS model itself—the primary focus of the article. The supply and demand for loanable funds are described, following which the working of the loanable fund market under PLS is briefly analyzed. Section six considers some extensions of the basic PLS model, relaxing the assumption of a purely intermediary role for banks.

Much of the literature on PLS banking is concerned with its operational details. These include the establishment and management of PLS banks; monetary policy and the operational relationship between central and commercial banks; the making of interest-free consumer loans; the creation of reserve funds and other schemes to insulate depositors from losses on paper; the criteria for making loans; issues dealing with short-term loans and discounting bills of exchange; the ways of dealing with bad debts; the mechanisms for providing security for banks; the outlets for appeals for those whose applications for loans were turned down; and the basis of international financial transactions in a PLS banking system.[2]

For the most part, the present paper ignores such operational issues, and is concerned with producer loans in a closed economy. As indicated above, most of the issues to be dealt with are analytical. These issues have received less attention in the literature.[3]

II. PROFITS

From an Islamic perspective, the concept of PLS can make sense only if the origin of that profit itself is not based on *ribā* but rather on some form of productive activity.

Clearly, a review of the various theories of profit is outside the scope of this paper, especially since several reviews already exist.[4] The broad view of profit, as residual income after all the (fixed) contractual payments, is utilized here. The views of two leading economists, whose theories fit into this mould, are used to briefly outline the framework underlying the PLS contract.

Schumpeter (1963) attributes residual income to entrepreneurial innovation. Profits, and in fact economic development, result from "new combinations" or innovations which are the outcome of entrepreneurial action.

Profits arise from innovation because of a lag in imputation. Entrepreneurs pay for resources at the prices set by previous uses. Innovations enable a more productive combination of those resources and hence lead to a surplus.

At least two issues need consideration. Given the assumption of perfect foresight normally made in the analysis of a perfectly competitive economy, there would not be the lag in imputation which is required by Schumpeter to explain profits. Furthermore, while Schumpeter's theory justifies a return to the entrepreneur (borrower), it does not justify, from the ethical perspective earlier referred to, the return to the lender. Interest in his larger theory [Schumpeter, (1963), pp. 155–211], is merely a tax on profits.

These issues can be dealt with by examining Knight's (1964) theory of profit. This is usually presented as an alternative theory, although it is actually an extension of, and a complement to, Schumpeter's theory. Knight (1964) relaxes the assumption of perfect foresight and defines uncertainty as a condition under which objective probabilities cannot bc assigned to a distribution of outcomes of an economic action. Knight goes on to argue that where uncertainty is absent, the imputation of product values to product services will always be perfect and exhaustive, and profit will be absent except stochastically [Knight, (1964), p. 98]. Profit is once again unimputable income, but it arises because, due to chance, there is a divergence of actual conditions from those that were anticipated. Factor incomes are determined by the competitive process on the basis of anticipated rather than actual conditions, and the residual value from sale of output, if positive, is profit [Knight, (1964), p. 98]. Profits, on average, will be positive due to innovations.

On the basis of this reasoning, Knight (1964) asserts that it is uncertainty which leads to profit. He does admit that the precondition of uncertainty is "change," which is defined in much the same way as in the Schumpeter model (pp. 141–173). It is for this reason that the two theories really complement each other; change is the source of the profit, while uncertainty is the basis of its realization.

Knight's (1964) breakdown of the entrepreneurial function into its various elements also serves to resolve the second of the two issues mentioned above. The two functions of the entrepreneur are control and guarantee [Knight, (1964), p. 284], both of which arise from the existence of uncertainty. Control is very closely tied to the innovative function of the Schumpeterian entrepreneur, since without that, a routine and purely managerial function for the entrepreneur would be adequate.

The guarantee function refers to the bearing of uncertainty. Since most productive resources require an *a priori* commitment to remuneration for their services (contract income), the guarantor shoulders the uncertainty in providing this contract income and settling for a return from the residual income if that is positive. This is in fact how PLS may be expected to operate, with the borrowers assuming the entrepreneurial role of innovation and control, and the lenders that of providing the guarantee. Since bearing uncertainty (tied to socially productive enterprise) is considered productive activity in Islam, the profit-share of the lender in his role of the guarantor would be legally justified.

Schumpeter's entrepreneur—in this case starting from the static state—is totally dependent on credit to be able to carry out his plans. Banks create the purchasing power or claims to resources by means of which entrepreneurs can bid away resources from their existing uses [Schumpeter (1963), p. 73]. A temporary increase in the price level is inevitable (length depending on gestation periods), but ultimately deflation would result from the new influx of goods and services onto the market. Banks thus play a very crucial role in the development process, and it is precisely this role which makes their characterization as mere intermediaries inaccurate, on Schumpeter's view.

This is the point where this analysis has to differ, for operational reasons, from Schumpeter's. We accept the assertion that reform of the banking sector along Islamic lines not only requires abolishing interest but also requires the conversion of banks into pure intermediaries. Not only does this deny the banks (as a whole) the ability to create purchasing power, but in every other way denies them any stake in profit. The reasons for this exclusion, according to Islamic scholars, are two fold. The first is based on the empirical observation that controllers of credit inevitably attain an unwarranted amount of influence and power. This would lead to *ribā* insofar as it would enable powerful bankers to dictate terms to comparatively weaker depositors and borrowers. Beyond this, where fractional reserve banking is permitted, bankers have the ability to draw profits on funds that they have in no way expended productive effort in earning.[5] However, the question that immediately arises is: Can an orderly functioning financial market continue to exist after these fundamental changes? Let us now outline the PLS system.

III. PROFIT AND LOSS SHARING MODEL

The two active agents to a PLS contract are the lenders of funds (also referred to as depositors) and the borrowers of funds (also referred to as entrepreneurs). Banks will in general be assumed to play the purely intermediary role of bringing the two parties to the contract together. This assumption will be dropped in section six, where banks will be considered active parties to the contract.

As a pure intermediary, the bank provides a service for both parties, and it covers its administrative expenses by charging both parties a fee. If in a conventional banking system, the difference between lending and borrowing rates of interest includes a profit margin, then this differential exceeds the total administrative fee by the extent of that margin.

This leaves the shares of the active parties to the contract to be determined. To begin with, the *muḍārabah* contract, where all funds are provided by the lenders, will be considered. In section six, the *mushārakah* contract, where the entrepreneurs also provide part of the funds for the project, say from retained earnings, will be analysed.

Let π be the average operating surplus (residual income, after all costs contracted on a fixed income basis have been subtracted from total revenue) that results from entrepreneurial activity. Let ρ be the share of this surplus forwarded to depositors in PLS accounts in the bank. We will illustrate in section five how ρ is determined in the market for loanable funds.

Given the above symbols, one can state the following:

$\rho\pi$ = share of the operating surplus forwarded to depositors in PLS accounts;

$(1 - \rho)\,\pi$ = share of the operating surplus retained by the entrepreneurs.

If κ represents the total funds forwarded by depositors, and the operating surplus accruing on these deposits is $\rho\pi$; then one can define a profit rate, r, where $r = (\pi/k)$. Hence, the profit rate for the depositors would be, $rd = (\rho\pi/k)$.

The most noticeable difference of PLS, as defined above, from the conventional debt financing for a fixed interest rate is that lenders are being constrained not only to shoulder the "risk" of project failures (which is always there) but also to settle for a variable return.[6] The implications of this constraint are analyzed in the next section.

IV. PLS VERSUS CONVENTIONAL BANKING

Two points are central to a comparison of PLS (equity financing) with conventional debt financing. First, what are likely to be the returns, on average, to the parties under these two contracts? Second, what is the incidence of risk borne by the parties under these two contracts? A convenient framework has been developed by Tobin (1958) to analyse these issues.

We proceed with the standard assumption that the contracting parties are risk averse. Then using the neo-classical portfolio balance framework to adjust for risk aversion (the best that can be done, given that uncertainty is not measurable), one can show that, irrespective of the value of ρ, the elimination of risk-free assets with a positive return (in a pure PLS system) is a constraint on the financial system that will inevitably make lenders less well off. To demonstrate this, the portfolio model as presented in Branson [(1979), pp. 251–258] is modified slightly to incorporate PLS.

Under PLS without risk-free assets, the lender has to bear the risk that is inherent in the productive activity itself. Thus, the two assets in this model are PLS claims and money, instead of bonds and money. Suppose risk under PLS is estimated from the probability distribution (normal) of expected returns on PLS deposits and represented by σ.[7] Then, if the total liquid wealth available for lending in PLS accounts is W, the total risk, σ_T, incurred on account of that lending must be σW, assuming all funds in PLS accounts are forwarded for use by entrepreneurs.

$$\sigma_T = \sigma W \tag{1}$$

Similarly, if r_{-1} is the profit rate that prevailed in the last period, then the current expected profit for depositors is

$$r_\epsilon = \frac{\rho\pi - 1}{k - 1} \tag{2}$$

and total expected return is

$$R = r_\epsilon W \tag{3}$$

(assuming that the lender's profit expectations are based on last period's profit rate). Substituting $W = \sigma_T/\sigma$ from equation (1) into equation (3) results in

$$R = r_\epsilon \frac{\sigma_T}{\sigma} \tag{4}$$

In Figure 1 below, the upper right quadrant shows the budget line representing the trade-off between risk and return. Its slope can be arrived at by differentiating equation (4) with respect to σ_T

$$\frac{\partial R}{\partial \sigma_T} = \frac{r_\epsilon}{\sigma} \tag{5}$$

The geometrical device in the lower right quadrant enables one to read the level of risk undertaken corresponding to the extent of liquid wealth a lender has in PLS accounts. That this is the case can be seen by differentiating equation (1) with respect to σ_T:

$$\frac{\partial W}{\partial \sigma_T} = \frac{1}{\sigma} \tag{6}$$

W max on the vertical axis of the lower quadrant represents the point where all funds are deposited into PLS accounts. Using equation (6), one can read off from the lower quadrant σ_T max as the maximum total level of risk that corresponds to (W max x $1/\sigma = \sigma_T$ max). Using equation (5), one can read off from the upper quadrant R max as

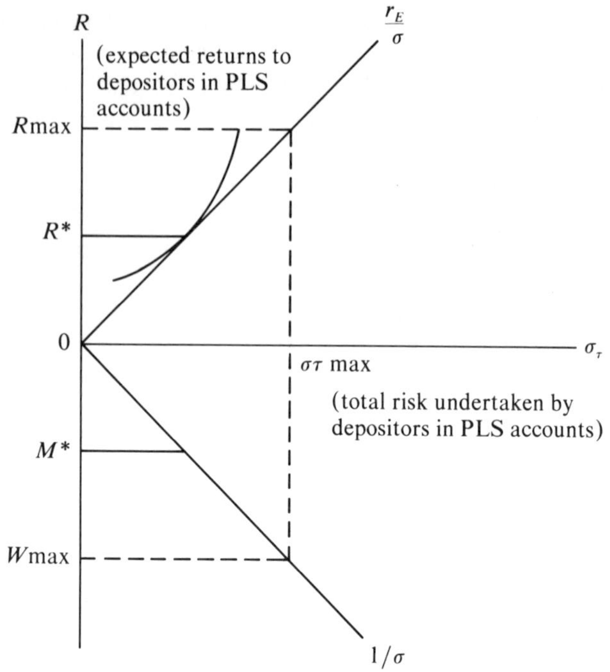

Figure 1
Portfolio selection between PLS and money

the maximum expected return which σ_T max corresponds to $[\sigma_T \max x(r_\epsilon/\sigma) = R \max]$.

So the information summarised in equations (5) and (6), when graphed, results in the two lines with the slope of (r_ϵ/σ) and $1/\sigma$. We can superimpose a preference ordering for a risk averse individual on the budget line represented by equation (5). The tangency of the budget line with the indifference curve represents the optimal portfolio balance between holding money and depositing it into PLS accounts as shown below, (see Figure 1).

The starred items below represent the optimal risk-return configuration for the lender. Corresponding to that is the optimal distribution of total wealth between PLS accounts (OM^*) and money (M^*W). Corresponding to OM^* in PLS accounts is OR^*, the expected return to the lender.

One result that follows from this analysis is that the supply of funds for profit-sharing accounts would vary positively with ρ given π_{-1}

(where $r_\epsilon = \rho \pi_{-1}/k_{-1}$). This result would come about because a higher ρ would lead to a higher budget line and hence show wealth diverted into the PLS accounts and away from checking accounts representing the demand for money to hold.

Let us now proceed to outline the argument that the addition of minimum risk assets within the PLS banking system would make the lenders better off within the context of a portfolio balance model. Let a guaranteed interest, *i*, on savings accounts be the additional asset. The third asset would now change the budget line into the budget-set $0iWx$ as shown in Figure 2 below. 0 represents a point of all money and zero risk. iW represents the maximum return (with zero risk) on savings accounts with a positive rate of interest. Finally, x represents the maximum return (with maximum risk) derived from putting all of one's funds into PLS accounts. The budget-set represents a linear combination of these three points. Since iWx dominates a linear combination of money and PLS, the lender is unambiguously made better off, as one might expect, from the introduction of a guaranteed interest saving account.[8]

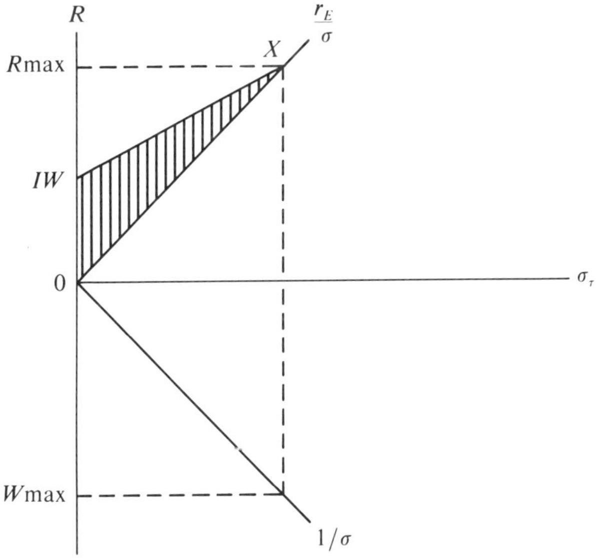

Figure 2

Portfolio selection between PLS., money and interest bearing saving accounts

Perhaps a more meaningful comparison would be that between PLS and a conventional financial system without PLS that offers the lenders a whole range of options (excluding PLS) to balance their risk and return depending on their preference function. This comparison is complicated due to an additional and qualitatively different element of risk that is introduced due to the possibility of realising capital gains or losses on financial assets. Under PLS, risk is related only to the variability of profit as arising from production and fluctuations in economic activity. Secondly, there is no way to relate *a priori* i with r. Thus, since the critical elements in the model are different, the comparison becomes difficult. Adding to this complexity is the likelihood that the aggregate preference function itself may change in a Muslim country due to the introduction of a *ribā*-free system.

Thus, it cannot be shown that the replacement of a conventional financial system by PLS would unambiguously leave the lenders better or worse off. However, the welfare of a lender would be higher under PLS if "risk-free" financial assets with a positive return were also available.

V. THE MARKET FOR LOANABLE FUNDS

a) Supply of Loanable Funds:

Due to the reasons adduced in section IV, little can be theoretically established about the position of the supply curve that would result from the substitution of PLS for a conventional banking system although it is likely that the supply of loanable funds would decline if the interest option were no longer available and lenders were constrained to take a risk to get a return, as in PLS.

Based on what was discussed in the last section, the supply function can be written as: $s = f(\sigma, r_\epsilon)$ (where r is the expected profit rate) and graphed with a positive slope with respect to ρ.

Some speculation about the supply of loanable funds under PLS is possible. One could argue that some funds will be drawn from hoarding into PLS accounts that claim to be *ribā*-free. On the other hand, some people will avoid committing their funds to such accounts due to the absence of "risk-free" returns on deposits; instead they may seek non-monetary forms of investment such as land, durable goods, real estate, jewelry, or seek havens for their capital abroad.

Apart from capital outflows and hoarding, it is not clear that the funds that are exchanged in the rest of the transactions mentioned above are diverted from the pool of funds available for productive investment in PLS accounts. This is so because there is always someone who ends up with the funds expended in these transactions. However, given that only part of these funds may be forwarded into PLS accounts (and part again expended on the above mentioned transactions), the flow of funds into PLS accounts, over time, will be reduced.

b) Demand for Loanable Funds:

The demand curve for loanable funds can be represented by function $D = f(\rho, r_\epsilon)$, (where $r_\epsilon = (1 - e)\pi_{-1}/k - 1$ is the operating surplus expected by the entrepreneur). This is based on current and anticipated choice of technology available, mix of government incentives and regulations, resource availability, product market demand conditions, and the political climate. An individual entrepreneur can be thought of as building these expectations into his calculations.

Different entrepreneurs attempt projects which yield different internal rates of return. These choices are based on differences in such factors as knowledge, experience, information, contacts, location, and taste for bearing uncertainty. Successful entrepreneurs may, however, be expected to diversify towards projects that yield a higher return. Given an adequate availability of entrepreneurs, one could envisage an investment schedule varying inversely with the internal rate of return, implying that the projects with the higher yield will be attempted first. Thus, an expansion of the scale of the investment coincides with less profitable projects being attempted.

This notion about the existence of a pool of entrepreneurs who differ as suggested can be used to explain the slope of the demand curve for loanable funds. The entrepreneurs are likely to compare the expected profits retained with the opportunity cost of their time, and their aversion to bearing the uncertainty of a project failure. The lower ρ gets, the higher will be the expected profits retained on the average and the greater the number of borrowers in the market for loanable funds. Conversely, the higher ρ gets, the lower the number of borrowers that will remain in the market.

c) A Comparative Static Equilibrium:

Using the demand and supply curve for loanable funds, the equilibrium profit share of lenders and the level of investment financed by PLS can be arrived at.

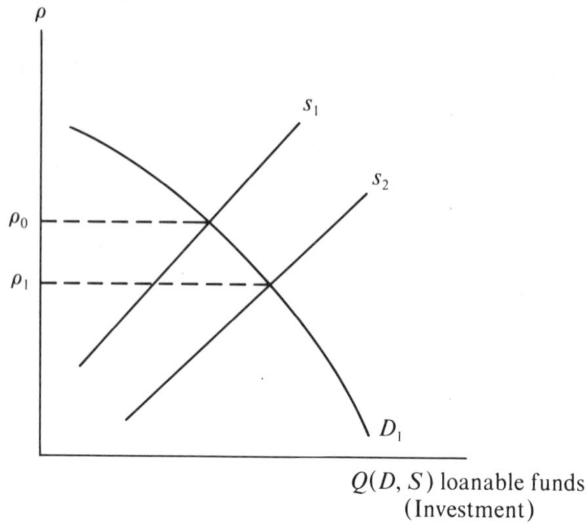

Figure 3
Comparative statics: capital inflow

A simple comparative static exercise is presented to illustrate the functioning of the loanable funds market. Figure 3 above illustrates a shift in the supply curve to the right (from s_1 to s_2) due to an injection of foreign remittances. It is assumed that part of this inflow finds its way into PLS accounts. As might be expected, an initial increase in funds in the market will reduce the returns forwarded to the PLS accounts on new contracts. This short-run change in ρ (from ρ_0 to ρ_1) will encourage investment as reflected by the movement along the demand curve below.

This is essentially a short-run model, though it is possible to ascertain some of the long-run forces that would be activated due to this initial change. The increase in investment would be associated with a decline in average profitability of investment even though the total operating surplus will rise. In the long run, to the extent that expected profits are based on past recorded profits, the demand for loanable funds may decline. Furthermore, if the rise in investment is associated with an increase in the cost of capital goods, recorded profits would be further reduced. Conversely, the whole investment schedule itself may shift out if the increase in income accompanying the increased investment sets into motion the accelerator, assuming that the structure of the economy allows one to become operative.

The analysis above shows that a competitive market for loanable funds can be theoretically relied upon to determine the equilibrium percentage profit-shares. A legislated profit share as an instrument of monetary policy, as suggested by some Islamic economists, would lead to a distortion and hence allocative inefficiency in the same sense that price-fixing does.[9] Another misconception in the literature states that abolishing interest will enable all potentially profitable projects (no matter how low the profit) to be financed.[10] Given that the supply of loanable funds for PLS is not infinite, but rather varies positively with ρ, the above clearly cannot be the case. Having presented a model for PLS banking and described its workings, we now turn to some possible extensions.

VI. SOME EXTENSIONS OF THE PLS MODEL

The extensions considered here are those that would follow from relaxing some of the assumptions of the model. So far, the *muḍarabah* contract, in which the lenders provide all the funds, has been analyzed. Let us now allow for the possibility of the entrepreneurs providing some of their own funds from retained earnings, as is the case in the *mushārakah* contract.

The working of the model remains essentially unchanged. The total funds forwarded for investment, now include the entrepreneurs' contribution.

$$\kappa = \kappa_e + \kappa_\ell$$

(where e and ℓ represent the entrepreneur and the lender).

It is assumed that there is no source of funds provided on a basis other than PLS. ρ is still determined in the market for loanable funds and can now be interpreted to be the return on funds utilized by entrepreneurs for the bearing of uncertainty. $(1 - \rho)$ continues to be the return for the entrepreneurial role of innovation and control. The return to capital provided from either source must be the same and so

$$\rho \frac{\pi}{\kappa} = \rho \frac{\pi_e}{\kappa_e} = \rho \frac{\pi_\ell}{\kappa_\ell}$$

or alternatively

$$r = r_e = r_\ell$$

In section II the reasons why *ribā*-free banking would require banks to be pure intermediaries were explained. It is instructive to analyze the consequence of relaxing the pure intermediary assumption.

When the banking sector is competitive, there would be little difference in reality between non-intermediary and pure intermediary PLS banking. Non-intermediary banks would be offering lenders one profit-share on deposits and requiring another from borrowers on loans. This in principle would be different from the straight administrative fee charged by the pure intermediary bank for its operations. In practice, competition would reduce the return of the non-intermediary bank to cover costs plus a normal profit which would amount to the administrative fee charged by the pure intermediary banks. In other words, competition would force the non-intermediary banks to play the role of pure intermediary.

When the banking sector is highly concentrated, banks are in a position to set profit-shares and thereby sever the direct link between the monetary and real sector. To explain this, some additional terminology has to be introduced and some issues reinterpreted.

Let $\rho\pi$ now be the bank's share of operating surplus since the bank is now effectively the lender. Part of this surplus has to be forwarded by banks to depositors in its PLS accounts. Let ϕ be the share of operating surplus forwarded in PLS accounts so that

$\phi\rho\pi$ = lender's share of operating surplus;

$(1 - \phi)\rho\pi$ = the share of operating surplus retained by the banks.

The two quadrant diagram below illustrates the determination of profit-shares to the lenders, banks, and entrepreneurs. The upper quadrant shows the determination of the equilibrium of profit-shares between the bank and its depositors and also the level of loanable funds the bank possesses to forward to entrepreneurs at the equilibrium level of profit-shares. This is shown to be carried down to the lower quadrant in the form of a fixed supply, which interacts with the entrepreneurs' demand for loanable funds to determine profit-shares between entrepreneurs and the banks (Figure 4).

Now, given that a bank faces a downward sloping entrepreneurs' demand curve for loanable funds, it can manipulate its supply to maximize its own share of operating surplus drawn from the entrepreneurs. It is no longer clear that a shift outward in the supply of loanable funds, say, due to more funds being brought into circulation as a

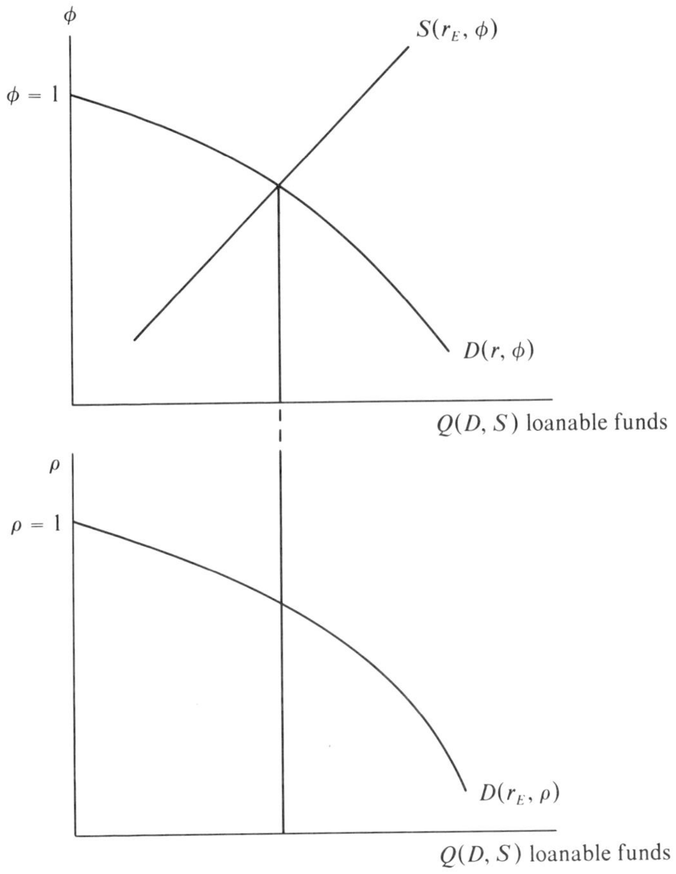

Figure 4
Determination of profit-shares with banks not being "pure-intermediaries"

consequence of dishoarding (in the upper quadrant), will mean an increased supply of funds to entrepreneurs and a lower ρ (in the lower quadrant).

This can be seen by analysing the condition under which it will not be in the banks' interest to increase the supply of funds. We can term the banks' net share of operating surplus π_β, so that

$$\pi_\beta = \rho\pi - c(k)$$

[where $c(k)$ is the variable cost of supplying funds].

The condition we are looking for is one that makes

$$\frac{d\pi\beta}{dk} < 0.$$

Now

$$\frac{d\pi_\beta}{dk} = \rho \frac{d\pi}{dk} + \pi \frac{d\rho}{dk} - \frac{dc}{dk}$$
$$\quad\quad\quad (+) \quad\quad (-) \quad (+)$$

The first term (on the right of the equality sign) shows that the total operating surplus will increase as more funds are utilized by entrepreneurs at a given rate of profit-sharing. The second term shows that the profit-share of banks, ρ, will decrease as more funds are supplied.
So

$$\frac{d\pi_\beta}{dh} \text{ will be} < 0, \qquad \text{If,} \qquad \pi \frac{d\rho}{dk} + \frac{dc}{dk} > \rho \frac{d\pi}{dk}$$

As one might expect, this says that the banks will not offer more funds if the fall of their share of operating surplus, due to a fall in their profit-share plus the marginal cost of supplying these loans, exceeds the increase in operating surplus accruing to them due to the increased funds forwarded to entrepreneurs.[11]

VII. CONCLUSION

The main object of this paper was to illustrate the workings of the market for loanable funds when PLS is substituted for interest. This analysis shows that essentially the same market forces are operative, and profit-shares (based on expectations) instead of interest equilibrate the market for loanable funds. Risk assumes a much more critical role in a financial market which allows PLS as the only form of investment since the returns are variable.

Perhaps the greatest challenge to PLS comes from the lack of an *a priori* guarantee that a comparable quantity of loanable funds will be available under PLS as in an interest based system. It was shown in section IV that lenders will be less well off unconditionally if risk free assets with positive return are eliminated from a system of PLS banking. However, it was not possible to theoretically establish how the welfare of lenders would be affected if conventional interest based banking (without PLS) is entirely replaced by PLS with no risk free assets with a positive return. Whether or not there would be an adequate supply of funds is therefore an empirical question. It does appear, however, that viewing PLS as a constraint on options available to lenders would adversely affect the supply of loanable funds. On the other hand, there is the possibility of tapping otherwise unavailable funds from devout Muslims.

Two findings emerge from the analysis of the market for loanable funds under PLS. First, that it would be inefficient to use profit shares as an instrument of monetary policy. Second, that it is a misconception to believe that interest-free banking would allow all profitable projects, no matter how low the profit, to be financed. The results of this paper also indicate that if the banking sector is concentrated, a non-intermediary PLS bank may restrict the supply of loanable funds to maximize its own return.

This analysis of risk is preliminary, and given the importance of the issue, more study is needed on how it affects both suppliers and demanders of loanable funds. Further research is also needed on the impact of PLS on both the likely composition and magnitude of aggregate investment.

A few general concluding remarks are tempting. Islamic proponents of PLS (or any other mechanism on which to base a *ribā*-free banking system) look for advantages primarily on the ethical and socio-religious level. In this regard, there is always scope for interpretation and discussion. The author's view is that the approach currently in operation in the Middle East, where patronizing interest-free banking is an option open to those so inclined, is preferable and consistent with Islam's religo-philosophical ethos. The above analysis also shows this to be the preferable option from an economic welfare maximization standpoint.

NOTES

1. See Schact (1939) for a definition of *ribā*. Also see Haque [(1980), p. 16].
2. For a general coverage of interest-free banking including details about operating principles, see Siddiqui (1983). For a different approach see Uzair (1978).
3. Some of the issues covered are analyzed in Siddiqui [(1983a), pp. 97–123], who describes a market for loanable funds. Siddiqui does not attempt to derive or explain the supply and demand schedules. Also there are some problems in the analysis which are dealt with in detail elsewhere, [Khan (1983)].

4. See Knight [(1964, pp. 22–50] and Weston (1954).

5. For an assertion of these arguments see Qureshi [(1974), p. 19].

6. Under conventional banking, uncertainty can be introduced into a financial contract by making the interest rate on a loan variable. This is a device used by banks to pass some of the uncertainty resulting from a change in the future cost of borrowing on to the borrowers. There is no change in the conditions of drawing funds from depositors. Under PLS, part of the uncertainty attached to the production process is shifted back to the depositors.

7. The representation of future returns as normally distributed and defined by two parameters (i.e., the mean and standard deviation) is a special case. The more general portfolio selection problem in which the choice is made over various distributions of return is subject matter for further research.

8. For details of differences of PLS from conventional equity as well as debt financing, see Khan [(1984), pp. 48–50].

9. See Siddiqui [(1983), pp. 121–123] and Uzair [(1978), p. 49].

10. See Rehman [(1979), p. 269].

11. Various alternative scenarios could be analyzed if the PLS contract is studied from the reference point of entrepreneurs rather than the banks. It does appear that not forcing a fixed interest (which is part of the variable cost like an excise tax) on the entrepreneurs and drawing a return from their profits (which like a profit tax may not affect price – output decisions) would have important effects on total investment. Moreover, the overall investment mix may turn towards the more risky which the change in risk-sharing the PLS contract implies. There are important areas for further research of the PLS financial mechanism.

6

Saving Behavior in an Economy Without Fixed Interest

Nadeem Ul Haque and Abbas Mirakhor

Nadeem Ul Haque is Economist, Development Research Department, World Bank; Abbas Mirakhor is Economist, Research Department, International Monetary Fund.

I. INTRODUCTION

Concerns have been expressed that the adoption of a financial system based on Islamic principles, which include notably the absolute prohibition of an ex ante fixed rate of return on borrowed money, may lead to a reduction of savings.[1] This assertion has been based on various arguments, the most convincing of which contends that uncertainty in the rate of return affects savings adversely. Heretofore, such assertions have been made without reliance on an analytic framework and have tended implicitly to compare the effects on saving of a fixed and certain rate of return with effects on saving of an uncertain return whose expected value is the same as the fixed rate of return. Although this conclusion is in line with the view that an increase in risk is of the same nature as an unfavorable change in the expected rate of return, its implicit assumption that the rate of return is kept constant while uncertainty is increased is not necessarily valid, since the main feature of a change to an Islamic financial system—i.e., the elimination of an ex ante fixed rate of return—may change the expected rate of return.

Even when it is assumed that the rate of return is more uncertain but has the same expected value, the conclusion that uncertainty will adversely affect savings is far from obvious. Although the question was raised by Marshall[2] who, on the basis of casual observation, maintained that an increase in uncertainty might lead to a reduction in savings, only recently has this question been subjected to rigorous theoretical analysis. Some studies have shown that the results obtained depend crucially on assumptions regarding the form of the utility function and its risk properties, e.g., the degree and the extent of risk aversion, the degree to which the future is discounted, the choice of a utility index, and the income and substitution effects of increased uncertainty regarding future capital income. It has been shown, for example, that when future noncapital income alone is subject to risk, decreasing temporal risk aversion is a sufficient condition for increased uncertainty about future income to decrease consumption and increase savings.[3] With respect to capital income, the total effect (income and substitution effects) of increased uncertainty on savings is shown to be indeterminate.[4] Other studies have shown that, under reasonable assumptions, in the face of uncertainty the precautionary demand for savings increases.[5]

In the present stage of the research few testable hypotheses are possible even in the case where the rate of return is kept constant. The problem becomes more complex if it is considered in the setting of an economy run entirely according to Islamic precepts; in such an economy not only the risk-return configuration but also the form of the utility function, as well as the institutional and behavioral rules affecting the consumer's decision, must correspond to that envisioned by Islam.[6] In undertaking an analysis of this problem, a first step should be to derive the conditions that must be satisfied in order for increased uncertainty to affect savings adversely and to determine whether or not these conditions can reasonably be expected to be satisfied within a system without fixed interest rates. Moreover, since the general problem in which the rate of return is allowed to vary along with increased uncertainty has not been treated in the literature,[7] it seems important that this first attempt be made in the framework of standard economic analysis so that the unambiguous results obtained will find general applicability. Once the problem is resolved in the traditional framework, its applicability to an Islamic system can be investigated.

Section II reviews the relevant literature on the effect of uncertainty on savings. Section III states the problem of eliminating interest from the economy as required by Islam and currently being implemented by some Islamic countries. This section considers the impact of the elimination of a risk-free asset for the economy. Section IV derives the optimal time paths of consumption, saving and wealth in the context of a deterministic infinite horizon, optimizing model. The optimal time paths of the same variables in a stochastic framework are derived in Section V, and the condition that must be satisfied in order for increased uncertainty to reduce savings is derived by comparing (in Section VI) the results obtained in Section V with those of Section IV. Section VII summarizes the main results of the paper and examines the reasonableness of the conditions derived in Section VI in the context of an economy without fixed interest.

II. SAVING AND UNCERTAINTY: A REVIEW

One of the first attempts of formulating the problem of choice between consumption and savings was made by Irving Fisher (1930), who introduced a two-period model in which the consumer has a preference ordering over present and future consumption. In this formulation, Fisher argued that income risk (uncertainty about future income) reduces the rate of time preference and thus increases current savings. Fisher's model was later reconsidered and reformulated by Hirshleifer (1958) and applied to various theoretical settings. In a later discussion of the problem, Boulding (1966, page 535) reached the same conclusion that the greater the risk of the future income, the greater is the impulse to provide for the future at the expense of present consumption. The Fisher-Boulding thesis seemed to have contradicted the casual observation made by Marshall that:

> ". . . The laborious and self denying peasant who had heaped up a little store of wealth only to see it taken from him by a stronger hand, was a constant warning to his neighbors to enjoy their pleasure and their rest when they could."[8]

Sandmo (1970) resolved this contradiction by suggesting that the difference between the two contrasting positions lay in the fact that they are not referring to the same kind of uncertainty and whereas

> "Boulding is concerned with uncertainty concerning future non-capital income, Marhall analyzes the effect of an uncertain yield

> on capital investment. The role of saving in the two cases is fundamentally different."[9]

Consequently, if capital holdings are not subject to risk and only future income is, then saving is increased (reduced) if relative risk aversion is greater (less) than unity and is non-increasing (nondecreasing). This case, which is referred to as "income risk," was considered by Boulding (1966), Phelps (1967), Leland (1968), Hahn (1970) and Sandmo (1970). Since accumulated savings are certain components of total resources available in the future, they provide a guarantee of a certain minimum level of consumption in the period ahead. Quite appropriately, therefore, an individual's response to increased income risk is to increase saving, and this response varies directly with risk aversion.

Much of the research on the effect of uncertainty on saving has been concerned with the effect of income uncertainty on saving and almost all studies have, under alternative assumptions about the behavior of the risk aversion function, confirmed the Fisher-Boulding position that income risk increases current savings.[10] In contrast to the problem of uncertainty about future income, the accumulated savings or individual capital holdings themselves may be subject to risk, as in the case of the peasant in Marshall's example. Studies that have dealt with this problem have found no clear direction for a change in saving behavior. In an analysis of this case, Sandmo (1970) derived a Slutsky-like expression and found that, given certain assumptions about the risk aversion function, when the rate of return to saving is uncertain there is first a substitution effect, which tends to reduce saving, but then there is also an income effect, which tends to increase saving. Hence, the total effect of increased capital risk was found to be indeterminate. Here too, later research has confirmed Sandmo's findings.[11] Moreover, other works have shown that the ambiguous results can be rendered unambiguous only if one is willing to allow certain restrictive assumptions regarding the utility function.[12]

It must be recalled that all of the studies mentioned have examined saving behavior in the context of a two-period model in which attempts were made to determine the direction of change in saving as a consequence of a mean preserving spread.[13] An exception is a study by Phelps (1967), who in the context of an N-period model attempted to determine the effect on consumption of variations in the riskiness and expected return from capital. While Phelps concludes that the conflict between substitution and income effects leads to indeterminate results, risk always "opposes" return: "where increase of the return raises (reduces) the propensity to consume, an increase in risk reduces (raises) it; and where return has no effect, neither does risk."[14] One objective of this paper will be to obtain conditions which lead to unambiguous results regarding this problem. In doing so, an optimization model of consumer behavior is constructed, first in the context of a deterministic infinite horizon (Section III) and then in a stochastic context (Section IV); the optimal time paths of saving resulting from these two models are then compared (Section V).

III. THE STATEMENT OF THE PROBLEM—THE IMPACT OF THE ELIMINATION OF THE RISK-FREE ASSET

The position which asserts that, as a result of the adoption of an Islamic financial system, savings will decline can be interpreted as implicitly assuming that the elimination of an ex ante fixed rate of return limits the menu of assets available to the saver and thereby increases risk, which in turn affects savings adversely. This view would therefore regard the move to an Islamic banking as equivalent to that from a system in which a wide range of assets with varying risk characteristics, including a risk-free asset, are present to a system where the only available assets are those representing risky equity-participation projects. If this interpretation of the argument is correct, the resulting conclusion seems unrealistically strong.

Consider a conventional system in which a whole range of assets is available to the saver (investor), such as those available in the United States. One such ranking of these assets in terms of their risk characteristics could be the following order (arranged in increasing order of risk): Certificates of Deposits, Treasury Bills, money market funds, mutual funds, blue chip stocks, other stocks, and finally future contracts and options. Given the availability of these assets, the investor can put together a portfolio of assets best suited to his needs. It must be kept in mind, however, that the higher the degree of diversification of the asset portfolio, the lower will be its risk. Now assume that by some process the society decides to eliminate the assets considered as risk free (CDs and Treasury Bills) from this menu. It can now be argued that the range of assets with a spectrum of risk starting from zero (for CDs) to some finite positive number has changed, so that the starting value on the risk spectrum is some positive number ϵ (for money market funds or perhaps more appropriately mutual funds, for example). There is nothing to bar the investor from organizing a new and well-diversified portfolio of assets, chosen from the available menu, which minimizes risk. How seriously this change will affect the risk characteristics of the investor's portfolio will depend on the magnitude of ϵ (which is not significantly large for money markets or mutual funds in the United States).

In an Islamic financial system the availability of assets with a variety of risk characteristics is a distinct possibility, and there is no reason to assume that there is a limit to the diversity of assets in such a system.[15] The saver, then, can organize a diversified asset portfolio which enables him to minimize risk in this system as in its counterpart. In an Islamic financial system, however, other assets representing profit-sharing arrangements will also exist that can affect the return property of the asset portfolio. The question now becomes what effects will this new risk-return configuration have on the saving behavior of the consumer. The problem can be stated as follows:

In an economy it is possible to rank all the returns to assets by the amount of risk that each carries. In such an economy, it can be argued that saving is a function of the rate of return on various assets and the risk associated with those assets. For simplicity, saving can be represented as a function of the average rate of return in the economy, as well as the average risk, i.e.,

$$S = S(\underset{+}{r}, \underset{-}{\sigma}) \tag{1}$$

The signs in equation (1) indicate that saving is positively related to the average rate of return and negatively related to the average risk in the economy. If a risk-free asset is allowed to exist, assets can be ranked from zero risk to some finite number, say $\overline{\sigma}$. But, when a society does not permit risk-free assets to exist, as is the case in some countries that have adopted the Islamic financial system, the ranking of assets is done over the interval $(\epsilon, \overline{\sigma})$ with $\epsilon > 0$, instead of $(0, \overline{\sigma})$ ranking. Consequently, the issue is to study how behavior might change when the minimum value of the range for risk is changed from zero to some small positive value that we have termed ϵ. Although it may be conjectured that since ϵ is likely to be small the impact on savings will be small, but further insight could be gained by studying, as is done in this and the following section, the polar cases of behavior in a risk-free environment versus that in a risky environment.

IV. THE DETERMINISTIC SAVING MODEL

Assume that an individual starts at an initial date μ, with an initial wealth endowment, W_μ, which grows at the rate of γ. In order to focus attention on pure saving behavior we assume that at each point in time, the individual, out of his income $\gamma W(t)$, makes a consumption-saving decision, with $C(t)$ being consumed and $S(t)$ added to wealth, $W(t)$.

In order to make the problem more tractable, it is also assumed that the individual possesses the following utility function[16]

$$U(C) = C^a \tag{2}$$

Designating r as the rate of time preference, the maximizing problem can now be stated as follows

$$J(W, \mu) = \underset{C}{\text{Max}} \int_{\mu}^{\infty} e^{-rt}\, C^a \, dt, \tag{3}$$

Subject to the constraints that

$$\dot{W} = \gamma W - C \tag{4}$$

and

$$W(\mu) = W_\mu > 0. \tag{5}$$

In this simple form the problem is readily solvable. Using the technique of dynamic programming[17] and the current value function, $[J(W, \mu) = e^{-r\mu}\, V(W)]$, the partial differential equation that optimizes the value function is,

$$rV(W) = \max_{C} \{C^a + V'(W)(\gamma W - C)\}. \tag{6}$$

Maximization of the LHS permits the control to be expressed as a function of the derivative of the value function, i.e.,

$$C = \left[\frac{V'(w)}{a}\right]^{1/a-1}. \tag{7}$$

Equation (4) can now be expressed as

$$rV(W) = \left[\frac{V'(W)}{a}\right]^{a/a-1} \frac{a-1}{a} + V'(W)\gamma W. \tag{8}$$

The solution to (8) is of the form

$$V(W) = BW^{\alpha}, \tag{9}$$

which yields

$$\alpha = a \tag{10}$$

and

$$B = \left[\frac{a(r - a\gamma)}{1 - a}\right]^{a-1}. \tag{11}$$

Thus we have

$$V(W) = \left[\frac{a(r - a\gamma)}{1 - a}\right]^{a-1} W(t)^{a} \tag{12}$$

and

$$C[W(t)] = \frac{a(r - a\gamma)}{1 - a} W(t) = AW. \tag{13}$$

Consequently, consumption at each point in time is shown to be proportional to wealth and to vary directly with the rate of time preference and negatively with the rate of return on wealth. Recognizing that current income is γW, the marginal propensity to consume out of income is A/γ. Thus in each period a constant proportion out of current income is consumed.

Substituting equation (13) into the state equation and solving we obtain the optimal time path of the state variable, W

$$W(t) = W_0 e^{(\gamma - A)t} \tag{14}$$

Consequently, wealth is accumulated whenever the rate of return on available assets is greater than the marginal propensity to consume out of wealth.

V. THE STOCHASTIC SAVING MODEL

In the last section it was assumed that all assets earned a known and constant rate of return γ. To introduce uncertainty into the model, we assume as before that an individual starting off with some level of wealth W^* chooses his consumption at each instant over an infinite time horizon. However the rate of return γ^*, rather than being constant, is drawn from a probability distribution with a known mean $\bar{\gamma}^*$ and a known variance $\sigma^2 W^{*2}$. At each instant, therefore, a rate of return is drawn from this distribution and may actually turn out to be negative thus reducing individual wealth. This is in line with the Islamic notion of equity participation requiring individuals to directly share in the risk associated with an investment.

To incorporate the above reasoning into the model, the differential equation in the deterministic form is now written in its stochastic version as follows[18]

$$dW^* = (\gamma^* W^* - C)\, dt + \sigma W^*\, dZ \tag{15}$$

where $Z(t)$ is a stochastic process (known as a Weiner process) defined on a probability space $(\pi, \mathcal{F}e, P)$ with the properties: (a) that increments in the process $Z(t) - Z(s)$, $(t \leqq s, t, s = 0, 1, \ldots)$ are independent random variables and (b) that $Z(t) - Z(s)$ is randomly distributed as a standard normal variable. The first property suggests that the past history of the process does not influence its future position. Thus similar to Markov processes, the future behavior of the process depends only on its present position and does not depend on how the process got there.

Dropping the stochastic term (i.e., setting $dZ = 0$) it can be seen that equation (15) is the same as the deterministic state differential equation (4) above. Since the properties described above denote that $E[dZ(t)] = 0$, the expected growth of wealth is the same as in the deterministic case. However, at each instant, a drawing of dZ from the Weiner process could increase or decrease this growth in wealth. In more formalistic terms, the instantaneous mean growth in wealth is still $(\gamma^* W^* - C)$ while the instantaneous variance of the growth in wealth is $\sigma^2 W^{*2}$. This formulation thus allows, given a large enough variance, a finite probability of the event that there could be a negative net addition to wealth.

Employing the same utility function as before the discounted sum of utility is maximized subject to (15). In this way the problem, analogous to the deterministic case encountered in the last section, becomes one of stochastic control. The problem can now be stated as follows:

$$L(W, \mu) = \underset{C}{\text{Max}} \int_{\mu}^{\infty} e^{-rt}\, C^a\, dt \tag{16}$$

subject to

$$dW^*(\gamma^* W^* - C)\, dt + \sigma W^*\, dZ. \tag{17}$$

To solve this problem dynamic programming is utilized once again.[19] The Hamilton-Bellman-Jacobi equation for this problem is

$$rV(W^*) = \underset{C}{\text{Max}}\, [C^a + V'(W^*)(\gamma^* W^* - C) + V''(W^*)\sigma^2 W^{*2}]. \tag{18}$$

Maximizing the right-hand side with respect to C, in terms of the derivatives of the value function, the control is

$$C = \left[\frac{V'(W^*)}{a}\right]^{1/a-1}. \tag{19}$$

Substituting equation (19) into equation (18) the Hamilton-Bellman-Jacobi equation can be written as,

$$rV(W^*) = \left[\frac{V'(W^*)}{a}\right]^{a/a-1} \frac{1-a}{a} + \gamma^* W^* V(W^*) + \frac{V''(W^*)}{2}\sigma^2 W^{*2}. \tag{20}$$

Here again positing a solution of the form $V(W^*) = BW^*$, it can be seen that $\alpha = a$ and

$$B = \left[a\left(\frac{r - \gamma^* a}{1-a} + \frac{a\sigma^2}{2}\right)\right]^{a-1}. \tag{21}$$

Therefore, the value function can be expressed as a function of current wealth and the parameters of the problem as follows:

$$V(W^*) = \left[a\left(\frac{r - \gamma^* a}{1-a} + \frac{a\sigma^2}{2}\right)\right]^{a-1} W^{*a}. \tag{22}$$

Similarly, the consumption as a function of the current wealth and the parameters of the problem can be expressed as:

$$C(W^*) = a\left[\frac{r - \gamma^* a}{1-a} + \frac{a\sigma^2}{2}\right] W^* = A^* W^*. \tag{23}$$

Hence, as in the deterministic model, in each period the individuals consume a constant proportion of their existing wealth, W^*. Moreover, optimal consumption varies directly with the rate of time preference and the riskiness of the rate of return and is negatively related to the rate of return on assets.

VI. A COMPARISON OF THE DETERMINISTIC AND STOCHASTIC MODELS

Since the consumption functions derived in the stochastic as well as the deterministic models show consumption to be a linear function of wealth, inferences about behavior can be drawn by comparing the marginal propensities to consume out of wealth for the two models. The difference between the marginal propensity to consume out of wealth in the deterministic case, i.e., A, and in the stochastic case, i.e., A^* is

$$A - A^* = a^2\left[\left(\frac{\gamma^* - \gamma}{1 - a}\right) - \frac{\sigma^2}{2}\right], \tag{24}$$

which is positively related to the difference between the mean return on assets in the two models and is negatively related to the variance (or riskiness) associated with the return on assets in the uncertainty case. It can be seen from this expression that if the expected return on assets in the case of uncertainty is equal to the rate of return when there is no uncertainty, i.e., $\gamma^* = \gamma$, then the marginal propensity to consume will be higher when there are no risk-free assets, i.e., $A < A^*$. However, it can also be seen that the marginal propensity to consume will remain unchanged when the risk-free asset is eliminated if

$$\gamma^* - \gamma = 1 - a\frac{\sigma^2}{2}. \tag{25}$$

That is, the expected rate of return on assets when the risk-free asset is eliminated is greater than the expected return when that asset is present; the difference between these two expected returns is equal to one minus the coefficient of relative risk aversion times one-half the variance (or riskiness) associated with the expected return on risky assets.

Since the wealth paths $[W(t)]$ in the two models are different, it is difficult to make any statement on consumption itself without solving for the wealth path in the stochastic problem. Using the optimized value of the control variable, i.e., consumption, this is tantamount to solving the stochastic differential equation (15), which can now be written as

$$\frac{dW^*}{W^*} = (\gamma^* - A^*)\, dt + \sigma dZ. \tag{26}$$

The solution to equation (26) is

$$W^*(t) = W_0^* \exp\left\{\left[\gamma^* - A^* - \frac{\sigma^2}{2} + \sigma Z(t)\right]\right\} \tag{27}$$

It is already observed from (15) or (26) that the stochastic shocks enter the consumption stream only via the time path of wealth. The marginal propensity to consume, which is unaffected by these shocks, is larger in the stochastic case than in the nonstochastic case. Consequently, inferences on consumption and hence on saving can be drawn on the basis of a comparison of the two wealth paths. However, since equation (27) retains the stochastic element, a meaningful comparison can only be made between the mean of $W^*(t)$ in the stochastic case with the time path of $W(t)$ in the nonstochastic case. Thus, whatever inferences are made, while valid in the mean sense, may not hold in terms of an actual time path because of the presence of the random disturbances. That is, the time paths of wealth and consumption may not be the same for the two cases being compared.

Since the instantaneous increments of the Weiner process are normally distributed, $W^*(t)$ in equation (25) is lognormally distributed with the mean

$$E[W^*(t)] = W_0^* \exp\{(\gamma - A^*)t\}. \tag{28}$$

The time path of the mean of $W^*(t)$ given by (28) can now be compared with that of $W(t)$ given by (14) using the following equation,

$$\frac{W(t)}{E[W^*(t)]} = e^{\{(\gamma-\gamma^*)-(A-A^*)\}t}. \tag{29}$$

It can be observed from this expression that the condition that must be satisfied in order for increased uncertainty, resulting from elimination of the risk-free asset, to adversely affect saving is that the rate of return remains unchanged. That is, if the rate of return is the same for both the deterministic case and the stochastic case (i.e., $\gamma = \gamma^*$), then wealth in the certainty case is greater than the expected wealth in the uncertainty case. If this condition in fact holds consumption will increase when the risk-free asset is eliminated.

On the other hand, if the rate of return on assest increases as the risk-free asset is eliminated, it is more difficult to meaningfully compare the two resulting wealth paths. If expression (24) holds, then the two marginal propensities to consume are equal, i.e., $A = A^*$. In this case, the path of expected wealth in the uncertainty case dominates that obtained in the certainty case. Consequently, when the risk-free asset is eliminated, consumption will decrease and savings will increase.

VII. CONCLUSIONS

Although the household's decision between consumption and saving has been considered in recent years, almost all the theoretical work in the area has examined only the effects of a mean-preserving spread upon saving. Even here the results have shown the conclusion that increased uncertainty regarding the rate of return to saving will lead to reduced savings to be far from obvious, and the best that can be said, in the absence of strong and restrictive assumptions about the risk aversion factor and/or the utility index, is that the effort is indeterminate. In any case, as has been argued in this paper, the move to an Islamic banking system cannot be analyzed as an a priori increase in uncertainty in the environment in which the consumer is operating. Haque and Mirakhor (1986) have shown that the move to an Islamic interest-free system, under certain conditions, could lead to increased rates of return on savings. Consequently, the increased level of uncertainty that could result from the elimination of the risk-free asset could be compensated for by an increased rate of return on savings, leaving the overall level of savings unchanged or perhaps even leading to an increase in savings.

It appears that if the traditional theory is to be relied upon to gain insights into this problem it is necessary, as a first step, to deal with the problem of variations in risk and return in a traditional setting and derive clear and unambiguous results that could then be used to draw inferences about a system without fixed-interest assets. This has been the primary objective of the paper, in which a straightforward condition has been derived that must be satisfied if, in the face of variation in riskiness *and* the rate of return, saving is to decline. This condition requires that the rate of return when risk is present must be no more than the rate of return when risk is absent. This result in itself is a contribution to traditional theory. But can the condition derived here be reasonably expected to be satisfied in an Islamic system?

Although one is tempted to suggest that the question must be answered empirically, there are *a priori* arguments that provide useful insights. For one thing, by prohibiting interest payments Islam requires investable funds to be utilized by agent-entrepreneurs on a profit-sharing basis. This requirement will in effect remove interest from the cost side, and both the saver and the entrepreneur become residual income earners.[20] It can reasonably be argued that, in the traditional system, rates of return to investment are on the average higher than the rate of interest paid on borrowed funds (since the rate has to be high enough to recover the cost of capital); therefore, as a result of adoption of the Islamic system in which the saver becomes an entrepreneur sharing in the profits earned, the rate of return to investable funds may be higher. Moreover, it can also be expected that, since the savers' reward will depend on the productivity of the investment undertaken, better quality investment projects, in terms of their rate of return, will be undertaken.

In conclusion it is useful to restate that this paper has been a first attempt at establishing a point of reference upon which meaningful theoretical discussions can proceed regarding the impact on saving of adopting an Islamic financial system. As such it has only tangentially dealt with the possible characteristics of consumer behavior if governed by Islamic precepts, which would need to be incorporated into the analysis if its conclusions were to be legitimately applied to an overall Islamic system. For example, no attempt was made to analyze the constraints that Islamic teaching may place on either the behavior or the utility function of the believer, an aspect to which Islamic scholars attach considerable weight.[21] Another factor that tends to influence consumer behavior is the effect of payments of compulsory levies constituting transfer payments to those in need and a 2.5 percent tax imposed on idle balances. Finally, no attempt was made to discuss the impact of adoption of an Islamic financial system on the degree and extent of individual's risk aversion, which could likewise be affected by the internalization of Islamic values by the consumer.

NOTES

The authors have benefitted from discussions with Mohsin Khan and Karl Voltaire on the subject.

1. See, for example, Pryor (1985) and De Rosa (1985).

2. Sandmo (1970).
3. See, for example, Phelps (1967).
4. See, for example, Sandmo (1970).
5. Leland (1968).
6. Among these are Islam's emphasis upon work and moderation in consumption, its exhortations against extravagance and waste in consumption, encouragement of thriftiness and transfer payments to the needy, and discouragement of accumulation of idle balances.
7. To the author's knowledge the only exception is Phelps (1967).
8. Marshall (1920), p. 226.
9. Sandmo (1970), p. 523.
10. See, for example, Leland (1968), Dreze and Modigliani (1972), and Menezes and Auten (1978).
11. See, for example, Block and Heineke (1972, 1975).
12. See, for example, Hanson and Menezes (1978) and Sproule (1985). Sproule, for example, has observed that by restricting the utility index the effects of a mean-preserving increase in interest-rate uncertainty can be shown to decrease the level of labor supply and decrease the optimal level of savings.
13. See Rothschild and Stiglitz (1970). A mean preserving spread denotes an experiment for the study of behavior under risk in which the expected rate of return of a prospect is kept constant while risk is increased.
14. Phelps (1976), p. 140 and pp. 149–53.
15. A variety of assets are available even in countries where an Islamic financial system has been adopted although this adoption has taken place relatively recently so that the range of asset availability is still limited (see Khan and Mirakhor (1985)). Theoretically, any asset whose return is not ex ante fixed and tied to the amount of money invested can be admitted into the menu of assets available in an Islamic financial system.
16. It is important to note that no claim is made here that such a function is in any way "Islamic." For concavity of the utility function it is required that $a < 1$. The coefficient of relative risk aversion for this utility function is $a - 1$.
17. Although dynamic programming is more convenient, the problem can also be solved using calculus of variations or Pontryagin's Maximum Principle.
18. *s are used to distinguish this case from the previous section.
19. For more information on the details of the solution technique employed here see Maliaris and Brock (1982).
20. See Haque and Mirakhor (1986), where this case has been analyzed and contracting conditions derived to show the possibility of both levels of savings and rates of return to be higher in the Islamic than in the traditional system. Whether or not the savers will actually receive higher returns will of course depend on the spread, between deposit rates and rates of return to capital, as a reward for financial intermediation.
21. Recently Toutounchian (1985) has analyzed a Muslim consumer's behavior taking into account Islamic exhortations with respect to sharing and has derived optimality conditions employing an interdependent utility function. See his forthcoming book, *Towards a Theory of Muslim Consumer Behavior.*

7

Optimal Profit-Sharing Contracts and Investment in an Interest-Free Islamic Economy

Nadeem Ul Haque and Abbas Mirakhor

Nadeem Ul Haque is Economist, Development Research Department, World Bank; Abbas Mirakhor is Economist, Research Department, International Monetary Fund.

I. INTRODUCTION

Despite a growing sentiment in Muslim nations for moving towards a system of economy-wide profit sharing and the fact that two countries have already adopted such a system, no serious attempt has yet been made to analyze in a rigorous manner its implications for economic behavior.[1] This paper is therefore the first attempt at modeling Islamic profit-sharing financial contracts and analyzing their implications. Models for both the case of certainty and the cases of uncertainty with and without complete information have been presented and analyzed, thus laying the basis for a more informed and rigorous discussion on the subject. It is shown that in a world of perfect certainty and full information, the elimination of interest would have no real consequences. When uncertainty is introduced, however, conditions are derived under which investment would increase or stay the same. Intuitively, the latter result can be explained by noting that when a fixed interest rate is replaced by profit sharing, the constant per unit cost to firms of borrowed capital is removed. Since in the profit-sharing system there are no debtors to the firm, only equity participants, the investors and the entrepreneurs now are all residual income earners. No prior claims therefore need to considered for the calculation of profit.[2]

Since observability has often been regarded as a factor that might preclude the efficient operation of such a system, considerable attention is paid to it here. An investor knows only that he will obtain a certain proportion of profits in return for the investment that he makes. As he may be unable to observe the output or the action of the agent, which influences the level of output, a moral hazard situation arises. Consequently, the investor will seek to contract on the basis of observable factors. For example, if the level of investment is observable and is a good indicator of profitability, the sharing ratio can be made a function of the observed level of investment. Moreover, in the writing of the contract, care would be taken to ensure that within the constraints, both optimal action and optimal amounts of information are elicited from the agent.

The treatment of the moral hazard problem in the manner described above and used in the paper below, is referred to as the principal-agent problem. The agency problem has recently been extensively used for analyzing wage-employment contracting and its implications for the aggregate economy.[3] To our knowledge that is the first application of the agency theory to the Islamic system of profit sharing. Nevertheless, recent research in economic theory, mainly in the applications of the agency literature, has suggested that the sharing of profit has significant resource allocational and macroeconomic implications. For example, recently Martin Weitzman has suggested that the profit-sharing system is superior to traditional capitalism because a

> profit-sharing system has the potential to automatically counteract contractionary or inflationary shocks—while maintaining the advantages of decentralized decision-making. And these desirable properties are robustly preserved throughout a variety of economic environments. At the very least, widespread profit sharing can be a valuable adjunct to traditional monetary and fiscal policies.[4]

Although Islam manifests a clear preference for an economy-wide application of risk and profit sharing, the attention in Muslim countries has thus far been concentrated in finance and banking applications. There has thus far been little rigorous analysis of the implications of increased uncertainty that would result from elimination of fixed interest and substitution of profit-sharing contracts in its place.[5]

The first section introduces the principal modes of Islamic financing and discusses the status of contracting in Islamic law; it is followed by a section that summarizes the principal-agent and the wage-contracting literature. These are followed by a characterization of the problem under certainty and then under uncertainty with complete information. Finally, the moral hazard problem in Islamic profit-sharing is considered. A summary of the main results of the paper and a discussion of some issues for future research are presented in the concluding section.

II. FINANCIAL CONTRACTS AND CONTRACTING IN ISLAM

The central feature of an Islamic financial system is the absolute prohibition of interest. Islam, however, encourages trade, which implies the permission to profit thereby.[6] To facilitate trade transactions Islamic law has developed specific forms of financial arrangements,[7] the most important of which are called *Muḍārabah* and *Mushārakah,* as principal means of earning profits without resort to charging of interest. In *Muḍārabah,* one party provides the necessary financial capital and the other (the agent-entrepreneur) the human capital needed for performance of the economic activity undertaken. The resulting profit is then shared between the parties in accordance with a sharing rule specified beforehand in the *Muḍārabah* contract. Under such an arrangement, the entrepreneur risks the loss of his time and manpower, but the owner of financial resources bears all the financial losses. Moreover, the entrepreneur is completely free to manage the project undertaken unless otherwise specified in the contract.

Muḍārabah traditionally has been applied to commercial activities of short duration. *Mushārakah,* on the other hand, is a form of business arrangement in which a number of partners pool their financial resources to undertaken a commercial-industrial enterprise and share in the resulting profits (or losses) corresponding to their share in the financial capital of the enterprise. These profit-sharing arrangements may be applied either to the whole firm or may have project-specific orientation.

Islamic law places a great deal of emphasis on contracts and the necessity for participants to remain faithful to the terms specified in the contract, so much so that faithfulness to the terms of contracts is considered a distinguishing characteristic of a Muslim. The maxim that "Muslims are bound by their stipulations" is recognized by all schools of Islamic thought.[8] Throughout the legal and intellectual history of Islam, a body of rules constituting a general theory of contracts—with explicit emphasis on specific contracts such as sales, lease, hire, and partnerships—were formulated based on the primary sources of Islamic Law.[9] This body of rules established the principle that, in matters of civil and economic dealings, any contract not specifically prohibited by the Law is valid and binding on the parties and most be enforced by the courts, which are to treat the parties to a contract as complete equals. The core notion of contract is understood in Islamic Law as meaning that the rights and duties between the two parties are specifically determined and fixed by their own voluntary and actual agreement.[10]

III. PRINCIPAL-AGENT THEORY

An agency relationship arises whenever one individual depends on the actions of another. The individual taking the action is called the agent and the affected party, the principal. In a *Muḍārabah* contract, for example, the owner of the financial capital is the principal and the entrepreneur, the agent. The two enter into a contract to undertake an economic activity. Accordingly, the agent takes an action a whose result is an outcome x, a random variable whose distribution depends on a. The two parties have agreed beforehand that the agent will receive a share, $S(x)$. If we assume x to be the profits resulting from the economic activity, then the principal's share will be $x - S(x)$. The choice of $S(x)$ depends on the attitude of the two parties toward risk and assumptions regarding the extent of the information available to both parties.[11] The Principal-Agent problem combines the two elements of risk sharing and differential information and has a first-best solution if all information is costlessly shared between the two parties or if the incentives of principal and agent can costlessly converge. However, such optimal risk sharing is not possible when along with uncertainty the two parties have unequal information, i.e., an information asymmetry exists. Given information assymmetry, a first-best solution is still possible if the principal can monitor the agent's action and obtain information perfectly and costlessly. If not, only second-best solutions are possible. This shortfall is referred to as an agency loss or agency costs.

The Principal-Agent literature has primarily focused on the case in which (1) the agent's action is not directly observable by the principal; and (2) the outcome is affected but not completely determined by the agent's action. If the principal can not observe the action taken by the agent but is able to make some observation, e.g., of the output, the reward or fee schedule can be set in advance stating that the agent's reward will be a function of the observation made by the principal. When the agent makes some observation not shared with the principal (and bases his action on that observation), but the principal cannot determine whether the agent has used his information in the way that best serves the principal's interest, moral hazard arises.[12] In this case the principal has to determine a contracting rule that will induce the agent to act in an optimal manner. This problem is referred to as incentive compatibility.

The attitudes of the principal and agent toward risk are crucial in the determination of optimal contracts. In general, second-best solutions involving risk sharing would obtain if both parties are risk averse. When the agent is risk-neutral, he bears all the risks. The principal receives a fixed amount while the agent receives the remainder, i.e., $S(x) = x - k$ where k is determined by the participation constraint.[13] But since all individuals are averse to sufficiently large risks, the simple solution of assigning all the risks to the agent alone fails when risks become large compared with agent's wealth. In the general case of a risk-averse agent, his share will be a function of the outcome in order to provide incentives, and risk will therefore be shared.

The following principles have emerged[14] from the theoretical literature on the Principal-Agent problem: (1) the agency loss is highest when the incentives of the principal and agent do not converge and when acquiring information is costly; (2) given the costs of monitoring, an optimal level of monitoring will be maintained by the principal; (3) when monitoring is expensive (or its substitutes are inexpensive), less monitoring (or monitoring of a poorer quality) will take place; (4) in a range of real world situations, effective monitoring of such indicators as output is relatively or fully successful in reducing agency costs even if the agent's information and action cannot be fully monitored; (5) values such as reputation, which could be lost through dysfunctional behavior or threat of legal action, are strong incentives for proper behavior on the part of the participants; (6) when the same action is repeated over time, the effect of uncertainty tends to be reduced, dysfunctional behavior is more accurately revealed, and the problem of moral hazard is alleviated, i.e., long-term relationships develop the stocks of values needed for enforcement and make limited monitoring more effective; and (7) when agency costs are reduced, the benefits are shared by both the agent and the principal, therefore, the principals and agents have a common interest in defining a monitoring and incentive scheme that yields outcomes as close as possible to ones that would be produced if information monitoring were costless.[15]

IV. THE DETERMINISTIC CASE: A SIMPLE GENERAL EQUILIBRIUM MODEL

We begin with setting out a simple model of profit-sharing in an environment of perfect certainty. Assuming perfect certainty and competitive conditions, the Islamic system described above requires entrepreneurs (agents) to obtain and use funds from individual savers (principals) in the first period, agreeing to return the funds in the second period for a promised ex ante share in the profits (losses), λ, to be returned along with the borrowed funds in the second period. For simplicity and without loss of generality, we shall assume only one consumer (principal) and one producer (agent). The return in the second period to the investors may therefore be expressed as:

$$r = \frac{\lambda \pi^*}{I^*} \tag{1.1}$$

where I^* is the optimal level of investment in the enterprise and π^* is the optimal profits obtained at that level of investment. The rate of return per unit of investment is then r. Since in this simple case there is only one consumer (principal) and one entrepreneur (agent), the firm's profit-maximizing problem may be expressed as:

$$\pi^* = \max_I f(I) - (1 + r)I = f(I^*) - (1 + r)I^* \tag{1.2}$$

and I is the total amount of funds borrowed by the entrepreneur (agent). Since the firm operates under competitive conditions, it treats r as the cost of capital.[16] Maximization of (1.2) yields the usual profit-maximizing condition equating marginal product to the cost of capital,[17]

$$f' = 1 + r. \tag{1.3}$$

Solving for the input demand function from the profit-maximizing condition yields

$$I^{*d} = I(r). \tag{1.4}$$

From the second order conditions for profit maximization, the investment demand schedule is downward sloping in r. The relevant parameter for our purposes, however, is λ, the profit-sharing ratio. Therefore, substituting (1.1) into (1.4)

$$I^{*d} = I\left(\frac{\lambda\pi^*}{I^*}\right) = \ell(\lambda). \tag{1.5}$$

To determine the effect of an increase in the sharing ratio on investment, differentiate (1.5) to obtain,

$$I^{*d} = \frac{dI^{*d}}{d\lambda} = I' \frac{\pi^*}{I^*} \frac{1}{1+\epsilon} \tag{1.6}$$

where $\epsilon = dI/dr\ r/I$ is the elasticity of the investment demand schedule from $\epsilon < 0$ from the second order condition of (1.3).

From (1.6) it can be observed that:

$$I_\lambda^{*d} \lesseqgtr 0 \text{ if } |\epsilon| \lesseqgtr 1 \text{ or } |f''| \lesseqgtr \frac{r}{I}. \tag{1.7}$$

Hence, investment as a function of the share parameter may be upward or downward sloping depending on the elasticity of investment demand with respect to the cost of capital or the rate of interest.

The consumer's problem is that of determining, out of his first period endowment, a certain amount to be saved in order to be made available for the entrepreneur's investment. In the second period, since there is no endowment, the consumer lives off the proceeds from his investment. Given Y, the problem can be stated as follows:

$$\max_{C_1, C_2} U(C_1, C_2), \tag{1.8}$$

subject to the constraints

$$Y - C_1 = I$$

$$(1 + r)I = C_2.$$

The first order condition for this problem is

$$\frac{U_1}{U_2} = 1 + r,$$

hence the supply schedule for investable funds is obtained as

$$I^{*s} = g(r) = g\left(\frac{\lambda\pi^*}{I^*}\right) = h(\lambda). \tag{1.9}$$

Differentiation of (1.9) yields

$$\frac{dI^{*s}}{dr} = \frac{(U_{12} - rU_{22})I - U_2}{A} \tag{1.10}$$

where $A = U_{11} - 2rU_{12} + r^2 U_{22} < 0$.

Since investment is foregone consumption in the first period, the first term in (1.10) is an income effect, which is negative, while the second is a substitution effect which is positive. This has been illustrated graphically in Figure 1, where

$$\text{the substitution effect} = AB = -\frac{U_2}{A} > 0,$$

and

$$\text{the income effect} = BC = \frac{U_{12} - rU_{22}}{A} < 0.$$

The supply schedule will have a positive slope, i.e., $g'(r) > 0$ and hence $dI/d\lambda > 0$, when the substitution effect dominates the income effect. In general,

$$\frac{dI^s}{d\lambda} \gtrless 0 \text{ if } |\epsilon^s| \lessgtr 1; \text{ where } \epsilon^s = g'(r)\frac{r}{I} \tag{1.11}$$

Equating I^{*d} and I^{*s} i.e., equations (1.5) and (1.9) yield the equilibrium sharing ratio.

It is not surprising that in a world of perfect information and certainty, it does not matter whether investment transactions take place on the basis of a fixed and predetermined rate or on the basis of a

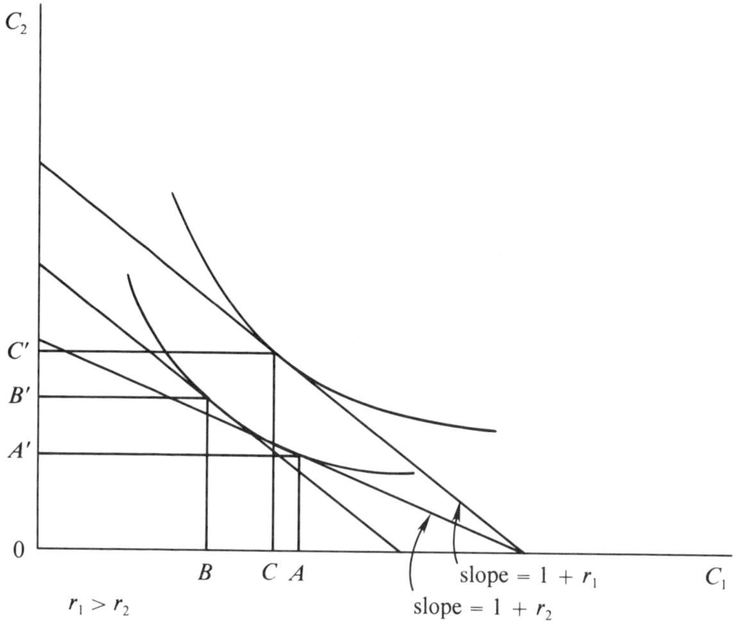

Figure 1

profit-sharing arrangement. Firms and agents recognize the availability of a market-determined opportunity cost of capital that is available and known with perfect certainty. Transactions are therefore based on this measure of opportunity cost, which also turns out to be the return to capital. In the case of uncertainty to which we now turn, this would no longer be true, since each firm and investor transacts in an environment where the outcome is not predetermined. The risk that now prevails has to be shared between the lender and the borrower.

V. INTRODUCING UNCERTAINTY: PERFECT INFORMATION

A convenient way to introduce uncertainty into the problem is to assume that some random factor θ influences the production function. For computational ease in later analysis, it is assumed that this factor is multiplicative. Hence the production function is writen as[18]

$$\theta f(I).$$

Since the profits of the firm are now simply revenues, i.e., $\theta f(I)$ minus the cost to the firm which is the borrowing of the firm (i.e., I), profits may be represented as $f(I) - I$. These profits are to be shared according to a predetermined sharing ratio λ. Thus, the firm retains $(1 - \lambda)(f(I) - I)$, while giving $\lambda(f(I) - I) + I$ to the investor.

Assuming the utility function $V(\ )$ for the entrepreneur (the agent), the combined problem for the economy may now be written as:

$$\text{Max } EU(Y - I, \lambda\theta f(I) + (1 - \lambda)I) \tag{2.1}$$

subject to

$$EV[(1 - \lambda)\{\theta f(I) - I\}] \geqq \overline{V} \tag{2.2}$$

The first order conditions, with γ as the Lagrange Multiplier for equation (2.2) are:

$$-EU_1 + EU_2[\lambda\theta f'(I) + (1 - \lambda)] + \gamma V'[(1 - \lambda)\theta f'(I) - 1] = 0 \tag{2.3}$$

$$E(U_2 - \gamma V')(\theta f(I) - I) = 0 \tag{2.4}$$

Equation (2.4) implies the Borch condition[19] of optimal risk sharing, i.e., the ratio of the marginal utilities with respect to λ of the two sharing parties is equal to a constant. This is the usual condition obtained in problems where full information enables optimal risk sharing.

Since in this case the firm borrows up to the point where the marginal productivity of capital is equal to 1 (i.e., $f'(I) = 1$), the third term in equation (2.3) is equal to zero, thus:

$$\frac{EU_1}{EU_2} = 1 \text{ for all } \theta. \tag{2.5}$$

Consequently, optimal risk sharing enables the consumer to equate expected marginal utilities across time periods.[20]

It is perhaps worth commenting on the first order condition for the firm, i.e., $f'(I) = 1$. This implies that the investment decision of the entrepreneur is independent of the profit-sharing ratio and depends only on the available technology. This result seems plausible since the prevalence of profit sharing leads to a situation where the respective roles of the lender and the entrepreneur are indistinguishable, as both are residual income earners. Unlike the fixed return case, there are no "fixed" costs to borrowing. Nor are there any bond holders whose claims take precedence. It can immediately be seen from the first order condition that investment is larger with profit sharing, since in this case the expected marginal revenue is equated to a constant 1, while in the traditional case it is equated to $(1 + r)$. Diagrammatically, this can be illustrated as in Figure 2.[21] The ray OC with slope $(1 + r)$ represents the cost of capital in the traditional case whereas in the profit-sharing case, OD with slope 1 represents the cost of capital. Consequently, a level of investment equivalent to OA obtains in the traditional case, whereas the profit-sharing case yields a higher level, OB.

VI. UNCERTAINTY AND UNOBSERVABILITY

The results obtained thus far have shown that a move from a situation of a known and fixed rate of return to one where only prean-

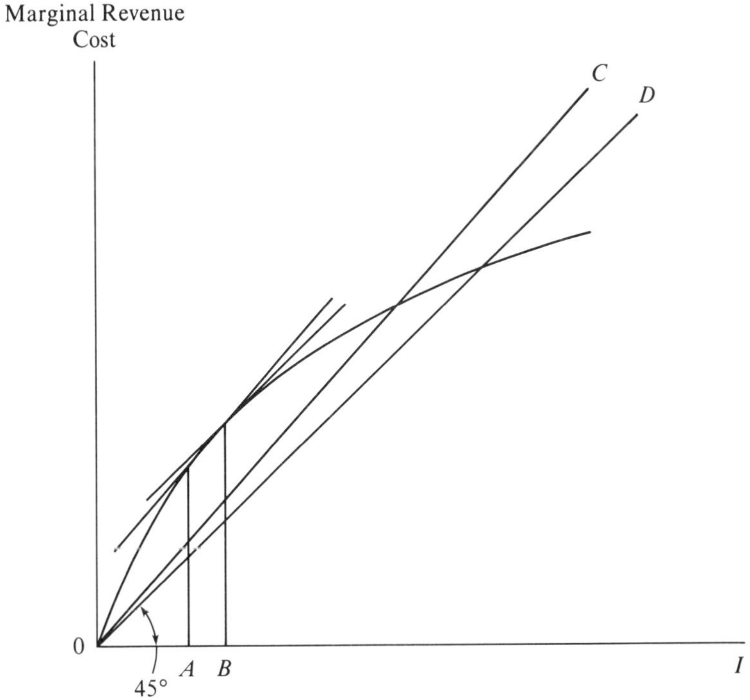

Figure 2

nounced profit-sharing rules are allowed does not necessarily lead to any observable sub-optimality. Both in the deterministic case and when uncertainty prevails with perfect information, i.e., all participants are able to observe all events as they occur, first-best solutions obtain. Information, however, may be asymmetric because certain events may either not be observable or the cost of observing them may be too high. For example, actions of the agent-entrepreneur that are important to the overall performance of the project undertaken may not be easily observable by the principal, or the production process itself may be subject to some uncertainties and not fully observable by the principal. In these situations there would be a moral hazard problem leading to a second-best solution. In their contracting, however, individual investors would attempt to account for this lack of information. It has been shown in the principal-agent literature[22] that the principal can use his knowledge of the prevailing uncertainty and the behavioral relationships in the contract in order to obtain optimal behavior from the agent.

A simple way to accommodate asymmetric information is to assume that realization of θ cannot be verified by the principal. In order to overcome the problem of asymmetric information, the individual would now need to write the contract such that all relevant information is used to deduce the state that is realized when, in fact, it is realized. To this end an incentive compatibility constraint, which is essentially like a truth-telling constraint, is utilized. Such a constraint can be written to ensure that in each state the desired level of investment takes place.[23] The profit sharing then becomes a function of the level of investment, which is observable. Using this reasoning the principal's problem can be written as:

$$\max_{\lambda()} EU(Y - I, \lambda\theta f(I) + (1 - \lambda)I) \tag{3.1}$$

subject to

$$EV[(1 - \lambda)(\theta f(I) - I)] \geqq V \tag{3.2}$$

and $I(\theta)$ is defined by the solution to

$$\max_{I(\theta)} EV((1 - \lambda)(\theta f(I) - I)), \tag{3.3}$$

which yields the optimal level of investment for the agent-entrepreneur. The principal, on the other hand, takes this level of investment as given and determines the optimal sharing ratio $\lambda(I)$. The equation

(3.3) is the truth-telling constraint which ensures that for a give state, the optimal level of investment is undertaken.

In the standard principal-agent problem where some output which is determined by the agent's action is to be divided, moral hazard is avoided by assuming a risk-neutral agent.[24] When the agent's effort (which determines the output) is explicitly entered in the principal's utility function, however, moral hazard is not eliminated and the first-best solution does not obtain.[25] The distinction between standard contracts analyzed in the principal-agent literature where a principal is to share in the output of an agent whose action is unobservable, and those embodying Islamic-type financial transactions where current savings are to be invested at an uncertain rate linked to profitability, were referred to earlier. Additionally, it is more than likely that the providers of investable funds, say investment depositors in an Islamic bank, would be small savers with little opportunity for diversification, whereas the principals are likely to be the banks or entrepreneurs with far greater opportunities for portfolio diversification. For these reasons, in addition to greater tractability, it is assumed here that the agent is risk-neutral.

For the solution of the problem presented in equations (3.1) to (3.3), it is more convenient to work in the state space by making the following transformation:[26]

$$k(\theta) = \lambda\theta f(I) + (l - \lambda)I = k(\lambda, I, \theta). \tag{3.4}$$

It may be noted that $k_I > 0$ and $k_\lambda > 0$[27] and hence k can be used, given either λ or I to obtain one or the other as a function of the state variable. Thus, if we can obtain k as a function of the optimal state θ and I as a function of θ we can obtain λ as a function of θ.

Transforming to the state space means that the incentive compatibility constraint should now serve to optimize behavior in each state. Consequently, this constraint in the state space is rewritten such that

$$\max_{\tilde{\theta}} \{\theta f(I(\tilde{\theta})) - k(\tilde{\theta})\} \text{ occurs at } \tilde{\theta} = \theta \tag{3.5}$$

The constraint is introduced in the problem by the statement that the first and second order conditions for that problem hold as identities in θ at $\tilde{\theta} = \theta$. In this manner, optimal behavior by the firm is ensured in all states. The first order conditions which ensure this optimal behavior are

$$\theta f'(I(\theta))I'(\theta) - k'(\theta) = 0, \text{ and} \tag{3.6}$$

$$\theta f''(I(\theta))I'(\theta)^2 + \theta f'(I(\theta))I''(\theta) - k''(\theta) < 0. \tag{3.7}$$

The problem in equation (3.1) to (3.3) may now be rewritten as

$$\begin{cases} \max EU(Y - I(\theta), k(\theta)) & \text{subject to} \\ E\theta f(I(\theta)) - k(\theta) \geqq \overline{\pi} & \text{and} \\ \theta f(I(\theta))I'(\theta) - k'(\theta) = 0 & \text{for all } \theta. \end{cases} \tag{3.8}$$

A further simplification may be made by letting $f(I(\theta)) = g(\theta)$ and rewriting the utility function of the principal,

$$U(Y - f^{-1}(g(\theta)), k(\theta)) = W(g(\theta), k(\theta)) \tag{3.9}$$

The derivatives of the two functions are then related as follows

$$U_2 = W_k; \qquad -U_1 = W_g f'.$$

Using g and k as state variables the problem can be written in a considerably simplified form, that is

$$\begin{cases} \text{Max } EW(g, k) & \text{subject to} \\ E(\theta g - k) \geqq \overline{\pi}, & \text{and} \\ \theta g' - k' = 0 & \text{for all } \theta. \end{cases} \tag{3.10}$$

Since the welfare function is concave and the constraints are linear, optimality is guaranteed by the fulfillment of the first order conditions. The Lagrangian expression for the problem may now be written out as[28]

$$\int_a^b \{W(g(\theta), k(\theta)) \begin{matrix} + \gamma(\theta g(\theta) - k(\theta) - \overline{\pi})\} y(\theta) \\ + h(\theta)(\theta g'(\theta) - k'(\theta))\, d\theta \end{matrix} \tag{3.11}$$

where $y(\theta)$ is the density function for the occurrence of the state θ, γ is the multiplier for the profits maximizing constraint and $h(\theta)$ is the functional multiplier for the incentive compatibility constraint. The Euler equations for the problem are:

$$y(W_g + \gamma\theta) = -\theta h' - h, \tag{3.12}$$

$$y(W_k - \gamma) = h', \tag{3.13}$$

$$\theta g' - k' = 0, \tag{3.14}$$

and the transversality conditions are

$$h(a) = h(b) = 0 \tag{3.15}$$

$$h(a)a = h(b)b = 0. \tag{3.16}$$

Under reasonable smoothness and differentiability assumptions, unique and continuous functions $h(\theta)$, $g(\theta)$, and $k(\theta)$ will be obtained as solutions. Combining equations (3.12) and (3.13) yields

$$W_g + \theta W_k + \frac{h}{y} = 0. \tag{3.17}$$

Equation (3.17) is the basic result that is derived in most of the principal-agent literature, in that there is a factor that drives a wedge into the first-best solution that would have obtained had there been no problem of unobservability. The factor h/y distorts the first-best sharing rule and dertermines the direction of the departure from efficiency. In terms of the sharing ratios, the rule can be stated as:

$$\frac{-U_1}{f'} + \theta U_2 + \frac{h}{y} = 0. \tag{3.18}$$

This expression illustrates more clearly the distortionary effects of the moral hazard problem since the first-best solution requires that

$$\frac{U_1}{U_2} = \theta f', \tag{3.19}$$

which is equivalent to

$$-\frac{Wg}{W_k} = \theta. \tag{3.20}$$

Since y is the probability of occurrence of state θ, it is positive. Hence the departure from efficiency is determined by the sign of the multiplier for the incentive compatibility constant. If $h > 0$, then $W_g + \theta W_k < 0$ implying that

$$-\frac{U_1}{U_2} > \theta f' \tag{3.21}$$

i.e., the marginal rate of time preference that is implicitly derived by the marginal rate of substitution between the two time periods is greater than the marginal product of capital in all states. Consequently, investment levels are greater than they would be in the first-best risk sharing arrangement of the previous section (2.5 in text). Alternatively equation (3.21) shows that the marginal cost of investment as measured by the loss in utility that arises from foregoing consumption in the first period is larger than the marginal return in the second period. Consequently, over-investment (under-investment) will result if $h > 0$ (<0). Differentiating equation (3.13) with respect to θ and using the incentive compatibility constraint (3.14) yields:

$$h'' = (W_{kk}\theta + W_{kg})g'y + y'\left(\frac{h'}{y}\right) \tag{3.22}$$

and substituting for θ from (3.17):

$$h'' = \left[\left(W_{kk}\left(\frac{-W_g}{W_k}\right) + W_{kg}\right) - \frac{W_{kk}}{W_k}\frac{h}{y}\right]g'y + \frac{y'h'}{y} \tag{3.23}$$

since normality of consumption requires that

$$U_{22}\left(\frac{U_1}{U_2}\right) - U_{21} < 0$$

and since $U_{22} = W_{kk}$, $U_2 = W_k$; $U_1 = -W_g f'$, $U_{21} = -W_{kg} f'$, and $f'(\theta) = g'(\theta)$, hence

$$\left[W_{kk}\left(\frac{-W_g}{W_k}\right) + W_{kg}\right]g' < 0. \tag{3.24}$$

Thus, the expression in round brackets in (3.23) is negative. Since $g' > 0$, $W_k > 0$, and $W_{kk} < 0$, if $h < 0$, the expression in the square brackets in (3.23) will be negative implying $h'' < (y'h'/y)$. If $h > 0$ then the relationship $h'' < (y'h'/y)$ may not hold.

Assuming that $h \leqq 0$ at some interior points of $[a, b]$; since h is continuous, it must attain a minimum in this interval. Call this minimum θ^*. At θ^* then by assumption $h'(\theta^*) = 0$ and $h''(\theta^*) \geqq 0$. But this contradicts $h'' < y'(h'/y)$. Therefore, $h \geqq 0$ and in particular $h > 0$ for all θ in the interior of $[a, b]$.

Since h has been proven to be positive, equation (3.17) suggests that $(W_g/W_k) > \theta$, i.e., the intertemporal marginal rate of substitution is greater than the marginal product of capital. Consequently, investment will be higher than the level that would have prevailed under complete observability when the first-best solution of perfect risk sharing was possible.[29]

In order to see the effect of moral hazard on the profit-sharing ratio, recall that any solution to our original problem defined in (3.1) to (3.3) defines $I(\theta)$ and $\lambda(I(\theta))$ for each θ. These optimal functions for I and λ can be used to define the optimal k and g that will optimize the problem in (3.10). Conversely, now that we have optimal $k(\theta)$ and $g(\theta)$, and $I(\theta)$ can be derived by inverting the production function, which is monotonic, to obtain a unique $I(\theta)$ if $I'(\theta)$ is monotonic. Since the incentive compatibility constraint (3.6) holds identically for all θ, differentiating it yields:

$$k''(\theta) = f'(I(\theta))I'(\theta) + \theta f''(I(\theta))(I'(\theta))^2 + \theta f'(I(\theta))I''(\theta). \tag{3.25}$$

Substituting this expression for $k''(\theta)$ in (3.10) the second order condition for the firm's problem becomes

$$\theta f'(I(\theta))I'(\theta) > 0. \tag{3.26}$$

Since $f'(I(\theta)) > 0$, $I'(\theta) > 0$. Consequently, for each θ, $I(\theta)$ can be determined uniquely from the optimal $g(\theta)$.

Recall from the definition of $k(\theta)$ in (3.4) that for each k and θ, $\lambda'(I) < 0$. Consequently, since the optimal level of investment in the moral hazard situation is greater than that which would obtain in the first best situation where perfect observability prevails, the return to capital in the moral hazard problem may be less than that in the first-best situation. However, since the level of investment has increased, the total profitability of the enterprise may be increased as observed earlier.

VII. CONCLUSIONS

The paper has studied behavior in a system where a profit-sharing rule of borrowing prevails. As discussed, the Islamic system of finance, which is gaining increasing importance in Muslim countries, requires the replacement of the current and traditional system of a guaranteed ex ante fixed rate of return to lenders by a system of profit-sharing between the lender and the borrower. The adoption of this system would therefore result in risk sharing between lender and borrower as well. Consequently, investment behavior and the level of aggregate investment may change as a result of this systemic change.

These issues have been examined in the case of certainty and in the case of uncertainty, both when information is available to all parties and when there is an observability problem. It has been shown that in the case of perfect certainty and full information, whether investment decisions are based on profit sharing or on a fixed rate of return does not have any real consequences for the economy. When uncertainty prevails, however, the level of investment may actually increase under certain conditions. Intuitively, this latter result seems plausible as the move to a profit-sharing system does away with the distinction between the entrepreneur and the lender. A fixed cost for capital is no longer required to be met as a part of the firm's profit calculations. The marginal product of capital can therefore be taken up to the point where maximum profits are obtained without the constraint of meeting a fixed cost on capital. Both the owners of the firm and the lenders to a firm are now residual income earners.

The paper also serves to illustrate how the view that unobservability may be an externality that precludes the smooth functioning of an Islamic system of profit sharing, may be incorrect. Contracting on the basis of observable indicators that may be correlated with the unobservable factors could prevent any market failure. Consequently, individual contracting and arbitrage would enable a market-determined sharing ratio for the economy to be determined. Since this form of contracting allows greater utilization of capital, profitability increases. The net return to capital, however, may or may not increase.

The conclusions of this paper are likely to be quite useful in economies that are currently making the transition to a profit-sharing system. First, the results are reassuring in that there is no market failure and individual investors and firms can continue to transact freely and openly in the usual decentralized manner. Second, it illustrates the importance of developing individual firm-specific or project-specific contracts that elicit optimal behavior in the presence of moral hazard. The use of monitoring or sharing rules that are a function of observables, which are in turn correlated with unobservable events or actions, should therefore be encouraged. The efficient working of the system in particular cases would of course depend, to quite an extent, on the ability of the domestic legal system to enforce these contracts in a speedy and judicious manner.[30]

Perhaps the most significant result of the paper is the disproving of the notion that investment levels must decline following the adoption of a profit-sharing system. The paper serves to illustrate that there is no immediately obvious conclusion on the effect of the adoption of profit-sharing system on investment. The models examined here have demonstrated an increase in investment under certain conditions. Before this result can be firmed up for policy purposes, however, further work would be required. First, an examination should be made of the sensitivity of the results that have been derived here to the assumption of risk aversion and to the sources of unobservability. Second, for the effective working of an interest-free Islamic system, efforts will need to be made to limit monitoring, enforcement and contract-design costs. Policy initiative in this direction would require the development of an extensive legal and institutional infrastructure that allows smoother transactions with enhanced monitoring and speedy enforcement. Third, efficiency will further improve if secondary markets develop for the trading of profit-sharing contracts. Although their project- or firm-specific nature would make these contracts imperfect substitutes, such trading would allow a near certain rate of return on capital to be determined. Finally, the issue of adverse selection when profit-sharing contracts are written would need examination.

NOTES

1. Two Muslim countries, the Islamic Republic of Iran and Pakistan, have opted for a comprehensive adoption of an Islamic-based financial system. While Pakistan has chosen a gradual approach towards Islamization, taking eight years to adopt an interest-free banking system in 1985, Iran completely transformed its economy in one move in 1983. Notwithstanding the different approaches, the two countries have faced similar problems. One of these, which is of relevance to this study, is the heavy concentration of bank asset portfolios in short-term trade transactions—probably an outcome of individual risk perceptions. However, this trend, if continued, would threaten longer-term growth prospects.

2. Since all investors are residual income earners, marginal productivity of capital is not equated to a fixed rate of interest plus one but to one—hence enabling greater profits to be obtained. This can be seen diagrammatically by observing that with a cost of capital, the profit-maximizing level of output is below the point where maximum obtains and the marginal product is one (see Figure 2).

3. See, for example, Holmstrom (1983), Kihlstrom and Laffont (1983), Grossman and Hart (1983) and Green and Kahn (1983).

4. Weitzman (1985). Addressing the question of profit sharing as an alternative to the wage system, Weitzman issues a "friendly challenge" for his critics saying "I challenge any one to cook up an empirical real world scenario, with reasonable number of specifications, where a profit-sharing system does not deliver significantly greater social welfare than a wage system."

5. One such attempt is a doctoral thesis by W.M. Khan (1984) in which he compares debt and equity instruments and, under a given set of assumptions, concludes

that where moral hazard is absent, variable rate of return instruments are superior. Arrangements on the basis of fixed rate of return (debt instruments) dominate when moral hazard is present. Khan concludes that one explanation for the dominance of debt instruments in the financial market may be that they minimize the cost of monitoring.

6. Khan (1986).

7. Khan and Mirakhor (1985).

8. In a very terse, direct and forceful verse, the Quran exhorts "O you who believe, fulfill (your) contracts" and directs Muslims to reduce their contracts to writing and have witnesses to the conclusion of their agreement. The faithfulness to one's contractual obligations is so central to Islamic belief that when the Prophet was asked, "Who is a believer?" he replied that a believer is one with whom the people can trust their person and possessions.

9. By primary sources of Islamic Law we mean the Quran and the actions and sayings of the Prophet which were meant to illustrate, explain, and exemplify the teachings of the Quran.

10. Consequently, Islamic Law as laid down early in Islamic history defines a contract in a manner quite similar to the modern notion of a contract.

11. For earlier work on principal-agent models, see Wilson (1969), Ross (1973), and Mirrlees (1976). For a good basic review of the theory see Rees (1985, 1985). For more recent work in this area see Harris and Raviv (1979), Holmstrom (1979), Shavell (1979), Gjesdal (1982), Hughs (1982), Grossman and Hart (1983), and Singh (1985).

12. See Pauly (1968), Zeckhauser (1970), Spence and Zeckhauser (1971). Arrow (1971) observes that in cases where there is possibility of moral hazard there is an advantage in behavior which is not motivated by narrow self-interest, i.e., moral behavior.

13. A participation constraint is the utility offered to the principal to a contract at least equal to what he could achieve in other activities.

14. See Pratt and Zeckhauser (1985).

15. The importance of "moral behavior" in reducing agency costs has been pointed out by Arrow (1971). It must be noted that behavior that would be in compliance with the stipulations of contracts is an ethical-legal requirement underlying the Islamic law of contracts. Adherence to and enforcement of these laws can minimize monitoring costs.

16. Contrary to the model that follows, this model exhibits naive behavior in that the entrepreneur does not use the knowledge that

$$r = \frac{\lambda \pi^*}{I^*}.$$

17. As shown later this may not be strictly correct since each firm's cost of capital depends on its own profitability and not on some general index of profitability in the economy. However, in this case of identical firms λ and π will be constant across firms. Primes indicate derivatives.

18. θ is a random variable with mean 1 and some standard deviation, say σ. This implies that $E(\theta f(I)) = f(I)$. Thus, for each realization of the state of the world, production is defined by $\theta f(I)$. In this manner, one can refer to θ as the variable that defines the state of the world for us.

19. Borch (1962).

20. If, as can be expected, a subjective rate of time preference is a part of individual preferences, equating marginal utilities will result in differing levels of consumption in the two time periods. The point can be made clearer by considering the case of separable utility function with an explicit time preference parameter, ρ. Then

$u'(C_1) = \rho u'(C_2)$

Thus, with the same utility function for the two time periods differing levels of consumption and hence marginal utilities are obtained because of the time preference parameter.

21. The illustration assumes certainty for greater clarity.

22. See for example Holmstrom (1972) and Grossman and Hart (1981).

23. See for example Grossman and Hart (1981) and Green and Kahn (1983).

24. See for example Harris and Raviv (1976).

25. Green and Kahn (1983).

26. The formulation of the problem in equations (3.1) to (3.3) is in terms of the sharing ratio λ. The term state space is used to indicate that the transformations allow us to work in terms of each realization of θ, i.e., the state of the world.

27. Assuming the firm is expected to be profitable.

28. In these terms the problem is now similar to the wage contracting problem studied by Green and Kahn (1983). The choice there was between labor and leisure in the same time period whereas in our problem, an intertemporal consumption investment decision is being considered.

29. Similar conclusions have been obtained in cases where employment contracts based on risk and profit sharing have been analyzed, under specifications similar to those utilized in this paper, using the principal-agent theory, i.e., increases in employment are possible when joint wage-employment contracts are signed (Green and Kahn, 1983). That profit-sharing arrangements have an employment-increasing characteristic has also been emphasized by Weitzman using a different methodology than the standard principal-agent framework (Weitzman, 1983). Weitzman concludes that "there are strong theoretical reasons for believing that were a share system in effect for large firms, the average worker, as well as the economy as a whole, would be better off because of the built-in bias toward eliminating unemployment, expanding production, and lowering prices." The analogy between investable funds as a factor of production as used in this paper and employment needs no elaboration.

30. An investigation of the process of transformation in the countries adopting an Islamic economic system reveals that bankers ascribe the problem of moral hazard or asymmetric information (real or perceived) to be an important explanation for individual preference for short-term liquidity. This perception of moral hazard is heightened by the unavailability of efficient monitoring systems and the lack of effective legal systems for enforcing contracts. Additionally, but to varying degrees, the lack of a clear definition of private property rights and of the role of private property increases the uncertainty in the environment.

8

*The Financial System and Monetary Policy in an Islamic Economy**

Mohsin S. Khan and Abbas Mirakhor

Mohsin S. Khan is Assistant Director, Research Department, International Monetary Fund; Abbas Mirakhor is Economist, Research Department, International Monetary Fund.

I. INTRODUCTION*

The central feature of an Islamic financial system is the absolute prohibition of the payment and receipt of interest. Thus, countries that have chosen to bring their economic systems into closer accordance with the rules prescribed by Islamic Law have had to restructure their banking systems to conform with the restriction on interest-based financial transactions. As Islamic Law, while rejecting the concept of a predetermined interest rate, permits an uncertain rate of return based on trade and profits, banks in an Islamic economy can strictly operate only on some type of profit and loss sharing basis.[1] Such arrangements for the conduct of financial transactions have been adopted in the Islamic Republic of Iran, Pakistan, and to a more limited extent, other Islamic countries.[2]

In broad terms, an Islamic banking system is essentially an equity-based system in which depositors are treated as if they were shareholders of the bank. Consequently, depositors are not guaranteed the nominal value, or a predetermined rate of return, on their deposits. If the bank makes profits then the shareholder (depositor) is entitled to receive a certain proportion of these profits. On the other hand, if the bank incurs losses the depositor is expected to share in these as well, and receive a negative rate of return. Thus, from the depositor's perspective an Islamic commercial bank is in most respects identical to a mutual fund or investment trust. Furthermore, to remain consistent with religious strictures, the bank cannot charge interest in its lending operations, but has to use special modes of investment and financing that are also based on the concept of profit and loss sharing.

The implementation of an equity-based financial system in which any type of fixed rate of return on transactions is excluded raises a number of complex issues. First, it is necessary to develop alternative financial instruments that do not have a fixed nominal value and bear a predetermined rate of interest. There are in fact a number of such alternatives proposed by Islamic scholars that satisfy such requirements. Second, there is the question of how monetary policy would be expected to operate in an interest-free economy. This is, of course, an issue of immediate relevance for the policymakers in Islamic countries. Obviously, instruments of monetary policy that rely in any way on the rate of interest would be removed from the arsenal of the authorities, and suitable substitutes would have to be found if monetary policy is to continue to play a role in Islamic economies.

Much of the literature on Islamic banking has focused on the creation and development of financial instruments that are regarded as permissible under Islamic Law.[3] The conduct of monetary policy in an Islamic economy has also been addressed recently in a number of papers.[4] The studies on monetary policy contain, in varying detail, descriptions of the instruments that the authorities could employ to change the quantity and rates of return on financial claims in the economy. Even though the use of the discount rate and open market operations with interest-bearing securities are precluded, there are a number of policy instruments available for controlling domestic liquidity. These include, for example, changes in reserve requirements, overall and selective controls on credit flows, changes in the monetary base through management of currency issue, and moral suasion. Furthermore, as pointed out by Akram Khan (1982) and Siddiqi (1982), open market operations could still be conducted with securities that do not bear a fixed rate of return. The monetary authorities also have the possibility of directly changing the rates of return on both deposits and loans by altering the ratios in which the banks and the public are expected to share in the profits and losses that are associated with the transactions, i.e., the profit-sharing ratios. However, this is still a somewhat controversial issue as there are certain scholars who believe it would be inappropriate for the central bank to unilaterally change a contractually-determined ratio. At the same time, other writers have argued in favor of regulating profit-sharing ratios to achieve the goal of monetary stability, provided such actions affect only new deposits and loans and not existing ones.[5]

While the existing studies provide a very useful inventory of the financial instruments that could substitute for interest-based instruments, they do not analyze how these would actually operate in an Islamic environment. Indeed, there is surprisingly little work of a formal nature on the financial system and the general role of monetary policy in an Islamic economy. The purpose of this paper is to first describe the main characteristics of an Islamic financial system. This part of the study relies on both the recent writings on the subject as well as the actual practice of Islamic banking in countries such as Iran and Pakistan. This description of the institutional framework sets the stage for the development of a simple theoretical model of the Islamic economic system. This model, while highly stylized, is nevertheless able to address some of the main issues of concern to the monetary authorities in Islamic countries. These issues include, in particular, the relationship between the instruments that a central bank in an Islamic economy has at its disposal and overall financial conditions in the economy, and the effects of monetary changes on macroeconomic variables. The focus in this paper will be primarily on determining whether such relationships are fundamentally altered when a country decides to move from a conventional financial system to an Islamic one.

In the next section (Section II) we describe the financial structure in an Islamic economy, paying particular attention to the types of transactions that would replace interest-rate transactions. The model that is based on this institutional structure is discussed in Section III. The concluding section brings together the main results of the paper, points out some of the limitations of the analysis, and finally, suggests areas where further research is needed to assist policymaking in Islamic countries.

II. INSTITUTIONAL CHARACTERISTICS OF AN ISLAMIC BANKING SYSTEM

The explicit injunction against the payment of interest implies that banks in an Islamic economy are denied conventional sources of funds, such as interest-bearing deposits, and cannot undertake lending operations on the basis of predetermined rates of return. However, although Islamic Law prohibits interest in any form, it permits profits arising from trade and business transactions. Consequently, profit sharing and equity participation are the principles on which Islamic banks have to operate. In the Islamic system savings are mobilized through direct participation of savers in entrepreneurial activities, including banking, and surplus funds are loaned out in various forms of (religiously) approved transactions. This section describes the methods that have evolved to enable banks to continue to serve their function as intermediaries between savers and investors, while at the same time remaining consistent with the guidelines of Islam.

We start by considering the liability side of the balance sheet of banks, and then turn to the asset side where we discuss in somewhat more detail the approved modes of lending and financing.

1. Sources of Funds

Besides their own capital and equity, the main sources of funds for Islamic banks would be two forms of deposits—transaction deposits and investment deposits.

a. Transaction Deposits

As the name suggests, such deposits are directly related to transactions and payments, and can be regarded as equivalent to demand deposits in conventional banking systems. Although a bank would guarantee the nominal value of the deposit, it would pay no interest on this type of liability. Banks would be expected to provide a variety of services to the holders of transaction deposits, the most important of which are checking facilities.[6] Generally speaking, funds mobilized through this source cannot be used for profitable investment by banks. As such, banks would presumably have to levy a service charge on deposit holders to cover the costs of administering this type of account.

It has been argued that transaction deposits should have a 100 percent reserve requirement placed on them, with the backing being in the form of currency, foreign exchange, or suitable government securities.[7] Obviously with a 100 percent reserve requirement the nominal value of these deposits would be automatically guaranteed. Aside from satisfying the desires of risk-averse individuals for a completely safe financial asset, this reserve requirement would also prevent the possibility of a banking crisis from interfering with the payments mechanism.[8]

b. Investment Deposits

The principal source of funds for banks would be deposits that more closely resemble shares in a firm, rather than time and savings deposits of the customary sort. The bank offering investment deposits would provide no guarantee on their nominal value, and they would not pay a fixed rate of return. The depositor instead would be treated as if he were a shareholder in the bank and therefore entitled to a share of the profits made by the bank. If the bank's operations resulted in an overall loss, such losses would also be shared by the depositor (and the bank) and the nominal value of the deposit would be written down. Unlike in conventional banking systems where the depositor is guaranteed the nominal value of his deposit, either by the bank or by the government through explicit or implicit deposit insurance,[9] the only contractual agreement between the depositor and the bank is the proportion in which profits and losses are to be distributed. This profit-sharing ratio has to be agreed in advance of the transaction between the bank and the depositor, and cannot be altered during the life of the contract, except by mutual consent.

While there are no firm rules on how profits would be shared, the basis of distribution would be presumably the overall profit and loss position of banks. Distributable profits would be calculated by setting off administrative expenses, provisions for taxes and reserves, and payments due to the central bank and other banks in respect of the financing provided by them, from total profits. The resulting net profits would be divided between the shareholders of the banks and the holders of investment deposits using a formula that took into account the relative contributions of capital and equity, and investment deposits, to the profitability of the bank.[10] There are, however, two crucial differences between investment deposits and common stock of the bank. First, deposit holders would typically not have any say in the management of the bank, and second, dividends on common stock would be discretionary on the part of bank management, whereas investment deposits would always yield a constant proportion of profits.[11]

Of course, in the absence of a single, or representative, interest rate there would be an increase in the information costs to those wishing to place funds in investment deposits. Individuals would have to evaluate the relative performances of various banks in order to decide where to invest, instead of simply going into time and savings deposits with a known interest rate. However, the information costs can be significantly reduced if there is a secondary market in which investment deposit certificates are traded. This market would provide the necessary signals to the public on the current and expected performance of banks through the pricing of these investment deposit certificates.

As shown in a recent paper by Khan (1985), this system of investment deposits is quite closely related to proposals aimed at transforming the traditional banking system to an equity basis made frequently in a number of countries, including the United States.[12] Since the nominal value of investment deposits is not guaranteed and will fluctuate according to the performance of the bank, any shocks to asset positions are absorbed by changes in the value of shares (deposits) held by the public. Therefore, an equity-based system of this type can respond more easily and rapidly in the face of a banking crisis. In the traditional banking system the bank is expected to guarantee the nominal value of the deposit, and a shock can cause a divergence between the real value of assets and liabilities. If the bank cannot absorb losses through its reserves and borrowings from the central bank, this divergence may well result in instability and possible collapse of the payments mechanism. With the value of deposits directly linked to the earnings, and therefore assets, of banks, such a possibility is excluded from the Islamic banking system.[13]

2. Lending Operations of Banks

Unlike the equity—participation schemes advocated by Simons (1945) and others, which focus exclusively on the liability side of the balance sheets of banks, Islamic banks also have to apply the same principles of profit and loss sharing to their loan operations. The two methods that fully satisfy the requirements of Islamic Law on the lending side are what are known in Arabic as *Muḍārabah* and *Mushārakah* arrangements.[14] Both these forms are essentially variants of partnership agreements in which risk and return are shared by the contracting parties.

a) Muḍārabah Financing

In general terms, in this transaction surplus funds are made available by the owner to the entrepreneur to be invested in a productive economic activity in return for a predetermined percentage of the profits earned. During the lifetime of the project the lender is the sole owner of the project and the borrower is the manager. Profits are to be shared between the lender and the borrower, but in contrast to the case of investment deposits, there is an asymmetry insofar as losses are concerned. In a *Muḍārabah* arrangement financial losses have to be borne exclusively by the lender. The borrower, as such, loses only the time and effort invested in the venture.[15]

In practice, under *Muḍārabah* rules banks would provide loans to business enterprises, but instead of receiving a specific return, would be entitled to a proportion of the profits earned by the borrower. For the purpose of profit distribution, the respective capital contribution of the parties concerned could be brought to a common basis by multiplying the amounts by the number of days during which each particular item, such as the equity capital of the firm, its cash reserves, financing provided by the bank and other sources, were actually employed in the business.[16] In the limiting case where a bank provides all the capital, it would be the sole owner of the project.

Banks can either engage in direct lending, or can make loans indirectly through companies set up specifically to engage in *Muḍārabah* financing.[17] Risk capital for the *Muḍārabah* company is provided by banks in the form of direct equity, or through loans with equity features. Banks receive *Muḍārabah* certificates with a specific face value from the company, and these certificates can be traded between banks. The *Muḍārabah* company, which can either be a specific-purpose company organized to finance a single project or type of activity, or a multipurpose company covering a variety of activities, is required to engage only in financial operations that are permitted under Islamic Law. In all other respects the *Muḍārabah* company is subject to the rules and regulations applying to nonfinancial enterprises.

b) Mushārakah Financing

A complementary method to *Muḍārabah* financing is a *Mushārakah* transaction in which there is more than a single contributor of funds. All parties invest in varying proportions and the profits and losses are shared strictly in relation to their respective capital contributions. The essential difference between the two forms of financing is the number of parties involved in the transaction, and indeed *Mushārakah* financing corresponds closely to an equity market in which shares can be acquired by the public, banks, and even the central bank and the government.

Since the dividends from *Mushārakah* claims will not be known in advance, and there is a possibility of a loss of the initial financial investment, this form of financing also satisfies the rules of Islamic Law against interest. Firms desiring to raise funds for investment could use this mechanism and offer *Mushārakah* certificates in the market. Such certificates would thus be in effect transferable corporate instruments secured by the assets of the company.[18] Their price, and the implicit rate of return, would be determined through market forces.

c) Other Modes of Financing

The recommended methods of financing through *Muḍārabah* or *Mushārakah* contracts would tend to be most feasible in the case of large borrowers where the investment projects could be clearly identified and evaluated by the lender. There would be practical difficulties, however, in utilizing the strict profit and loss sharing approach to small-scale borrowers or for consumption loans.[19] As such, a number of alternative instruments for investment and financing that are not expressly forbidden by Islamic Law are available to banks. In the remainder of this subsection we discuss some of these.

(i) *Deferred Payment Sale, or "Mark-up".* This method allows for the sale of a product on the basis of deferred payments either in installments or in a lump sum. The price of the product is agreed to between the buyer and seller at the time of the sale and cannot include any charges for deferring payments. Insofar as banking transactions are concerned, this method, known in Arabic terminology as *Bay' Mu'jjal* or *Murābaḥah,* implies that the bank would purchase the product and resell it to the ultimate buyer, including in its price a profit margin or mark-up. This mark up has to be negotiated with the buyer (borrower) and cannot be set unilaterally by the bank.

Because of its inherent simplicity the mark-up method has become the most frequently used mode of financing in Islamic countries.[20] However, it is considered to be a second-best method in comparison to profit sharing. For the mark-up system to be consistent with Islamic Law the transaction must satisfy two conditions. First, the financier has to take physical possession of the goods being financed for the borrower. This ensures that the lender is exposed to some measure of risk. Second, the rate of mark-up should not be tied to the length of the period over which the financing is to be provided. This second condition means that there is an incentive to keep the maturity of the transaction fairly short.

(ii) *Purchase with Deferred Delivery.* In this transaction, known as *Bay' Salām,* the buyer pays the seller the full negotiated price of a product which the seller agrees to deliver at a specified future date. Obviously the transaction would be limited to goods whose quality and quantity is known at the time of the contract. Because of this characteristic, this future delivery method is particularly suited for agricultural financing. Essentially the bank enters into an agreement with the farmer for the future purchase of agricultural products and makes the payment when the contract is determined. The assets of the farmer could be used as collateral for the loan as a guarantee against fraud or negligence, but any financial losses incurred in the operation would have to be fully borne by the lending bank.

(iii) *Leasing.* A bank can purchase the product and lease it to the borrower for a specific sum and a specific period of time. The borrower can also negotiate for lease-purchase of the product, where the payments include a portion which can be applied towards the final purchase and transfer of ownership of the product. The bank, as in a normal leasing arrangement, can expect to receive payment for the cost of the product, as well as a share in the net rental value of the item. The risk also has to be shared between both parties in the event of any damage to the leased item.[21] The leasing method can be particularly helpful to enterprises in the acquisition of capital equipment, as well as for loans to households for purchases of consumer durables.

(iv) *Service Charges.* Islamic Law allows a lender to recover the costs of operation over and above the principal amount from the borrower. Thus, banks are legally able to impose a service charge or commission on the loans they make, as well as when they serve as trustees. There is one important condition attached to such charges. To prevent the commission or service charge from becoming equivalent to interest, the amount of the service charge cannot be made proportional to the size of the loan. The maturity of the loans of this type would necessarily tend to be short and the main beneficiaries of the method of lending would generally be consumers and other small-scale borrowers.

3. Islamic Banks and the Role of the Central Bank

Under the Islamic system, banking operations will undoubtedly be more varied and complex, as compared to the traditional banking system. The criterion of creditworthiness of the borrower that underlies conventional banking systems will have to be changed to place more emphasis on the viability and profitability of the specific project being proposed. In addition to a term structure of rates of return, there will be a structure of returns for different economic activities that banks have to consider. Project evaluation and appraisal, determination of profit-sharing ratios, and the establishment of a procedural framework for the processing, monitoring, supervision, and auditing of various projects will create new demands on commercial banks. On the liability side, banks would have to attract depositors on the basis of profits and dividends, rather than through interest rates. In short, commercial banks in an Islamic system would have to be transformed into institutions that would closely resemble investment banks in Western financial systems.

The monetary authorities operating in an Islamic framework would continue to have the power to regulate banking and financial operations in the economy to both allocate resources in conformity with the priorities of the society, as well as to direct monetary policy towards specific goals. To achieve its policy objectives, the central bank has control over the supply of high-powered money, the reserve ratios on the different types of liabilities, and the maximum amounts of assets which the banks can allocate to their profit-sharing activities. A further opportunity for enhancement of the control over the banking system is available to the central bank through its purchases of equity shares of banks and other financial intermediaries. Through performance of its regulatory, supervisory, and control functions, as well as its lender-of-last-resort role, the central bank can continue to exert substantial influence on the financial system. Moreover, opportunities will exist for the central bank to invest directly in the real sector on a profit-sharing basis, as well as to take equity positions in joint ventures along with other banks. The ability to buy and sell securities in the financial market, that is, open-market operations, will still be available to the central bank as long as these securities do not have par value features and a non-zero coupon rate.

Additionally, the suggestion has been made that the central bank could regulate profit-sharing ratios between the banks and borrowers on the one hand, and the banks and depositors on the other. Variations in these ratios will change the rates of return and could have the same impact as interest rates on the overall and sectoral flows of financial resources. There is, however, debate on whether such a policy is valid, since it represents a limitation on the freedom of contract and may be inequitable.[22] The issue of inequity would arise if the profit-sharing rules imposed by the central bank required, say, a lower return from profits than the share in losses.

III. A THEORETICAL MODEL OF THE ISLAMIC FINANCIAL SYSTEM

In order to study the design and effects of monetary policy we develop a simple macroeconomic model that incorporates the principal characteristics of Islamic banking outlined in Section II. This model is basically a variant of the general equilibrium financial models of Brainard (1967), Tobin (1969), and Modigliani and Papademos (1980), that have become standard in monetary theory. Specific attention is paid to the financial relationships in this model, since as argued by Modigliani and Papademos (1980), to properly analyze the role of monetary policy in affecting the actions of market participants, and the consequent effects on the spending behavior of firms and households, one has to employ a framework that takes explicitly into account the structure of financial markets. As will be shown, the model formulated here, despite its simplicity, is a useful representation of the basic Islamic financial system, and thus proves to be a convenient device for the study of monetary policy in an Islamic economy.

This section discusses the basic accounting structure of the model, the underlying behavioral relationships, and finally, the effects of monetary policy.

1. Structure of the Model

The financial side of the economy is assumed to be composed of commercial banks, which are the only financial intermediaries, the central bank, and the nonbank public.[23] In addition to financial assets, the model contains a single (composite) commodity that is both produced and consumed domestically. For simplicity, the economy is assumed to be closed so that there is no trade or capital movement.

a) Banking Sector

Commercial banks are assumed to offer only investment deposits (Db) to the public which, as discussed in the previous section, are not guaranteed by the banks and do not yield a predetermined rate of return. At this level of abstraction the exclusion of transactions deposits does not materially affect the analysis. The banks are assumed to pay depositors a rate of return (r_b) that is based on profits from their operations.[24] These profits are shared between the depositor and the bank in some mutually-agreed proportions determined prior to the transaction, so that r_b is the depositor's share of the profits as a proportion of his deposit. In other words, if π represents distributable profits of banks, and λ is the share of the depositor, then

$$r_b = \frac{\lambda\pi}{Db} \qquad \lambda > 0; \pi \lesseqgtr 0$$

Of course, should the bank incur losses, that is if $\pi < 0$, the rate of return to the depositor would be negative and the nominal value of the deposit (Db) would be reduced accordingly.

Unlike in the case of the traditional banking system, commercial banks in the Islamic system cannot borrow from the central bank through the customary mechanism of rediscounting at a given official discount rate. Any such borrowing has to be based on a profit and loss arrangement. We assume here that banks can borrow from the central bank only on a equity-participation basis. That is, the central bank purchases equity in the bank when it wishes to expand reserves in the system, and vice versa. Therefore, an additional source of funds for commercial banks becomes the sale of equity shares (Eb) to the central bank.[25] As in the case of investment deposits, the rate of return on equity shares (r_e) would depend on the overall profit position of banks, so that in contrast to an official discount rate, it would not be determined directly by the central bank.

On the lending side banks engage in only risk-return sharing *Muḍārabah* arrangements with the public. *Muḍārabah* financing (Fb) in this case is assumed to subsume all other types of similar arrangements, such as *Mushārakah* financing.[26] As in the case of investment deposits, the profits earned from the projects financed by the bank (π) are shared between the bank and the entrepreneur on a prearranged basis specified in the contract between the two before the financing is provided. Since the stock of *Muḍārabah* credit is defined to be the only income-yielding asset of the bank, its overall rate of return will be equal to the rate of return on *Muḍārabah* financing—r_b. If the profit-sharing ratio in favor of the bank is γ, then

$$r_b = \frac{\gamma\pi}{Fb} \qquad \gamma > 0; \pi \lesseqgtr 0$$

and the return to the borrower would consequently be equal to $(1 - \gamma)\pi/Fb$.

Banks are also required to hold a certain proportion of their liabilities to the public (Db) in the form of reserves with the central bank (Rb). There has been some discussion in the literature on Islamic banking as to whether investment deposits should be subject to legal reserve requirements or not.[27] In the present case, however, we assume that banks hold reserves at the central bank without necessarily implying that such holdings are mandatory.

b) Central Bank

The central bank's liabilities in this simplified system consist solely of reserves of commercial banks (Rc). Since there is no currency held by the public in the model, high-powered money in the economy is definitionally equal to the stock of bank reserves. On the asset side the central bank holds equity shares of commercial banks (Ec), and the rate of return (r_e) on these is market determined. The supply of reserves is changed by the central bank through variations in its stock of bank equity shares ($\Delta Ec = \Delta Rc$), which in turn alters the cost of borrowing for the banks.

c) Public Sector

Since commercial banks are the only financial intermediaries in the economy, investment deposits in the banking system represent financial wealth of the public. Total wealth of the public is, thus, equal to financial wealth and its stock of capital (K).[28] The public has basically two sources of funds: first, *Muḍārabah* financing obtained from banks (F_b), and second, its own savings (S). In the absence of a debt market, any desired increase in assets (financial or total) has to be accommodated through one of these sources.

The basic structure of the model that we have described above can be conveniently summarized in the flow of funds account (Table 1).

While Table 1, which defines the aggregate budget constraint of the economy,[29] is a very simple representation, it does nevertheless point out the main accounting relationships that can be expected to exist in an Islamic economy. Any model that attempts to explain this type of economy would necessarily have to ensure consistency with the flow of funds accounts.

Table 1. Flow of Funds Accounts of the Islamic Financial System

	Public		Banks		Central Bank	
	Uses	Sources	Uses	Sources	Uses	Sources
Investment deposits	ΔDp			ΔDb		
Mudarabah credit		ΔFp	ΔFb			
Equity of banks				ΔEb	ΔEc	
Reserves			ΔRb			ΔRc
Investment	I					
Savings		S				

2. Behavioral Relationships

The particular model that we utilize in the study of monetary policy in an Islamic economy is a variant of the standard IS-LM model. While relatively simple in structure the model developed is sufficiently general to incorporate the balance sheet restrictions outlined in Table 1.

In specifying this macroeconomic model we make three important assumptions. First, there is no attempt to an explicit price-output breakdown in the determination of national income. If prices are assumed to be fixed, as would be the case if a strict version of Keynesian model were employed, then all changes in income will reflect variations in real output. Here no distinction between nominal and real changes in income is considered as it is not essential to the argument. Second, the model does not feature any role for expectations. In other words, we assume here that expectations of economic agents are fully realized. Finally, the economy and the financial sector are assumed to be in continuous equilibrium and the analysis is essentially comparative static in nature.[30] Each economic variable is, thus, defined as a deviation from its respective equilibrium value.[31]

The real side of the economy is represented by a function relating the excess of investment over savings to the rate of return on bank (*Muḍārabah*) financing, the level of national income, and total net wealth of the public:

$$(I - S) = -a_1 r_b - a_2 Y + a_3 W_{-1} \quad (1)$$

where,

I = investment;
S = savings;
r_b = rate of return on bank financing;[32]
Y = national income; and,
W_{-1} = total net wealth of the public, defined as $K + Dp$, at the beginning of the period.

Equation (1) will be recognized as being simply an IS relationship, derived assuming that investment is a negative function of the rate of return on *Muḍārabah* financing, and savings a positive function of income. Net wealth at the beginning of the period is assumed to affect both investment and savings, with the former effect dominating.[33] Given the underlying relationships all the parameters in equation (1) are written to be positive.

The derivation of the LM part of the model is somewhat more complicated, since in contrast to the real sector where there was a single commodity, there are three financial assets in the model: bank loans, investment deposits, and equity shares of commercial banks. Starting with the loan market, the public's demand for *Muḍārabah* financing is specified as a function of the banks' required rate of return, and net wealth at the beginning of the period:

$$\Delta Fp = -f_1 r_b + f_2 W_{-1} \tag{2}$$

The banking sector's supply of *Muḍārabah* financing can be specified as a positive function of the rate of return, and a negative function of the cost of borrowing for banks. This cost will be effectively the rate of return on the banks' equity shares held by the central bank (r_e). The sale and repurchase of its equity is the only way a bank is assumed to be able to augment or reduce its resources. This operation, as pointed out earlier, is equivalent to the use of a rediscounting mechanism, where r_e is the quasi discount rate. The supply equation has the form:

$$\Delta Fb = s_1 r_b - s_2 r_e \tag{3}$$

Changes in the public's demand for investment deposits is derived from the balance sheet constraint:

$$\Delta Dp = \Delta Fp - (I - S) \tag{4}$$

Substituting equations (1) and (2) into equation (4), we obtain:

$$\Delta Dp = -(f_1 - a_1)\, r_b + a_2 Y + (f_2 - a_3) W_{-1} \tag{5}$$

The reserves of the banking system are given by the following definition:

$$\Delta Rb = k \Delta Dp \tag{6}$$

where k is the reserve ratio.

If the banking system passively meets the demand for deposits, $\Delta Db = \Delta Dp$, we are left with the following four markets:

$$(I - S) + (\Delta Fb - \Delta Fp) + (\Delta Rb - \Delta Rc) + (\Delta Ec - \Delta Eb) \equiv 0 \tag{7}$$

We can, thus, take advantage of Walras' Law to eliminate any one market, and here we have chosen to drop the equity shares market, $(\Delta Ec - \Delta Eb)$.

As mentioned earlier, the central bank adjusts the supply of reserves to the system by varying its holdings of equity shares of banks:

$$\Delta Rc = \Delta Ec \tag{8}$$

Given that the equity shares market is determined through (7), the equilibrium conditions of the model, that is,

$$\Delta Fp = \Delta Fb \tag{9}$$

$$\Delta Rc = \Delta Rb \tag{10}$$

$$I = S \tag{11}$$

allow us to solve for the three endogenous variables, namely the rates of return on *Muḍārabah* financing (r_b) and equity shares (r_e), and the level of national income (Y). Using these equilibrium conditions, the system of equations can be written as:

$$-(f_1 + s_1) r_b + s_2 r_e = -f_1 W_{-1} \tag{12}$$

$$-k(f_1 - a_1) r_b + k a_2 Y - \Delta Rc = -k(f_2 - a_3) W_{-1} \tag{13}$$

$$a_1 r_b - a_2 Y = a_3 W_{-1} \tag{14}$$

The system is closed by specifying an equation for the intermediate target for monetary policy, which then allows ΔRc to be determined.

c) Solution of the Model

We can now solve the model for two specific types of monetary policy. In the first, we assume the authorities wish to control the money supply itself; then we consider an alternative case where ceilings are placed on *Muḍārabah* financing.

If the intermediate target of monetary policy is the total money supply, which in turn is achieved by variations in the reserves of banks (Rc), the furth equation in the model becomes:

$$-(f_1 - a_1)r_b + a_2Y = \Delta M - (f_2 - a_3)W_{-1} \tag{15}$$

where ΔM is the change in the money supply, and as there is no currency in the hands of the public, $\Delta M = \Delta Dp$. Equation (15) is taken directly from equation (5), and basically says that the authorities adjust the supply of money to meet demand.

Solving the system of equations (12)–(15) we obtain the equilibrium values of r_b, r_e, Y, and Rc.[34] These are:

$$r_b^* = \frac{f_2}{f_1} W_{-1} - \frac{1}{f_1} \Delta M \tag{16}$$

$$r_e^* = \frac{s_1 f_2 W_{-1}}{s_2 f_1} - \frac{(f_1 + s_1)}{s_2 f_1} \Delta M \tag{17}$$

$$Y^* = \frac{(a_3 f_1 - a_1 f_2)}{a_2 f_1} W_{-1} + \frac{a_1}{a_2 f_1} \Delta M \tag{18}$$

$$\Delta Rc^* = k\Delta M \tag{19}$$

Given the assumed signs of the relevant parameters, an increase in the rate of monetary expansion will lower the rates of return on financial assets, and will raise the level of national income. This corresponds to the result obtained in the familiar *IS-LM* model when there is an outward shift in the *LM* curve.

Suppose the central bank, instead of choosing to target the overall money supply, decides to use *Muḍārabah* financing (ΔFb) as the operative variable and again adjusts ΔRc to achieve its target. In this case the central bank would have to ensure that the supply of *Muḍārabah* financing is equated to the demand. Equation (15) would, therefore, be replaced by equation (3) as follows:

$$-s_1 r_b + s_2 r_e = \Delta Fb \tag{15a}$$

The equilibrium values of r_b, r_e, Y, and ΔRc, from equations (12), (13), (14), and (15a) would be:

$$r_b^* = \frac{f_2}{f_1} W_{-1} - \frac{1}{f_1} \Delta Fb \tag{20}$$

$$r_e^* = \frac{s_1 f_2}{s_2 f_1} W_{-1} - \frac{(f_1 + s_1)}{s_2 f_1} \Delta Fb \tag{21}$$

$$Y^* = \frac{(a_3 f_1 - a_1 f_2)}{a_2 f_1} W_{-1} + \frac{a_1}{a_2 f_1} \Delta Fb \tag{22}$$

$$\Delta Rc^* = k \Delta Fb \tag{23}$$

The solutions of the model clearly show that it is a matter of indifferences as to whether the authorities attempt to influence monetary conditions directly, through changing the money supply, or use the flow of *Muḍārabah* financing as an intermediate objective. Both types of monetary policy measures yield identical effects on the financial rates of return in the system, and on the level of national income. Indeed, there is what one would expect to observe in a closed economy, where there is no economic difference whether the monetary authorities choose to focus on the liability or asset side of the balance sheet of the banking system. What is more important is that exactly the same solutions would have been obtained if one were working with a traditional financial system with a predetermined rate of interest on deposits. As long as lending rates are fully flexible, the two systems turn out to be formally equivalent from the standpoint of monetary policy. This result, while obtained for a closed-economy, also carries over to the more realistic case where trade in goods and financial claims is possible. As is well known, in an open economy with a fixed exchange rate, the money supply can no longer be treated as an exogenous policy instrument, as variations in it can be brought about through balance of payments surpluses and deficits. Consequently, it is the domestic component of the money stock, i.e., domestic credit, that becomes the relevant instrument of policy. In the Islamic system *Muḍārabah* credit is the counterpart to domestic credit, and accordingly can be used in the same manner to alter domestic financial conditions to achieve the desired results on macroeconomic variables in an open economy.

IV. CONCLUSIONS

The establishment of an economic system based on Islamic values requires fundamental changes in the operations of financial institutions. Since interest rates are not allowed, alternative mechanisms that rely primarily on a notion of profit sharing or equity participation have had to be developed to replace the system of interest-based transactions. The purpose of this paper was to describe some of these alternative methods of conducting financial transactions in an Islamic economy, and then to analyze the role of monetary policy in such an environment.

In very broad terms, the use of profit-sharing arrangements in place of interest rates makes commercial banks in an Islamic economy more akin to investment banks. Depositors receive a share of the profits made by the bank, rather than a predetermined rate of interest, and banks in turn receive a rate of return based on profits made by the borrower. At the simplest level, the Islamic financial system replaces debt financing by equity financing, and predetermined rates of return by returns that are a direct function of profits. Of course, this transformation requires the creation of a variety of financial institutions and instruments that have the profit-sharing characteristics, and in this paper we have discussed a number of those proposed in the literature.

To obtain a better understanding of how the Islamic financial system would function, and how it would interact with the real side of the economy, we developed a simple macroeconomic model that explicitly incorporated the main elements of an Islamic system. This model, which is really only a generalization of the standard *IS-LM* model, yields some useful insights on the determination of financial rates of return in the economy and how monetary policy is conducted. The principal conclusion to emerge from the analysis is that there is apparently no fundamental change in the way monetary policy affects economic variables in an Islamic economy. The authorities can achieve the very same results through controlling the supply of profit-based bank lending as they can through variations in the total money supply. While institutions and financial instruments may be quite different in an Islamic economy, the standard macroeconomic result, namely that an expansionary monetary policy would reduce rates of return and increase output in the short run, carries through.

What the authorities do lose in the process is the ability to directly set financial rates of return. Such practices are fairly commonplace in developing countries, and in one sense the financial system is more market oriented in an Islamic economy.

There are, of course, a number of limitations associated with the model utilized in this paper, so the analysis should be viewed only as suggestive. A more realistic model would have to take into account at least the following: first, the effects of uncertainty created by the elimination of a predetermined interest rate on the basic behavioral relationships. Second, the role of expectations, particularly as economic decisions in an Islamic financial system rely heavily on the expected rates of return and expected profits. In the present model this issue was sidestepped by assuming that expectations were fully realized. Third, the model would have to allow for some sort of dynamic behavior to understand how the system would move out of equilibrium. Finally, it would be necessary to allow for an explicit role for the government in order to see how its actions would affect the real sector, and through the financing of fiscal deficits, monetary conditions in the economy. Such issues are admittedly quite difficult to handle analytically, but have to be addressed to gain a proper understanding of the workings of the Islamic financial system.

In conclusion, policymakers in Islamic countries face a number of difficult problems as they move towards transforming their economies to accord with religious principles. There are many macroeconomic issues that are as yet unresolved. These include, among others, the respective roles of monetary and fiscal policies, exchange rate policies, and the effects of changes in the system of savings and investment, and thereby on growth and development. During the transition many seemingly *ad hoc* and second-best policies have been adopted, but this is only to be expected as Islamization of the economy involves a learning process. How the Islamic financial system will look when it achieves all of its objectives should not be judged from the current practices of Islamic banking in certain countries. Considerably more theoretical analysis and actual experimentation is required to reconcile the rules and codes of economic behavior that have evolved over fourteen hundred years with the functioning of a modern-day economy. The fact that so much progress has been achieved already in implementing Islamic values and ideals in the economic sphere is a tribute to scholars and policymakers. However, economists still have much to contribute concerning the direction that the Islamization of economies takes.

NOTES

*The authors are grateful to Nadeem Ul Haque and Peter Montiel for helpful comments. The views expressed in this paper are the sole responsibility of the authors.

1. Useful descriptions of Islamic banking are contained in Ahmad (1984), Karsten (1982), and Pryor (1985).

2. In Iran and Pakistan all banks are now legally prohibited from engaging in interest-based transactions; in other countries interest-free banks co-exist with conventional banks. For a discussion of the growth of Islamic banking, see Fahim Khan (1983).

3. A sampling of writings on the subject include, among others, Ahmad (1952), Kahf (1978), Ahmad (1984), and the papers in Ahmad *et al.* (1983).

4. See, for example, Siddiqi (1982), Kahf (1982), Chapra (1982), Akram Khan (1982), Uzair (1982), and Ahmad (1984).

5. For a discussion of this issue, see Ahmad (1984).

6. Other services would presumably include the transfer of funds, foreign exchange facilities, the issue of bank drafts and letters of credit, and share brokerage.

7. See Khan (1986).

8. Any losses incurred by a bank would not affect its transaction deposit liabilities as these would be fully covered.

9. Even in cases where there is no official deposit insurance scheme, the government is likely to step in to compensate depositors when a bank faces a crisis and potential bankruptcy.

10. For a discussion of the type of formula that could be used, see Ahmad (1984).

11. This does not imply that the return on investment deposits will be constant, since profits will normally fluctuate.

12. These are basically variants of the system advocated by Henry Simons (1945) in connection with the banking crisis of the 1930s. A similar proposal has been made more recently by Kareken (1985).

13. For a formal analysis of the process, see Khan (1985).

14. As shown by Ahmad (1984), these types of transactions can be strongly defended on religious grounds, and there is no dispute among scholars on their consistency with Islamic Law. There is less certainty regarding the other forms of financing discussed later.

15. This arrangement, therefore, effectively places human capital on par with financial capital.

16. This method of converting to a daily product basis is suggested by Ahmad (1984).

17. Such companies have been established in Pakistan.

18. The "participation term certificate" instituted in Pakistan since 1981 is one example of such instruments.

19. Some Muslim scholars argue that short-term consumption loans should be made by banks to needy borrowers on an interest-free basis, presumably using the resources obtained from transaction deposits. But as not all borrowers can be classified as "needy," and as it is unlikely that the resources from transaction deposits would be sufficient to meet demand, alternatives to profit sharing must be developed.

20. The mark-up method is also employed in financing of foreign trade by the Islamic Development Bank in Jeddah. In Pakistan this technique has been used for

bank financing of commodity operations of the government and public sector agencies.

21. Assuming, of course, that the item has not been insured by a third party.

22. See Ahmad (1984).

23. The government does not appear explicitly in the model. One can either assume that the government is part of the public or the central bank.

24. More precisely the rate of return received by depositors would be equal to the rate of return earned by banks, less their operating and other costs. The costs are assumed to be constant.

25. The public cannot participate in this market.

26. Financing schemes involving mark up, deferred delivery, or leasing, as discussed in Section II, are not considered.

27. See Khan (1986).

28. Changes in the stock of capital would be equal to investment, i.e., $\Delta K = I$.

29. This budget constraint is given by:

$$(\Delta Dp + I - \Delta Fp - S) + (\Delta Fb + \Delta Rb - \Delta Db - \Delta Eb) + (\Delta Ec - \Delta Rc) \equiv 0.$$

30. A more simplified dynamic version of this model is presented in Khan (1986).

31. As the behavioral equations in the model are assumed to be linear, this assumption allows us to drop the constant terms.

32. Recall that the rate of return on bank loans is equal to the rate of return on investment deposits.

33. Strictly speaking, the sign of the parameter a_3 is ambiguous, but this assumption does not affect the analysis.

34. Even with this simple system of four equations the analytical solutions are quite difficult and time-consuming to obtain. Any increase in the number of equations to take into account other financial assets would probably make the system impossible to solve.

9

Short-term Asset Concentration and Islamic Banking

Abbas Mirakhor

Abbas Mirakhor is Economist, Research Department, International Monetary Fund.

In discussions of Islamic financial systems a distinction is made between Islamic banking and interest-free banking. Accordingly, Islamic banking has been defined as "banking in consonance with the ethos of the value system of Islam," whereas "interest-free banking is a mechanical concept, denoting a mode of banking which steers clear of interest."[1] Islamic banking is expected not only to avoid transactions on the basis of interest, but also to participate actively in achieving the goals and objectives of an Islamic economy.[2] Ideally, a banking system which can be considered as Islamic is one in which all transactions are based on risk-return sharing on an equitable basis among the participants, and one in which the basis of any bank transaction is that of partnership with the client rather than one of the creditor-debtor relationship.[3] The implication here is that, while avoiding interest is a necessary condition for a banking system to be Islamic, it is not sufficient.

Although interest-free banking has been adopted in a number of countries, only the Islamic Republics of Iran and Pakistan have elected to implement Islamic banking. In both countries a number of Islamically approved modes of transaction have been adopted according to which banks may conduct their business.[4] The consensus among Muslim economists, however, is that even among these approved modes of operation, some can be considered strongly

Islamic (in that they conform to Islamic objectives both in form and in substasnce) and some only weakly so (in that they conform to Islamic norms in form only but not in substance). The basis for judgment as to the strength or weakness of a given mode of operation is the extent to which that mode contributes toward achievement of the objectives of the Islamic economy. Thus, only those modes of operation which permit risk-return sharing between providers and users of financial capital can be considered as strongly Islamic. These scholars consider only two modes of transactions among the approved modes, namely *Muḍārabah* (commenda) and *Mushārakah* (partnership), to be strongly Islamic.[5] The remaining modes of operation, namely *Bay' Mu'jjal* (usually translated as mark-up), *Ijārah* (leasing), *Ijārah* was *Iqtinā* (lease-purchase), *Bay' Salām* (pre-purchase agreements) and *Ju'alah* (service charge),[6] are recommended only in cases where risk-return sharing (i.e., *Muḍārabah* and *Mushārakah*) cannot be implemented. In all other instances these scholars advise against employment of these methods, warning that the banking system may come to rely too heavily on weakly Islamic modes, such as mark-up, which, because of their simplicity, minimal risk, and predetermined fixed rate of return, preserve the status quo associated with traditional banking, with its emphasis on creditworthiness of the client and maintenance of creditor-debtor relationship.[7]

The Muslim monetary authorities, on the other hand, argue that adoption of fully Islamic banking on the basis of risk-return is embarking "on an uncharted course"[8] and that steps toward full implementation of Islamic banking must be taken cautiously and carefully, lest the financial structure "collapse under its own weight."[9] They assert that in addition to being compatible with Islamic norms the banking operations adopted must be viable because:

> The bank's money belongs to a number of depositors of all shapes and sizes: the big shots are there, but also ordinary people who make deposits as small as Rs. 1000 in their accounts. That money is channeled to borrowers by the bank, which is also a trustee of that money. The system should be such that it protects the depositor and also gives him an adequate rate of return. Unless we safeguard the interest of the depositor, the system will be totally unfair because it will be lacking in *Adl* [justice], which is essential in any Islamic system.[10]

Clearly, although the Muslim monetary authorities agree that ideally the Islamic financial system should be based on risk-return sharing, as trustees of public money, they are concerned with the safety of the banks first and wish to avoid bankruptcy and failure of the banks. The fact that the fear of bank failure is what concerns the policymakers is evident from the following statement:

> The point is that a balance must be maintained among the borrower, the bank, and the depositor; it is this balance which will safeguard the interest of the depositor, provide him some earnings, and also provide incentive for savings. . . . Now if we weight things too much in favor of the borrower and say that banks should depend upon his word when he reports profits, then we will be doing a great disservice to the banking system. In a few years the banks will be bankrupt, and that will not serve the cause of any economic system. Therefore, whatever system we evolve, we have to be very cautious that it will not collapse beneath its own weight.[11]

The statement elsewhere warns that ". . . the structure which we have should be a viable structure which will protect the banking system itself and which does not lead to the collapse of the banking system."[12]

This cautious concern with the safety of the banking system is essentially based on a type of moral hazard argument that, in the absence of Islamic ethical values functioning in the business community,[13] engaging in risk-return activities such as *muḍārabah* and *mushārakah* by the banks without adequate safeguards may lead to the bankruptcy of the banks. This legitimate concern of the authorities translates into policies which approach the idea of risk-return sharing, so essential to the adoption of Islamic baning, with utmost caution, thus resulting in heavy reliance on weakly Islamic modes of finance, such as mark-up, which have minimum probability of risk. And this may lead to policy tools such as limits on the bank's rate-of-return, moral suasion, and credit rationing being used to steer the banks away from risk-return sharing projects through *muḍārabah* and *mushārakah*.

The purpose of this paper is to suggest that, even in the transition to full Islamic banking, the policy of heavy reliance on weakly Islamic measures as a means of minimizing risk of bankruptcy may not be optimal. And that, aside from the consideration of social benefits (e.g., financial deepening, development of an active entrepreneurial class, reduction of financial repression, and contribution to economic growth, income and employment) of adopting strongly Islamic measures, on purely rational economic grounds the policy of restricting the banks from engaging in risk-return sharing may, in fact, be a suboptimal policy.[14] Our argument assumes that the monetary authorities are concerned with safety, and that ultimately the risk of bankruptcy of the banks is what concerns them the most.[15] Correspondingly, the probability of a bank's going into bankruptcy (or at least getting into serious difficulty) is assumed to be based on the ability of the bank's capital to absorb a given level of losses; the focus in this paper, therefore, is on risk and return per unit of bank's capital.[16] We assume further that, in order to safeguard against the risk of bankruptcy, the authorities set a minimum capital to asset ratio. It is apparent that since the bulk of transactions seem to be concentrated in mark-up activities,[17] it is *muḍārabah* and *mushārakah* transactions which in the impression of authorities (intensified by a perception of sizable elements of moral hazard involved) are considered risky. For simplicity of analysis two classes of assets, mark-up (denoted by H) and *muḍārabah* (denoted by M), are selected as representatives of weak and strong Islamic measures. The suggestion of this paper is that since the concern of the authorities is the risk of bankruptcy, they should consider the riskiness of bank's total portfolio of assets. In line with this expectation, the risk of an asset should be considered according to its contribution to the variation of overall portfolio returns rather than on its own variability (risk) considered in isolation. The thesis presented here is that it is impossible to judge the riskiness of *muḍārabah* transactions in a bank's portfolio without considering how the returns on these transactions covary with the rest of the bank's return, and that the effect on risk of adding a *muḍārabah* transaction to a bank's portfolio is based on the covariability between returns on *muḍārabah* transactions and its overall portfolio returns.

Given the two assets, the decision problem facing a bank involves the choice of the optimal portfolio and the distribution of this portfolio between the two assets.

Definition of symbols used:

f_H = fraction of bank capital committed to mark-up;
f_m = fraction of bank capital committed to mudarabah;

π = overall portfolio return per unit of bank's capital;
k = bank's capital to asset ratio;
π_H = net return per unit of mark-up assets;
π_M = net return per unit of mudarabah assets;
σ_H^2 = variance of π_H[18];
σ_M^2 = variance of π_M;
σ_{HM} = covariance between π_H and π_M;
σ_π^2 = variance of overall portfolio return.

The bank's degree of leverage (assets per unit of capital) is assumed constrained by the capital to asset ratio, k, hence:

$$f_H + f_M = \frac{1}{k} \text{ or } f_H = \frac{1}{k} - f_M \tag{1}$$

In accordance with modern portfolio theory, the bank's overall portfolio return and its variance are given by[19]:

$$\pi = f_H \pi_H + f_M \pi_M, \text{ and} \tag{2}$$

$$\sigma_\pi^2 = f_H^2 \sigma_H^2 + f_M^2 \sigma_M^2 + 2 f_h f_M \sigma_{HM} \tag{3}$$

To derive a measure of the probability of bankruptcy one must define bankruptcy itself. Accordingly, bankruptcy is defined as when the bank's losses exceeds its total capital (i.e., $\pi < -1$). This definition of bankruptcy is well known[20] and, following several authors,[21] Chebyshev's inequality can be used to derive a measure of probability of bankruptcy. According to Chebyshev's inequality, if y is a random variable with a mean m and variance σ^2, then

$$P_r(|y - m| \geq d) \geq \frac{\sigma^2}{d^2}$$

when d is any positive number and $P_r(|y - m| \geq d)$ is the probability that y will differ from m by at least $\pm d$. Substituting in the relevant parameters and rearranging terms, the following boundary is obtained on $P_r(\pi \leq -1)$, i.e., the probability that the bank will go bankrupt is:

$$P_r(\pi \leq -1) \leq \frac{\sigma_\pi^2}{(\pi + 1)^2} \tag{4}$$

Where $\overline{\pi}$, the expected mean overall return equals

$$\overline{\pi} = f_H \overline{\pi}_H + f_M \overline{\pi}_M \tag{5}$$

where $\overline{\pi}_H$ and $\overline{\pi}_M$ are, respectively, the expected returns from mark-up and from *muḍārabah*.[22] Substituting (3) and (5) in (4) we obtain:

$$P_r(\pi < -1) < \frac{f_H^2\, \sigma_H^2 + f_M^2\, \sigma_M^2 + 2\, f_H f_M\, \sigma_{HM}}{[f_H\, \overline{\pi}_H + f_M\, \overline{\pi}_M + 1]^2} \tag{6}$$

This expression shows the relationship between expected returns to mark-up and *muḍārabah* activities, the variability and covariability of those returns, the breakdown between the two activities, the bank's capital position (since $f_H = (1/k) - f_M$), and the probability of the bank's going bankrupt.

The narrowness of focusing primarily on the risk of *muḍārabah* is evident here. It can be seen that the impact on bank's risk of increasing the proportion f_M of *muḍārabah* assets is a function of current level of f_M as well as the variance-covariance structure of asset returns and their means. This implies that there may be an optimal level of *muḍārabah* assets—even in the absence of any consideration of religious imperatives or the social benefits which may accrue as a result of expansion in these activities—depending on the bank's objective function.

The authorities can force the banks, for example, to choose f_H and f_M so as to minimize the variance of overall returns. The values of f_M and f_H which will minimize (3) can be obtained by taking its partials with respect to these parameters and setting them equal to zero:

$$\frac{\partial \sigma_\pi^2}{\partial f_H} = 2 f_H\, \sigma_H^2 + 2 f_M\, \sigma_{\mathrm{HM}} = 0 \tag{7}$$

$$\frac{\partial \sigma_\pi^2}{\partial f_M} = 2 f_M\, \sigma_M^2 + 2 f_H\, \sigma_{HM} = 0 \tag{8}$$

from (7) and (8) the optimal f_M and f_H are found to be[23]:

$$\tilde{f}_{\mathrm{H}} = \frac{\sigma_M^2 - \sigma_{HM}}{k\,(\sigma_H^2 + \sigma_M^2 - 2\sigma_{HM})} \tag{9}$$

$$\tilde{f}_{\mathrm{M}} = \frac{\sigma_{HM} - \sigma_H^2}{k\,(\sigma_{HM}^2 + \sigma_M^2 - \sigma_H^2)} \tag{10}$$

However, since the probability of bankruptcy is a function of the expected return as well as its variance, minimizing the return variance could increase the risk of bankruptcy. The alternative is to have the banks choose f_M and f_H such that the right-hand side of (4), i.e., σ_π^2, is minimized. This occurs at the point $(\overline{\pi} + 1)^2$.[24]

$$f_H^* = \frac{\sigma_M^2\,(\overline{\pi}_H + k) - \sigma_{HM}\,(\overline{\pi}_M + k)}{k\,[\sigma_H^2\,(\overline{\pi}_M + k) + \sigma_M^2\,(\overline{\pi}_H + k) - 2\sigma_{HM}\,(\overline{\pi}_H + \overline{\pi}_M + 2\,k)]} \qquad (11)$$

As can be seen from (11), f_H^* is an increasing function of σ_M^2 and $\overline{\pi}_H$ and a decreasing function of σ_H^2 and $\overline{\pi}_M$. The opposite is true of $f_M^* = 1/k - f_H^*$. On the other hand, f_H^* is an increasing function of σ_{HM} if, and only if, $(\overline{\pi}_H + k)\,\sigma_M^2 > (\overline{\pi}_M + k)\,\sigma_H^2$. A major implication of the analysis is that attempts to restrict the banks from engaging in risk-return sharing such as *muḍārabah* activities in order to reduce the variance of bank returns could actually increase the probability of bankruptcy if the expected returns from risk-return sharing activities exceed the expected return from mark-up,[25] i.e., $\overline{\pi}_M > \overline{\pi}_H$. Thus in determining whether regulating or otherwise imposing limits on the fraction of a bank's portfolio committed to risk-return sharing activities will succeed in lowering bankruptcy risks, the effect of these limitations on overall portfolio return and its variance and covariances of expected returns from various assets in the portfolio must be taken into account. If the expected returns from mark-up and *muḍārabah* assets are different, the values of f_H and f_M will affect the level of overall portfolio return. Consequently, refusal by banks to consider *muḍārabah* activities solely because of their risk may lead to a lower overall expected return than could otherwise be achieved; thus, such a decision would be nonoptimal for the banks. To the extent that financial transactions policies of individual banks are affected, financial intermediation in the aggregate and concomitantly, the allocation of real resources in the economy is affected. Hence, what is not optimal for the banks may also not be optimal for the society.[26]

Additionally, allowing the banks to engage in risk-return sharing presents them with additional opportunities to diversify their assets, and a bank's asset diversification affects its overall expected net earnings as well as its variance.[27] A more diversified bank represents a more stable source of funds and a more stable place for depositors. Given the desirability of diversification, the banks should be the primary source of determination of the appropriate trade-off between risk and return as well as the method of diversification. It is the bank which has to assess how the various modes of asset acquisition are related in their prospects for timely payment of returns and principal. If the banks are constrained to concentrate their portfolios heavily in favor of one type of asset (e.g., mark-up) only, then that portfolio must be considered very risky. To discourage banks from engaging in risk-return sharing activities, either through fiscal-monetary tools or through institutional constraints such as unfavorable laws, simply because of the perceived risk of these activities may not be an optimal policy.[28] It has been pointed out in this paper that the relevant factors which must be considered are the overall earnings of the banks and the riskiness of the bank's total portfolio.

There seems to be little doubt among Muslim economists and professional bankers that, given a favorable fiscal-monetary and institutional framework, the banks would undertake the financing of risk-return sharing projects. Thus to restrain the banks, through imposition of rate-of-return ceilings, credit rationing, moral suasion, unfavorable fiscal measures, or unfavorable laws, from engaging in risk-return sharing projects because of a perception of high risks associated with these activities, without sufficient analysis of risks and returns involved, may discourage the Islamic measures from taking root and the banks from playing an effective role in the development process.[29] The banks themselves should be in a position to assess the risk-return trade-off in asset acquisition. The authorities' legitimate concerns should be directed at the safety of the bank's overall portfolio of assets rather than the risk of a particular mode of financing considered in isolation.

NOTES

1. Ahmed (1984) p. 1, see also CII report on Elimination of Interest (1983), p. 183.

2. Ahmed, ibid., p. 8 and pp. 11–12.

3. Ahmed, ibid., p. 9–12, Siddiqi (1982), Siddiqi (1983).

4. Bank Markazi Jomhouri Islami Iran (1983) and State Bank of Pakistan (1984).

5. Siddiqi (1982), pp. 25–38, Mohsin (1982), pp. 187–203, Qureshi (1984, 1985) and Chapra (1982) pp. 145–176. Mohsin argues (p. 203) that "Islam recognizes the productivity of capital but at the same time does not allow it prior claims on productive surplus. It insists upon a fair distribution of risk and reward." Qureshi (1985, p. 4) asserts that "the proposed Islamic model of financial intermediary is in the nature of venture capital. Under this system the bank guarantees no fixed return to the saver, and on the investment side, the bank does not require any fixed return from the investor."

6. For definition and explanation of these terms see State Bank of Pakistan (1984), Bank Markazi Jomhouri Islami Iran (1983) and Khan (1984). For detailed discussion of "Profit/Loss Sharing" system (Muḍārabah and Mushārakah) in Islam and its eco-

nomic implications see Siddiqi (1982), Qureshi (1985), Ahmad (1984), Chapra (1982), CII (1983), Abu Saud (1980), and Siddiqi (1980).

7. Ahmed (1984, pp. 10–11), for example, argues that the weakly Islamic "techniques, though far simpler to operate than profit/loss sharing, cannot be recommended for widespread use as they cannot be of any material assistance in achieving the socio-economic objective of an Islamic economy. The fact that replacement of interest by *Bay' Mu'jjal* (mark-up), for example, does not represent any substantive change becomes apparent if one views it in the perspective of the philosophy behind prohibition of interest. As mentioned earlier, the interest system is disallowed by Islam because intrinsically it is a highly inequitable system. The feature that makes the interest system inequitable is that the provider of capital funds is assured a fixed return while all the risk is borne by the user of these capital funds. Justice, which is the hallmark of the Islamic system, demands that the provider of capital funds should share the risk with the entrepreneur if he wishes to earn profit. It is easy to see, therefore, that the mark-up system, and for that matter all other devices which involve a fixed predetermined return on capital, are no real substitutes for interest." For similar sentiments see also Siddiqi (1983) and the CII Report (1983). A group of Muslim economists who were invited to comment on the CII Report (see Ahmed, et al., 1983, p. 12) strongly cautioned "against the danger that such methods could open a back door to interest," and they emphasized that "keeping in view the rationale for the condemnation and prohibition of interest in Islam, no mechanism other than profit/loss sharing really conforms to the spirit of Islam." Moreover, there is evidence to suggest that these scholars were justified in their concern. Qureshi (1985, p. 15) comments that mark-up transactions "have been the subject of acute criticism because [this kind of arrangement] is tending to encompass the bulk of financial transactions." The fear that this would happen had been expressed earlier by Siddiqi (1983, p. 225).

8. Kazi (1984) p. 9.

9. Ibid., p. 13.

10. Ibid., p. 13.

11. Kazi (1984) p. 13.

12. Kazi (1984) p. 10.

13. Qureshi (1984, p. 89) argues that "the successful functioning of the profit and loss sharing system will depend on the existence of a high degree of business ethics and the moral fabric of the society leaves much to be desired"; he concludes that "initially, therefore, recourse may have to be taken to techniques which are not predicated on the maintenance of proper books of accounts."

14. In this paper, by "risk" is meant the variability of expected returns. Although, as was stated earlier, Muslim economists are in agreement that the ideal Islamic financial system is based on risk-return sharing, there has been no explicit attempt to define risk in an Islamic context. However, given the strong position which Islam takes against gambling, forward transaction and lottery [see, for example, Siddiqi (1980, pp. 341)], as well as its emphasis on the necessity for full information regarding the nature of transaction and the products which are subject of the transaction, and its requirement regarding safety and security of credit transactions (see Quran 2:82), it is clear that risk in Islamic context is not the same as is generally understood. In fact, where there is any element of uncertainty regarding the nature of the transaction, or the products and services which are the subject of the transactions, and where there is a chance that either one or both parties may be defrauded, the transaction is said to contain *gharār* (usually translated as 'risk') and is not allowed (see Khamenei 1979, p. 105). On the other hand, uncertainty regarding the future events is recognized (see, for example Quran 31:34: "No soul knoweth what it will earn tomorrow"); in fact permissibility of *muḍārabah* and *mushārakah* makes sense only in face of uncertainty regarding the magnitude and the probability of expected return [see Zarqa (in Ariff,

1982, p. 100); also Mohsin (in Ariff, 1982, p. 189)]. Consequently, it seems reasonable to interpret risk in Islamic context as variability of expected returns. Qureshi (1983, p. 6) seems also to interpret risk the same way; he states, "The smaller the variation in earnings, the smaller the degree of business risk, assuming other things remaining constant."

15. This does not seem to be a very strong assumption given the position taken by Mr. Kazi, the Governor of the State Bank of Pakistan, quoted above (see n. 1 and n. 2, p. 5).

16. A digression may help clarify the reasonableness of this assumption. It is generally thought that it is because financial markets are imperfect that financial intermediaries have an economic role to play (see Stigler, 1967). These imperfections include imperfect divisibility of financial claims, transaction costs of search, acquisition and diversification by lenders and borrowers, regulatory restrictions of various types and the local nature of the markets. The intermediaries through exploitations of these imperfections alter relationships between borrowers and lenders. Thus, by their action, intermediaries provide higher returns to lenders and lower costs to borrowers than would be possible with direct finance. In the process of intermediation, a bank becomes unsound if it cannot liquidate enough assets to supply deposit withdrawals. Thus, if a bank has suffered severe losses so that its asset value has declined below the level of its debts to depositors (i.e., so that it finds itself in a negative capital position), then under massive withdrawal, the bank may fail. The insolvency reflects a decrease in asset market values. In other words, a bank may not be able to withstand deposit withdrawals if there are not enough assets to liquidate. It seems reasonable that the regulations should be concerned mainly with the riskiness of the bank position (which is related to its portfolio composition), its profitability, and its asset liquidity as key factors for determining the soundness of a bank. In general, the greater the risk of a bank's assets, the higher the level of capital required to avoid potential failure due to asset losses. In this context bank earnings are important since a profitable operation is the bank's first line of defense against occasional shrinkage in asset value and because profitable banks have higher capacity to attract deposits and can better raise new capital when desired in order to take advantage of profitable investment opportunities. This paper suggests that the profitability and asset composition of a bank's portfolio, rather than the risk of *muḍārabah* transactions alone, should be considered.

17. Qureshi (1985, p. 15) and Ahmed (1984).

18. Even though mark-up resembles interest, it is not riskless. See Khan (1983, p. 254).

19. Babcock (1972, p. 700), Tobin (1966, p. 20), Markowitz (1959, p. 88), and Allen (1983, p. 86).

20. Morgan (1984, p. 145), Blair and Heggestad (1978), and Koehn and Santomero (1980).

21. Roy (1952), Telser (1955), Koehn and Santomero (1980), Blair and Heggestad (1978), Allen (1983, p. 142) and Kahane (1977). Graphically, this upper bound on the probability of failure can be seen as the square of the reciprocal of the slope of a ray in mean-variance space [see Roy (1952) for proof]. The ray has intercept of -1.

22. It should be pointed out that portfolio theory is based on the assumption that the investor is risk-averse. This assumption is interpreted as meaning that (a) if two portfolios have the same standard deviation of return and different expected returns, the one with the larger expected return is preferred, (b) if two portfolios have the same expected return and different standard deviations of return, the one with the smaller standard deviation is preferred, and (c) if one portfolio has a smaller standard deviation of return and a larger expected return than another, it is preferred. Graphically, this implies that as long as expected return is desired and standard deviation is not, every indifference curve in the return-standard deviation space will be upward-sloping

and each curve, generally, will become steeper as expected return and standard deviation increase, as in the following graph, [see Sharpe (1970, p. 26), Tobin (1966), and Allen (1969)]:

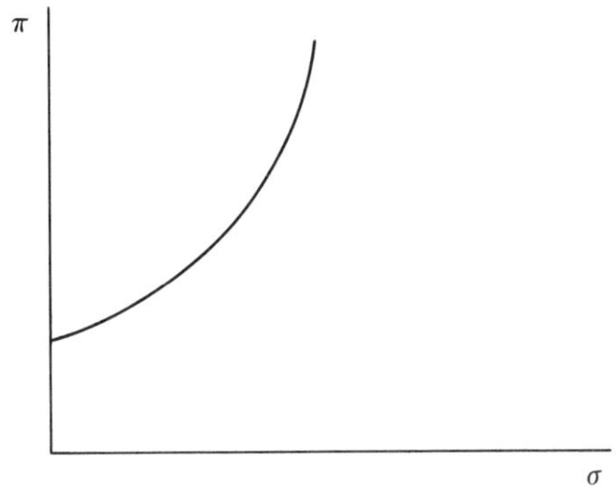

Figure 1

The curve represents the locus of all portfolios between which the investor is indifferent. Although it is believed that this is not a strong assumption and that most people are risk averters, this assumption becomes particularly meaningful in an Islamic context. Given the fact that a Muslim believes in the omniscience of Allah, the day of judgment, that Allah has endowed man with intelligence and free will, and that the Divine Law has provided man with a spectrum of valuation containing Divine judgment as to man's actions being obligatory (*wājib*), recommended and meritorious (*mandūb* or *mustaḥab*), permitted (*ḥalāl*), forbidden (*ḥarām*), reprehensible (*makrūh*) and indifferent (*mubāḥ*), each having comensurate reward and punishment, as well as the belief that Allah has given man the knowledge of the "straight path" and what is expected of him, a Muslim has to be risk averse in his general behavior. This conclusion is strengthened by the attitude of Islam toward "risky" transactions (see footnote 1, page 6). Indeed, it is reported that once a bedouin questioned the Prophet (SAWA) regarding the meaning of the phrase Tawakkaltu 'Ala Allah (I put my trust in Allah), asking if it meant that he could get off his camel and, by saying the phrase, let it roam freely while he himself went about his business knowing that God would take care of his camel so that on his return he would find his camel safe and sound. The prophet (SAWA) is reported to have said that the phrase meant that he should first tie up his camel safely and then say: I put my trust in God.

Generally, portfolio theory is applied to cases where the investor has to allocate his portfolio between a risk-free and risky assets. In the Islamic context, however, there are no risk-free assets; therefore, the investor has to choose between all risky assets. The problems can be stated as follows: for N assets, all of which are assumed risky, choose f_i (i.e., the percent of the portfolio invested in the ith asset) such that the risk of the portfolio is minimized. In other words, the problem is one of constructing an efficient portfolio of all risky assets, where an efficient portfolio is defined as the locus of feasible portfolios that have the smallest variance for a prescribed expected return subject to the conditions that:

$$\sigma^2 = \sum_{i}^{N} \sum_{j}^{N} f_i f_j \sigma_{ij} \qquad (1)$$

$$\pi = \sum_{i}^{N} f_i \pi_i \tag{2}$$

$$\sum_{i}^{N} f_i = 1 \tag{3}$$

where σ^2 is the variance of the overall expected portfolio return and measures the riskiness of the portfolio, π_i denotes expected return from the ith asset, $i = 1, 2, \ldots, N$, and σ_{ij} denotes the covariance of return between the ith and jth asset. This problem has been solved by various authors [see Allen (1983, p. 146), Sharpe (1970, p. 244), Fama and Miller (1972, p. 282), Fama (1971), Martin (1955), Morton (1972), and Black (1972)]. The solution provides an efficient frontier with a unique minimum point in the expected return-standard deviation plane. The application of portfolio theory should be particularly fruitful in an Islamic context where there are no risk-free assets. Bashir (1983) has applied portfolio theory to Islamic banks under conditions of certainty [but see Zarqa (1982) who suggests it is un-Islamic to assume certainty], and S. R. Khan (1983) has applied portfolio theory to a case where the choice is between cash and risky assets [see also Tobin (1966) for similar ideas]. A particularly useful paper by Hart and Jaffee (1974) applies portfolio theory to depository financial intermediaries in the absence of a riskless asset [see also Sealy (1980), Koehn and Santomero (1980), and Santomero (1984) for application of portfolio theory to financial intermediaries]. Given the efficiency frontier in expected return-standard deviation plane and a set of indifference curves, the optimal portfolio is represented as the point of tangency between the efficiency frontier and one of the indifference curves as shown in Figure 2.

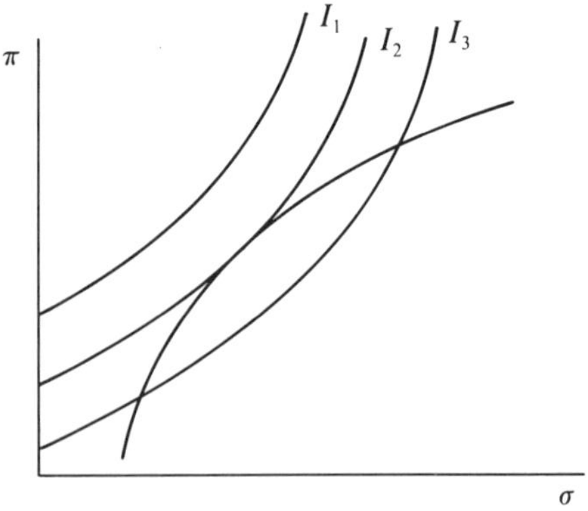

Figure 2

23. It can be shown that (9) and (10) satisfy the condition that $f_H + f_M = 1/k$. A sufficient condition for $\tilde{f}_H$ to be an interior point (i.e., $0 < \tilde{f}_H < 1/k$) and thus yield a global minimum is $\sigma_H^2, \sigma_M^2 > \sigma_{HM}$.

24. From (11) it can be seen that:

$f_H^* = \tilde{f}_H$ if $\pi_H = \pi_M$

$f_H^* > \tilde{f}_H$ if $\overline{\pi}_H > \overline{\pi}_M$

$f_H^* < \tilde{f}_H$ if $\overline{\pi}_H < \overline{\pi}_M$

25. It is not unreasonable to expect that, in fact, the rate of return on risk-return sharing activities will be higher than the rate of return from mark-up, since generally the rate of return on the average is higher than the rate of interest, and since mark-up rates have closely tracked interest rates.

26. Pringle (1975).

27. It has long been recognized that, depending on the degree of correlation between returns, portfolio risk (variance) can be reduced by diversification. For proof see Samuelson (1967), Lintner (1965), Evans and Archer (1968), Mao (1970), and Allen (1983). The Muslim economists too have recognized the need for diversification. Qureshi (1985, p. 4) states that in an Islamic system, "if the banks act in the best interest of the depositor, they must pursue an active financing strategy. More specifically, under this system all capital is risk capital since all funds are received and provided on the basis of sharing in the profits and losses of the enterprises." Moreover, arguing that banks in an Islamic system are investment banks he says (p. 5), "Investment banking can be successful if the investment bank can achieve a perfectly diversified portfolio." Siddiqi (1982, p. 30) maintains that in Islamic banking the "bank undertakes two kinds of businesses: (a) it offers banking services earning fees and commissions, and (b) it assumes the role of a financier-entrepreneur making judicious selection of businessmen who seek capital from it, stipulating that it share in the profit of their productive enterprise. Liability to loss in a *Muḍārabah* contract rests with the financier. It follows that the loss incurred by an individual entrepreneur working with capital advanced by the bank is borne by the bank. The bank, however, advances capital to a large number of entrepreneurs, diversifying its investments as far as possible. Thus, losses incurred on some advances are likely to get absorbed by the profit resulting from some other advances." It should be pointed out that the possibility of a deposit insurance scheme as well as allowing banks to maintain loss-compensating reserves out of their earnings has been discussed by Muslim economists and bankers [see Siddiqi (1982)].

A simple example can illustrate the effects of diversification on overall expected return and its variance. Consider two risky assets with the following assumed characteristics:

$\overline{\pi}_1 = 0.659 \quad \overline{\pi}_2 = 0.450;$ expected value of returns on the two assets
$\sigma_1^2 = 0.482 \quad \sigma_2^2 = 0.267;$ variance of the returns
$\sigma_{12} = -0.099 \quad \rho_{12} = -0.275;$ covariance and correlation coefficient
f_i = proportion of total portfolio allocated to asset i, $i = 1, 2$
$\overline{\pi}_p$ = overall expected portfolio return
σ_p = variance of overall expected return

and where

$$\overline{\pi}_p = f_1 \overline{\pi}_1 + f_2 \overline{\pi}_2$$
$$\sigma_p^2 = f_1^2 \sigma_1^2 + f_1^2 \sigma_2^2 + 2 f_1 f_2 \sigma_{12}$$
$$\sigma_{12} = E\{[\overline{\pi}_1 - \overline{\pi}_1]\,[\pi_2 - \pi_2]\}$$

i.e., the covariance of π_1 with π_2 is the expected value of arithmetic mean of the cross products of deviations. And

$$\rho_{12} = \frac{\sigma_{12}}{\sigma_1 \sigma_2},$$ which is an expression of the degree to which π_1

and π_2 are related [for proof see Markowitz (1959, pp. 82–91)]. For this problem the relevant facts are:

$$\overline{\pi}_p = 0.659 f_1 + 0.450 f_2 \tag{1}$$

$$f_1 + f_2 = 100 \text{ percent} \quad (2)$$

$$f_1 \geq 0 \text{ and } f_1 \geq 0 \quad (3)$$

$$\sigma_p^2 = 0.482 f_1^2 + 0.267 f_2^2 - (2)(0.099) f_1 f_2 \quad (4)$$

Here asset 1 offers the highest expected return (66 percent) but also has the largest risk (its variance = 0.482). The opposite is true of the second asset. The problem is to choose f_1 and f_2 such that (4) is minimized subject to constraints (2) and (3); hence,

$$\text{Min } L = f_1^2 (0.482) + f_2^2 (0.267) + 2 f_1 f_2 (-0.099) + \lambda (f_1 + f_2 - 1) \quad (5)$$

The first order conditions are:

$$\frac{\delta L}{\delta f_1} = 2 (0.482) f_1 + 2 (-0.099) f_2 + \lambda = 0 \quad (6)$$

$$\frac{\delta L}{\delta f_2} = 2 (-0.099) f_2 + 2 (0.267) f_1 + \lambda = 0 \quad (7)$$

$$\frac{\delta L}{\delta \lambda} = f_1 + f_2 - 1 = 0 \quad (8)$$

Solving these equations simultaneously one obtains

$$f_1 = 0.614, \qquad f_2 = 0.386 \text{ and } \lambda = -0.251$$

$$\bar{\pi}_p = (0.659)(0.386) + (0.450)(0.614) = 0.531$$

and

$$\sigma_p^2 = (0.386)^2 (0.482) + (0.614)^2 (0.267) + 2 (0.386)(0.614)(-0.099) = 0.1255$$

The solution can be illustrated graphically as follows:

Hence, by adding the second asset and dividing the portfolio between the two assets (with 61.4 percent and 38.6 percent of the portfolio invested in assets 2 and 1, respectively), the overall portfolio risk is reduced compared to the situation where the portfolio would be entirely composed of the second asset only. This problem illustrates the point that within a portfolio an asset's riskiness is not properly measured either directly or simply by the variance of its return. Even though asset 1 is nearly twice as risky as asset 2, both the overall portfolio return as well as its variance were improved by adding asset 1 to the portfolio.

28. A point of contention is that, even if one were to consider the risk of *muḍārabah* and *mushārakah* activities in isolation from their expected returns and their covariance with other assets, the perception of the riskiness of these assets may represent an overestimation on the part of the authorities. The risks which a bank takes in entering into a risk-return sharing project with a specific firm can be divided into risks which relate to the general market conditions (including socio-political conditions and general economic fluctuation in the economy) and risks which are firm-specific. The first type of risk will exist regardless of whether the bank engages in mark-up or risk-return activities. The firm-specific risks can be broken down into investment risk and fraud risk. The investment risk is clearly a function of the viability and the profitability of the proposed project as well as the ability of the entrepreneur.The banks should be able to develop the expertise necessary for project appraisal, thus allowing them to assess this component of firm-specific risks. The risk of fraud, which is especially worrisome to the authorities, seems to have two sources. One is the possibility of under-reporting of profits earned by the entrepreneur, e.g., through maintenance of two sets of books, which is in turn apparently motivated by a desire to evade taxes. Although there are no precise measures of the extent of the presence of this practice, it appears that this risk can be minimized through a system of audit stipulated by the *muḍārabah* contract. The other source of risk of fraud is that since in risk-return sharing arrangements the banks will have to carry the entire burden of financial losses should they occur, there is an element of moral hazard involved in these transactions. There is no practical way of determining the magnitude of this risk due to the fact that so far banks have not engaged in risk-return sharing activities. But this residual risk may in practice be minimized since hardly any bank is expected to undertake to finance a risk-return sharing project without having sufficient information regarding the ability and the character of the entrepreneur. Moreover, as was stated earlier (see footnote 1, page 17), possibilities of collective insurance schemes with the participation of central bank and commercial banks as well as maintenance of loss-compensating reserves have not been ruled out by Muslim scholars.

29. Karsten (1982, p. 132) states that "The process of financial intermediation could be affected if Islamic banks were somehow constrained in carrying out the task of transforming short-term liabilities into long-term advances."

Appendix I
Islamic Interest-Free Banking: A Theoretical Analysis

Mohsin S. Khan

DYNAMIC PROPERTIES OF THE TRADITIONAL BANKING SYSTEM WITH LIABILITY MANAGEMENT

The Islamic banking model developed in the text of the paper can, with suitable alterations, be used to represent the traditional banking system as well. Once the hypothesis of liability management is introduced, however, the dynamic properties of the two systems turn out to be quite different. This Appendix analyzes the dynamics of the traditional banking model in the presence of liability management for the cases of fixed and flexible prices.

Fixed-Price Model

The explicit guarantee provided for the nominal value of shares in a traditional banking system does not affect the long-run properties of the model. Thus, the following identity, which ensures equilibrium in the capital market, will continue to hold:

$$\bar{S}/P = y/r. \tag{9}$$

This is the same as equation (1a) of the text, where $\bar{S}$ is the exogenously determined nominal value of shares.

Equilibrium in the money market is given by[25]

$$\gamma(r) \cdot m = y/r, \tag{10}$$

where $\gamma(r) = 1/g(r)$. This equation implies that the demand for shares relative to real money balances in the long run is a positive function of the real rate of return on shares.

In the goods market, real aggregate demand y^d is defined as

$$y^d = C(r, w^*) + I(r)$$
$$C_r < 0, \qquad C_{w^*} > 0, \qquad I_r < 0, \tag{11}$$

where $C(r, w^*)$ is the consumption function and $I(r)$ is the investment function. The variable w^* is long-run wealth; that is,

$$w^* = m + (y/r), \tag{12}$$

which can differ from measured real wealth, $w = m + \bar{S}/P$, if y/r does not equal $\bar{S}/P$.

The adjustment function for the goods market is

$$dy/dt = \dot{y} = \beta[C(r, m + y/r) + I(r) - y], \qquad \beta > 0, \tag{13}$$

which is the same as equation (6) of the text and where the expression in brackets is excess aggregate demand. As in equation (7), this can be written as a reduced-form equation:

$$\dot{y} = f(r, y; m)$$
$$f_r < 0, \qquad f_y < 0, \qquad f_m > 0, \tag{14}$$

where m is exogenous. Equations (9), (10), and (14) define the model for the traditional banking system; as can be seen, it is virtually the same as the Islamic banking model.

Suppose for some reason that there is a fall in the earnings of banks. In the Islamic banking system, the liabilities of the banks would be immediately written down to ensure continuous financial market equilibrium. In the traditional banking system, however, the nominal value of deposits is predetermined in the short run, so that changes in y are not necessarily reflected in the real value of shares unless there is a corresponding change in r. If banks try to prevent bankruptcy by resorting to liability management—that is, they raise interest rates to retain deposits—this practice can set in motion an unstable process. Liability management can be approximated by a simple adjustment function suggested by Fernandez (1984), which says that if the amount banks are willing to pay depositors for any reason exceeds the income of banks (y), then the banks would try to increase the public demand for shares by increasing the real return to depositors; that is,[26]

$$(d/dt)[\gamma(r) \cdot m] = \alpha\{[\gamma(r) \cdot m \cdot r] - y\}, \qquad \alpha > 0. \tag{15}$$

This equation can also be written as

$$\dot{r} = \{[\alpha\gamma(r)/\gamma_r] \cdot r\} - \alpha y/m\gamma_r. \tag{16}$$

The second equation in the system is the adjustment function for the goods market:

$$\dot{y} = f(r, y; m), \tag{17}$$

the same as equation (7) of the text.

The steady-state solutions of equations (16) and (17)–that is, when $\dot{r} = \dot{y} = 0$–are

$$m = g(r) \cdot y/r, \tag{16a}$$

$$f(r, y; m) = 0. \tag{17a}$$

These are exactly the same as the steady-state solutions obtained in the Islamic banking version of the model. In other words, the two systems are identical in long-run equilibrium.

The short-run dynamics, however, turn out to be quite different.[27] Whereas the Islamic system has a stable solution, this is not true in the traditional banking model represented by equations (16) and (17). The characteristic matrix of the system (K) is defined as[28]

$$K = \begin{vmatrix} [\alpha\gamma(r)/\gamma_r] + \alpha r & -\alpha/m\gamma_r \\ f_r & f_y \end{vmatrix}. \tag{18}$$

Since $|K| < 0$, the two eigenvalues are real, with one positive and the other negative. This implies that the solution of the model is a saddle point.

The potential saddle-point properties of the traditional banking system are illustrated in Figure 3. This phase diagram gives the steady-state solutions for r and y, with full equilibrium being defined, as in the case of Islamic banking (Figure 1 of the text), at point A. Note, however, that a movement away from A to a point such as X will cause the system to become explosive, with $\dot{r} > 0$ and $\dot{y} < 0$.

Repeating the experiment conducted in the Islamic banking case—that is, assuming that real income falls from y^* to y_1—one finds that a unique solution will be obtained if the real return on shares declines

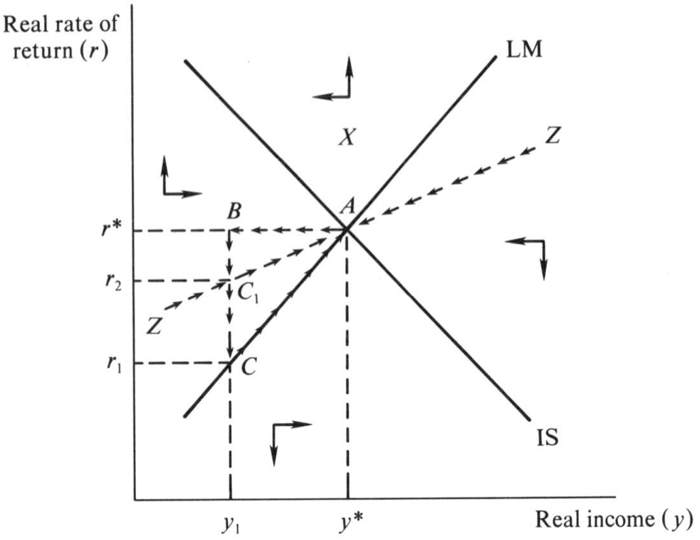

Figure 3
Traditional Banking System with Fixed Prices

to r_2 (point C_1) and then rises along the saddle path ZZ to A. In the case of Islamic banking, the real rate of return on shares would have been pushed down initially to r_1 (point C) with the fall in real income. Since $r_1 < r_2$, the excess aggregate demand created by the fall in output is clearly greater in the Islamic system than in the traditional banking system.[29] Therefore, the adjustment of real income to its steady-state value—that is, from y_1 to y^*—will be faster in the case of Islamic banking than in traditional banking.

Flexible-Price Model

The basic change in this case is in the adjustment equation for the goods market, which in terms of real money balances is written as

$$\dot{m} = -f(r, m; y^*)$$
$$f_r < 0, \qquad f_m > 0, \qquad f_{y^*} < 0, \tag{19}$$

and which is the same as equation (8) of the text, where $\dot{m}$ is the change in real money balances and $f(r, m; y^*)$ is the excess demand function for an exogenously given level of (long-run) real income, y^*.

For the flexible-price model, equation (19) replaces equation (14) so that the system now becomes

$$\dot{m} = -f(r, m; y^*) \tag{19}$$

$$\dot{r} = [\alpha\gamma(r)/\gamma_r \cdot r] - \alpha y^*/m\gamma_r. \tag{20}$$

For the traditional banking system with flexible prices, one once again obtains a saddle point as a solution to equations (19) and (20). The characteristic matrix is given by

$$K = \begin{vmatrix} -f_m & -f_r \\ \alpha y^*/m^2\gamma_r & [\alpha\gamma(r)/\gamma_r] + \alpha r \end{vmatrix} \tag{21}$$

Because $f_r < 0$ and $f_m > 0$, one can see that $|K| < 0$ and that the roots of the characteristic equation are real and of opposite sign.

If there is a sudden drop in real income, one would observe that both the $r_{y*} = 0$ and $m_{y*} = 0$ schedules would shift as shown in Figure 4, yielding a new saddlepoint equilibrium at C. In the Islamic bank-

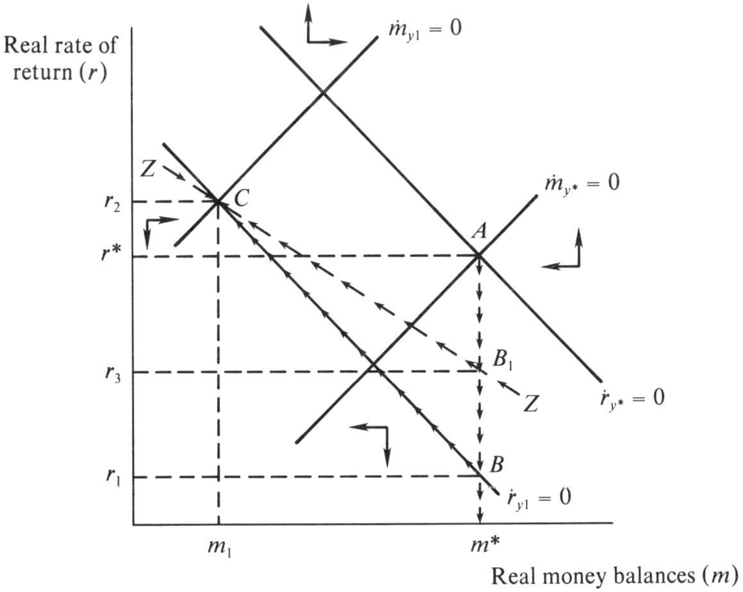

Figure 4
Traditional Banking System with Flexible Prices

ing system, this fall in real income would result in an instantaneous movement of r from A to B, and then a gradual movement along $\dot{r}_{y1} = 0$ toward C. In the case of traditional banking, however, to achieve a unique adjustment path the real rate of return on shares has to fall from r^* to r_3 (given by point B_1) and then rise along the saddle path ZZ. Along this path prices rise in response to excess aggregate demand, and real money balances fall. Again, since B_1 is above B, excess aggregate demand will be larger in the case of Islamic banking, so that the adjustment of prices to the new steady-state equilibrium (C) will be more rapid.

NOTES

25. The same long-run money demand function discussed in the text continues to be used.

26. An alternative adjustment function that directly relates the change in the rate of return to the difference between real assets and liabilities,

$$\dot{r} = \alpha[(\bar{S}/P) \cdot r - y],$$

yields the same qualitative results.

27. For the dynamic analysis, the linearized versions of equations (16) and (17) were used; further, it was assumed that $\gamma_{rr} = 0$ in equation (16).

28. The characteristic equation is $\lambda^2 - tr(K)\lambda + |K| = 0$.

29. For simplicity, the analysis has abstracted from wealth effects.

Appendix II
Towards an Interest-Free Islamic Economic System

Waqar Masood Khan

LEMMA-1: Let P_z be a sequence of identically and independently distributed random variables with mean $LE(P_z)$ and variance zL var (P_z); then

$$P_z \rightarrow LE(P_z) \text{ as } z \rightarrow 0$$

Proof: For a fixed e positive, by Chebysheve's inequality we have

$$Pr[|P_z - LE(P_z)| \geq e] \leq (1/e^2)[\text{var } (P_z)]$$
$$= (1/e^2)zL \text{ var } (P_{zi})$$

which goes to zero as z goes to zero.

LEMMA-2: Let P_z be a sequence of I.I.D. random variables which converges to $E(P_z)$ in probability. If U_b is a continuous function, then

$$U_b(P_z) \rightarrow U_b(E(P) \text{ as } z \rightarrow 0, \text{ where } P = E(P_z)$$

Proof: Fix η, a positive number. Let I be an arbitrary interval such that

$$Pr[P \in I] = 1 - \eta/2$$

Now since P_z converges to P in probability, there exists an z_0 such that for all $z \leq z_0$ we have

$$Pr[|P_z - P| \leq \delta] = 1 - \eta/2 \qquad \text{for all } P \in I \text{ and any}$$

positive δ. Since U_b is continuous we have for any e positive

$$|U_b(P_z) - U_b(P)| \leq e \quad \text{if} \quad |P_z - P| \leq \delta$$

$$\begin{aligned} \text{hence } Pr[|U_b(P_z) - U_b(P)| \leq e) &\geq Pr[|P_z - P| \leq \delta, \qquad P \in I] \\ &= Pr[|P_z - P| \leq \delta] \\ &\quad - Pr[P \in I^c] \\ &= 1 - \eta/2 - \eta/2 \\ &= 1 - \eta \end{aligned}$$

But η is arbitrary and hence the result follows by letting

$\eta \longrightarrow 0$

LEMMA-3: Fix D and let $a\epsilon(0, 1)$, then there exists an a^* such that

$$E(P^F) = E(P^V)$$

Proof: Define:

$$\begin{aligned} h(a) &= E(P^F) - E(P^V) \\ &= L[E(\min(R_i, D) - (1 - a)E(R)] \end{aligned}$$

Now

$$h(1) = L(E(\min(R_i, D))) \geq 0$$

and

$$h(0) = L[E(\min(R_i, D)) - E(R)] \leq 0$$

since $E(R^i) \geq E(\min(R_i, D))$

Furthermore, since h is continuous there exists an a^* such that

$h(a^*) = 0$ as required.

COROLLARY-1: For all $a \leq a^*$ the lender strictly prefers the VRS.

Proof: Consider again $h(a)$. Now for $h(a) \leq 0$ the VRS dominates whereas for $h(a) \geq 0$ the FRS dominates. Since $h(a^*) = 0$ and $h(0)$ is a decreasing function of a, $h(a) \leq h(a^*)$ for all $a \leq a^*$.

PROPOSITION-1: (Miller-Modigliani). If investors are risk neutral then the choice of a financial contract is irrelevant.

Proof: If investors are risk neutral then they look at their expected return from the two schemes. Now there exists (D^*, a^*) such that

$$E(P^F) = E(P^V)$$
$$E(Y^F) = E(Y^V)$$

The existence is assured by the fact that both of the functions are continuous, and by appropriately defining the joint map we can appeal to the fixed point theorem.

Thus the return across both schemes is the same for both the lender and the investor, so there will be no basis for a preference for either of the two schemes. This means that the choice of the kind of contract is irrelevant.

PROPOSITION-2: Let

$$S^*(R) = \min(R, D')$$

and

$$S_*(R) = \max(R - D, 0)$$

Fix a and pick D and D' so that $S^*(R)$ and $S_*(R)$ are a-sharing rules. Then for all concave utility functions U and any a-sharing rule $S(R)$

$$EU(S^*) \geq EU(S) \geq EU(S_*)$$

Proof: Let $\Lambda = [S(R){:}ES(R) = aE(R); \quad 0 \leq S(R) \leq 1]$

Thus Λ defines the class of a-sharing rules. Suppose also that $R \leq M$ where M is a sufficiently large constant.

The proof requires two things:

*) $EU(S^*(R)) \geq EU(S(R))$ for all $S(R) \in \Lambda$ and U concave.

**) $EU(S_*(R)) \leq EU(S(R))$ for all $S(R) \in \Lambda$ and U concave.

i.e. $S^*(R)$ is the upper bound and $S_*(R)$ is a the lower bound for the class A under all concave functions.

Thus we will prove the above two statements separately. We will make use of the following two lemmas by Rothschild and Stiglitz (1970).

LEMMA-a: Suppose X and Y are two random variables with the same expected value. Y is riskier (or more variable) than X if any of three conditions are true:

i) $Y = X + Z$ with $E(Z|X) = 0$ and X and Y are identically distributed.

ii) $EU(X) \geq EU(Y)$ for all bounded and concave utility functions.

iii) If f is the density of X and G is that of Y then $g = f + s$ where $\int s(x)\,dx = \int xs(x)\,dx = 0$
i.e. the density of Y can be obtained from that of X by a single mean-preserving spread.

LEMMA-b: Let G be the distribution function of Y and F be the distribution function of X. Define

$$S(x) = G(x) - F(x)$$

then G is riskier than F iff S satisfies the following two conditions (called the integral conditions):

$$\text{i) } T(1) = \int_0^1 S(x)\,dx = 0$$

$$\text{ii) } T(y) = \int_0^y S(x)\,dx \geq 0 \qquad \text{for all } 0 \leq y \leq 1$$

Proof of (*): $S^*(R)$ is not the most preferred payoff, rather $S(R)$ has this property (such a payoff exists since Λ is a member of the bounded class of function). We will establish a contradiction.

Since $S(R) \in \Lambda$

$$ES(R) = aE(R)$$

and $0 \leq S(R) \leq R$

Second, since $S(R)$ is most preferred

$$EU(S(R)) \geq EU(S'(R)) \qquad \text{for all } S'(R) \in \Lambda$$

and in particular we have

$$EU(S(R)) \geq EU(S^*(R)) \tag{1}$$

Given that U is concave (1) implies that $S(R)$ is less risky than $S^*(R)$ (by lemma-a above). Again by lemma-a (iii), this means that the distribution of $S^*(R)$ can be obtained from that of $S(R)$ through a single mean-preserving spread. Thus for (1) to be true the difference of the distribution functions of $S(R)$ and $S^*(R)$ should satisfy the integral conditions of lemma-b.

Thus we need to find the distribution functions of $S(R)$ and $S^*(R)$.

Let $F(r)$ be the distribution function of R and $H(r)$ be the distribution function of $S^*(R)$, then

$$H(r) = \begin{bmatrix} 0 & r \geq 0 \\ F(r) & 0 \leq r \geq D' \\ 1 - F(D') & D' \leq r \geq M \\ 1 & M \leq r \geq r \end{bmatrix} \tag{2}$$

Define $S(R)$ as follows:

$$S(R) = \begin{bmatrix} t_1(r) & r \leq D' \\ t_2(r) & r \geq D' \end{bmatrix} \tag{3}$$

where, given D', $t_1(r)$ and $t_2(r)$ are chosen so that:

$$ES(R) = aE(R) \quad \text{and} \quad 0 \leq S(R) \leq R$$

Thus $S(R)$ is an arbitrary payoff function that belongs to Λ. Let $G(r)$ be the distribution function of $S(R)$, then:

$$G(r) = \begin{bmatrix} 0 & r \geq 0 \\ F(t_1^{-1}(r)) & 0 \leq r \geq D' \\ F(t_{21}^{-1}(r)) & D' \leq r \geq M \\ 1 & M \leq r \end{bmatrix} \tag{4}$$

Finally, let:

$$K(r) = H(r) - G(r) \tag{5}$$

Thus we need to check if $K(r)$ satisfies the integral conditions of lemma-b.

The first condition is trivially true since both of the payoffs belong to the class Λ.

For the second condition let:

$$\begin{aligned} T(r') &= \int_0^{r'} K(r)\, dr \\ &= \int_0^{r'} [H(r) - G(r)]\, dr \end{aligned}$$

Thus it should be true that:

$T(r') \geq 0$ for all $r' \in (0, M)$

Let $r' = D'$, then

$$T(D') = \int_0^{D'} [H(r) - G(r)]\, dr$$
$$= \int_0^{D'} [F(r) - F(t_1^{-1}(r))]\, dr$$

Since F is monotonic and $r \leq t_1^{-1}(r)$ we have

$$F(r) \leq F(t_1^{-1}(r))$$
$$T(r) = \int_0^{D'} [F(r) - F(t_1^{-1}(r))]\, dr \leq 0$$

contradicting that $S(R)$ is the most preferred *a*-sharing payoff.

Proof of (**): Though a rigorous proof along the same lines of (*) can be given, here we argue by a simple method that is fairly intuitive.

Since $S^*(R)$ is the most preferred payoff, the residual payoff should be the least preferred payoff. The residual payoff is given as:

$$S^0(R) = \begin{cases} 0 & R \leq D \\ R - D & R \geq D \end{cases}$$

where D is determined by the constraint that $S^0(R)$ must belong to Λ. But

$$S^0(R) = S_*(R)$$

and as such

$$EU(S^*(R)) \leq EU(S(R)) \qquad \text{for all } S \in \Lambda$$

COROLLARY-2: A risk averse investor strictly prefers the VRS over the FRS.

Proof: We need to show that:

$$EU(Y_i^V) \geq EU(Y_i^V)$$

at the point where:

$$E(Y_i^V) = E(Y_i^F)$$

Note that both Y^V and Y^F are a-sharing rules since:
$E(Y_i V) = aE(R)$ and both of these payoffs are bounded by M. Therefore the corollary follows by letting:

$$S_*(R) = Y^F = \max(R_i - D, 0)$$

in proposition-2.

THEOREM-1: Corresponding to each FRS there is a VRS which improves everyone's welfare.

Proof: From Corollary-2 each investor prefers VRS. We show that the lender can be made better off through the VRS arrangement.
Since U is continuous there is an e positive such that:

$$EU\{(a^* - e)R = EU(\max(R_i - D, 0))\}$$

Therefore it is possible to give, say, $\frac{1}{2}eR_i$ to the lender without changing the investor's preference for the VRS. From corollary-1, it follows that for $a = a^* - \frac{1}{2}e$ lender strictly prefers the VRS. This shows that the VRS improves everyone's welfare.

Appendix III
Towards an Interest-Free Islamic Economic System

Waqar Masood Khan

PROPOSITION-1: Let (P^V, Y^V, g, h, C^V) be the game defined above for the VRS. The Nash Solution of the game is given by the pair

$$(g^*, h^*) = [r - b/1 - a, 1 - \exp - \{(1 - a)(1 - g(r)) - b\}/b]$$

and minimizes the expected cost of monitoring.

Proof: The investor chooses $g(r)$, for a given $h(g(r))$, to maximize:

$$Y^V = r - (1 - a)g(r) - h(g(r))(1 - a)(r - g(r))$$

The first order condition is:

$$\frac{dY^V}{dg(r)} = -(1 - a) - h'(g(r))(1 - a)(r - g(r))$$
$$+ (1 - a)h(g(r)) = 0$$

$$g(r) = r + \{1 - h(g(r))\}/h'(g(r)) \qquad (1)$$

On the other hand the lender maximizes, for a given $g(r)$:

$$E(P^V) = \int_d^1 \{(1 - a)g(r) + h(g(r))$$
$$\cdot [(1 - a)(r - g(r)) - b]\}\, mdr \qquad (2)$$

where $m = 1/1 - d$.

This is equivalent to maximizing the integrand in (2). We will justify this procedure below. Since (2) is linear in $h(g(r)$ for a given $g(r)$, we have:

$$h(g(r)) = \begin{cases} 0 \text{ if } (1-a)(r-g(r)) \leq b \\ 1 \text{ if } (1-a)(r-g(r)) \geq b \end{cases} \tag{3}$$

A corner solution is clearly inefficient in terms of cost of monitoring. If lender has access to randomized monitoring technology then he chooses $h(g(r))$ such that:

$$h(g(r)) \in (0, 1) \text{ and } (r - g(r)) = b/1 - a \tag{4}$$

This is the Nash Equilibrium condition for the lender. But the problem is how to find $h(g(r))$ from (4).

From (1):

$$r - g(r) = -[1 - h(g(r))]/h'(g(r)\text{-})$$

So the Nash Solution is given by the two equilibrium conditions:

$$r - g(r) = -[1 - h(g(r))]/h'(g(r)) = b/1 - a \tag{5}$$

From the second equation in (5) we get:

$$[1 - h(g(r))]/h'(g(r) = -b/1 - a$$

or

$$-(\mathrm{b}/1 - a)h'(g(r)) + h(g(r)) = 1 \tag{6}$$

(6) is a linear differential equation which has the solution:

$$h^*(g(r)) = 1 - \exp\{[-(1-a)(1-g(r)) - b]/b\}$$

where $h(1 - b/1 - a)$ is the initial condition. Note that the lender's optimal strategy does not have r as its argument since he does not observe r. This justifies our procedure of maximizing the integrand in (2)

$h^*(g(r))$ forces $g(r)$ to be:

$$g^*(r) = r - b/1 - a \tag{7}$$

It can be seen that $g^*(r)$ is invertable in r, but the reporting space $(0, 1 - b/1 - a)$ is different from $(d, 1)$, the original space. We see that $d = b/1 - a$.

Thus we have shown that:

$$(g^*, h^*) = [\mathrm{r} - b/1 - a, 1 - \exp\{[-(1 - a) \cdot (1 - g(r)) - b]/b\}]$$

is Nash equilibrium solution of the game under the VRS.

It remains to be shown that this also minimizes the expected monitoring costs.

Given (g^*, h^*):

$$E(C^V) = \int_0^{1-b/1-a} b[1 - \exp\{-[(1 - a)g(r) - b]/b\}]\, mdg(r)$$
$$= b[1 - (b/1 - a - b)(1 - \exp - (1 - a - b)/b)] \qquad (8)$$

Thus $E(C^V) \leq b$. The only other equilibrium is $h(g(r)) = 1$. But then $E(C^V) = b$. Thus (g^*, h^*) minimizes the monitoring costs.

PROPOSITION-2: Let (P^F, Y^F, g, h, C^F) be the game defined above for the FRS. The Nash Solution of the game is given by:

$$(g^*, h^*) = [\min(r, D) - b, 1 - \exp\{-(D - g(r) - b)/b\}]$$

and minimizes the expected cost of monitoring.

Proof: In this case the investor chooses $g(r)$, for a given $h(g(r))$, to maximize:

$$Y^F = r - g(r) - h(g(r))[\min(r, D) - g(r)] \qquad (9)$$

Maximizing (9) over $g(r)$ gives:

$$\frac{dY^F}{dg(r)} = -1 - h'(g(r))[\min(r, D) - g(r)] + h(g(r)) = 0$$

which gives:

$$g(r) = \min(r \cdot D) + (1 - h(g(r))]/h'(g(r)) \qquad (10)$$

On the other hand the lender maximizes, for a given $g(r)$:

$$E(P^F) = \int_d^1 [g(r) + h(g(r))\{\min(r, D) - g(r) - b\}] \qquad (11)$$

As we argued in Proposition-1, this is equivalent to maximizing the integrand in (11). Since (11) is linear in $h(g(r)$, we get:

$$h(g(r) = \begin{cases} 0 & \text{if } \min(r, D) \leq b \\ 1 & \text{if } \min(r, D) > 0 \end{cases} \qquad (12)$$

Again a corner solution is inefficient in terms of cost of monitoring. If the lender has access to a randomized technology he will choose $h(g(r))$ so that:

$$h(g(r) \in (0, 1) \quad \text{and} \quad \min (r, D) - g(r) = b \tag{13}$$

This is the Nash Equilibrium condition for the lender under the FRS. Now combining (10) and (13), we get:

$$\min (r, D) - g(r) = -[1 - h(g(r))]/h'(g(r) = b \tag{14}$$

From the second equation in (14) we get:

$$-bh'(g(r)) + h(g(r)) = 1 \tag{15}$$

(15) is a linear differential equation having the solution

$$h^*(g(r)) = 1 - \exp \{-[D - g(r) - b]/b\} \tag{16}$$

where we have imposed the initial condition:

$$h(D - b) = 0$$

On the other hand the optimal $g(r)$ is given as:

$$g^*(r) = \min (r, D) - b$$

It is easy to show in the same way as in Proposition-1 that this Nash equilibrium minimizes the cost of monitoring.

PROPOSITION-3: Given a uniform distribution of return R and $(1 - a)$ and D, such that:

$$E(P^F) = E(P^V)$$

with no monitoring costs, then the expected monitoring costs under the VRS are greater than under the FRS.

Proof: The expected costs for the VRS are given by:

$$E(C^V) = b[1 - (b/1 - a - b)[1 - \exp \{-(1 - a - b)/b\}]]$$

while under the FRS the costs are given by:

$$E(C^F) = (b/1 - b)[D - b(2 - \exp \{-(D - b)/b\})]$$

We need to show that:

$$E(C^V) > E(C^F)$$

$$b[1 - (b/1 - a - b)[1 - \exp\{-(1 - a - b)/b\}]]$$
$$> (b/1 - b)[D - b(2 - \exp\{-(D - b)/b\})]$$
$$1 - (b/1 - a - b)[1 - \exp\{-(1 - a - b)/b\}]$$
$$> D - b(2 - \exp\{-(D - b)/b\})$$
$$(b/1 - a - b)[1 - \exp\{-(1 - a - b)/b\}]$$
$$> b(2 - \exp -(D - b)/b)$$

since $D < 1$

$$1 - \exp\{-(1 - a - b)/b\} < 2 - \exp\{-(D - b)/b\}$$
since $1 - a - b < 1$ $\exp\{-(1 - a - b)/b\} >$
$$\exp\{-(D - b)/b\} - 1 \tag{17}$$

Since $0 < \exp(-k) < 1$ for all non-negative k, (17) is true for all a, D, and b. This means that in particular it is true for the pair (a, D) such that:

$E(P^V) = E(P^F)$ with no information costs.

LEMMA-1: Let $(1 - a)$, $(1 - a')$, D and D' denote the share and fixed return of the lender without and with the information costs. Then if the lender equalizes his return across two shemes under both situations then:

$$a' < a$$

and

$$D' > D$$

Proof: The payoff to the lender under the FRS with information costs is:

$$E(P'^F) = (1/1 - b)[D(1 - \tfrac{1}{2}D) - \tfrac{1}{2}b^2)] - b \tag{18}$$

while the payoff to the lender under the FRS with no information costs is:

$$E(P^F) = (1/1 - b)[D(1 - \tfrac{1}{2}D) - \tfrac{1}{2}b^2] \tag{19}$$

Equalizing (18) and (19) we get:

$$D'(1 - \tfrac{1}{2}D') - b(1 - b) = D(1 - \tfrac{1}{2}D)$$

or

$$D'(1 - \tfrac{1}{2}D) = D(1 - \tfrac{1}{2}D) + b(1 - b)$$

Since $b(1 - b) > 0$, we have:

$$D' > D$$

On the other hand the lender's payoffs under the VRS with and without the information costs are:

$$E(P'^{V}) = \tfrac{1}{2}(1 - a')[1 + b/1 - a'] - b \tag{20}$$

$$E(P^{V}) = \tfrac{1}{2}(1 - a)[1 + b/1 - a] \tag{21}$$

respectively.

Equalizing (20) and (21) we get:

$$(1 - a') = (1 - a) + 2b/1 + b(1 - b)$$

Since $b/1 + b(1 - b) \geq 0$, we have $(1 - a') > (1 - a)$ or $a' < a$ as required.

PROPOSITION-4: The choice between financial schemes depends on the attitude towards risk of the investor. For a sufficiently low degree of risk aversion the FRS dominates the VRS.

Proof: It is clear that in order to determine the investor's choice of type of contract we have to look at his expected utility under each of the alternatives. Thus, his choice depends on the degree of risk aversion. The proof of exact dependence is fairly tedious; therefore, we shall ignore it here. We show the dominance of the FRS under the linear case.

The proof follows from Proposition-3 and Lemma-1. From Proposition-3 we know that expected monitoring costs are higher for the VRS, and Lemma-1 establishes the transfer of these costs to the investors. Since the payoff to the lender is equalized across both schemes and in both situations, the investors ultimately bear these monitoring costs. But these costs are smaller in the case of the FRS since there is a smaller deadweight loss. Therefore, the investor's payoff is higher under the FRS, and he would accordingly prefer the FRS over the VRS.

Bibliography

Abdul-Rauf, Muhammad, *The Islamic Doctrine of Economics and Contemporary Economic Thought,* published in *Capitalism and Socialism: A theological Inquiry,* Michael Novak, ed., The American Enterprise Institute for Public Policy Research, Washington 1978. pp. 129–151.

Abu-Bequer de Tortosa, *L'ampara de los principes,* translated into Spanish and edited by M. Alarcon, Madrid 1930 (2 volumes).

Abu Saud, Mahmud, *Money, Interest and Qirad,* published in Khurshid Ahmad, ed., *Studies in Islamic Economics,* London, Islamic Foundation, 1980.

Abul Qasem Muhammad, *The Ethics of al-Ghazali,* University of Edinburgh, 1973.

Abū-Yūsuf, *Kitāb al-Kharāj,* translated into Persian by Ali Asghar Shu'a'.

Adler, Michael, *On the Risk-Return Trade-off in the Valuation of Assets,* published in *Journal of Finance and Quantitative Analysis* (vol. 4, N. 4, pp. 493–512), December 1969.

Afnan, Soheil, M., *Avicenna: His Life and Works,* George Allen and Unwin 1958.

Agarwal, P., *Financial Markets in Developing Countries: A new Analysis with Transaction Costs,* Stanford University, Economics Department, Ph D Thesis (Chapter 2), 1982.

Agnides, N. P., *Muhammadan Theories of Finance,* Premier Book House, Lahore 1961.

Ahmad, Khurshid, ed., *Studies in Islamic Economics,* The Islamic Foundation, Leicester, U.K. 1980.

Ahmad, Shaikh M. *Economics of Islam: A Comparative Study,* Sh. Muhammad Ashraf, Lahore 1952.

Aḥmad, Khālid, *al-Tafkīr al-Iqtiṣādī fi al-Islam̄,* Dar al-Da' wah al-Islāmīyah, Beirut 1397/1976.

Ahmed, Ziauddin, *Concept and Models of Islamic Banking: An*

Assessment, paper presented at the seminar of Islamization of Banking, Karachi, November 1984.

Ahmed Ziauddin et al., ed., *Money and Banking in Islam,* Institute for Policy Studies, Islamabad 1983.

Albach, M., *Risky Capital, Business Investment and Economics Cooperation.* Paper presented at the International Symposium *Islamic Banks and Strategies of Economic Cooperation,* in Baden-Baden, West Germany, 1981.

'Alī, Mu'aẓẓam, ed., *Islamic Banks and Strategies of Economic Co-operation,* New Century, London 1982.

Allen, David E., *Finance: A Theoretical Introduction,* Martin Robertson, Oxford 1983.

Amīn, Aḥmad, *fajr al-Islām,* Beirut 1969.

Anṣārī, Murtaḍā, *al-Makāsib,* (for a list of editions, see: Hossein Modarresi, Ṭabāṭabā'i, *An Introduction to Shīī Law, A Bibliographical Study* (p. 174), Ithaca Press, London 1984.

Anṣārī, Zafar Isḥāq, *Some Reflections on the Quranic Legal Verses,* published in *Hamdard Islamicus* (vol. 4, No. 2, pp. 13–29).

Arberry, A. J. *The Koran Interpreted,* McMillan Publishing Company, New York 1976.

Ariff, Muhammad, ed., *Monetary and Fiscal Economics of Islam,* International Center for Research in Islamic Economics, Jeddah 1982.

Arinm Felix, *Opérations usuraires aléatoires en droit musulman,* A. Pedone, Paris 1909.

Arrow, K. J., *Uncertainty and the Welfare Economics of Medical Care,* published in *American Economic Review* (vol. 53, pp. 941–973), 1963.

———. *Essays in the Theory of Risk-Bearing,* North-Holland Publishing Co., Amsterdam, 1970.

———. *Insurance, Risk and Resource Allocation,* published in *Essays in the Theory of Risk-Bearing,* Markham, Chicago 1971.

Azariadis, C., *Employment with Asymetric Information,* published in *Quarterly Journal of Economics* (supplement, vol. 98, pp. 157–172), 1983.

——— and J. Stiglitz, *Implicit Contracts and Fixed Price Equilibria,* published in *Quarterly Journal of Economics* (supplement, vol. 98, pp. 1–22), 1983.

Babalbālī, Maḥmūd, *al-Māl fi al-Islām,* Beirut 1975.

Baḥr al-'Ulūm, Maḥammad ibn Muḥammad Taqī al-Ṭabāṭabā'ī,

(It is included in the author's *Bulghat al-Faqīh,* Tabriz 1325/1907, Tehran 1329/1911, Najaf 1389/1969).

Bank Markazi of the Islamic Republic of Iran, *The Law of Usury (Interest) Free Banking,* Tehran, August 1983.

Bashir, B. A., *Portfolio Management of Islamic Banks: Certainty Model,* published in *Journal of Banking and Finance* (vol. 7, pp. 339–354), 1983.

Bernardelli, H., *The Origins of Modern Economic Theory,* published in *Economic Record* (37, pp. 320–338), 1961.

Bihbahānī, *Risālah fi Buṭlān al-Qarḍ bi Sharṭ al-Mu'āmalah al-Muḥabatiyah,* (for the list of catalogues, see: Hossein Modarresi Ṭabāṭabā'ī, *An Introduction to Shi'i Law, A Bibliographical Study,* Ithaca Press, London 1984.

Bihbahānī, *Risālah fi anna al-Aṣl fī al-Mu'āmalāt al-Ṣihhah,* manuscript, Danishgah Tehran Library 713/3 (catalogue V, p. 1777); Huqūq Library of Tehran 247/4j (catalogue p. 348).

Beheshti, Sayyid Muhammad Husayn, *Bankdārī wa Qawānīn -e Mālī -e Islām,* (for reference, see: *Fihrist -e Mawḍū'ī -e Bakhshī az Āthār -e Shahīd -e Maẓlūm,* Tehran 1361/1982.

Black, Marshall, *Capital Market Equilibrium with Restricted Borrowing,* published in *The Journal of Business* (vol 45, No. 3, pp. 444–455), July 1972.

Blair, Roger D. and Arnold A. Heggestad, *Bank Portfolio and the Probability of Bank Failure,* published in *Journal of Money, Credit and Banking* (vol. 10, No. 1, pp. 88–93), February 1978.

Block, M. K., and J. M. Heineke, *Factor Allocation Under Uncertainty: An Extension,* published in *Southern Economic Journal,* (vol. 41, pp. 526–30), 1975.

———, *A Comment on Uncertainty and Household Decisions,* published in *Review of Economic Studies,* (vol. 39, pp. 5233–5), 1972.

Borch, K., *Equilibrium in Reinsurance Market,* published in *Econometrica* (vol. 30, No. 3, pp. 424–444), 1962.

Brainard, William C., *Financial Intermediaries and the Theory of Monetary Control,* published in D. D. Hester and J. Tobin, eds., *Financial Markets and Economic Activity,* New York 1967.

Branson, William H., *Macroeconomic Theory and Policy,* second edition, Harper and Row, New York 1979.

Burns, Robert I. S. J., *Mudejar History Today: New Directions,* published in *Viator* (vol. 8, pp. 127–151), 1977.

Butterworth, Charles E., *New Light on the Political Philosophy of Averroes,* published in Hourani, F. G., ed., *Essays on Islamic Philosophy and Science,* pp. 118–127.

Chapra, M. Umar., *The Economic System of Islam,* The Islamic Cultural Center, London 1970.

———. *Money and Banking in an Islamic Economy,* published in Ariff, Muhammad, ed., *Monetory and Fiscal Economics of Islam,* International Center for Research in Islamic Economics, Jeddah 1982.

Chari, V. V., *Involuntary Unemployment and Implicit Contracts,* published in *Quarterly Journal of Economics* (vol. 98 supplement, pp. 107–122), 1983.

Chejne, Anwar, *Muslim Spain,* Minneapolis, 1974.

Copleston, F. C., *A History of Medieval Philosophy,* Harper and Row, New York, 1972.

Coulson, N. J. *Succession in the Muslim Family,* Cambridge University Press, 1091.

Coulson, N. *Conflicts and Tensions in Islamic Jurisprudence,* University of Chicago Press 1969.

———. *A history of Islamic Law,* Edinburgh University Press, 1978.

Council of Islamic Ideology, *Report on Elimination of Interest,* published in Ahmed Ziauddin et al., ed., *Money and Banking in Islam,* Institute for Policy Studies, Islamabad 1983.

Daoualibi, M., *La théorie de l' usure en driot musulman,* published in *Travaux de la Semaine Internationale de Droit Musulman,* Sirey, France 1953.

Dar al Maal al Islami. Dar al Maal Al Islami and Islamic Economic and Financial Institutions, *New Century, London 1982.*

De Rosa, D. A., *Islamic Financial Policies and Domestic Resources Mobilization, Savings and Developments,* unpublished 1985.

Diamond, P., and J. Stiglitz, *Increasing Risk and Risk Aversion,* published in *Journal of Economic Theory,* (vol. 3, pp. 337–60), 1974.

Drāz, Shaikh, *L'usure en driot musulman,* published in *Travaux de la Semaine Internationale de Driot Musulman,* Sirey, France 1953.

Dreze, J., and F. Modigliani, *Consumption Decisions Under Uncertainty,* published in *Journal of Economic Theory,* (vol. 5, pp. 308–55), 1972.

Evans, John L. and Stephen H. Archer, *Diversification and Reduction of Dispersion: An Empirical Analysis,* published in *Journal of Finance* (vol. 23, No. 5, pp. 761–767), December 1968.

Fama, Eugene F., *Risk, Return and Equilibrium,* published in *Journal of Political Economy* (vol. 79, No. 1, pp. 30–55), January-February 1971.

——— and Merton H. Miller, *The Theory of Finance,* Dryden Press, Handsdale Illinois 1972.

Fernandez, Roque B., *Implicancias dinamicas de la propuesta de Simons para reforma del systema financiero,* published in *Ensayos Economicos,* Banco Central de la Republica Argentina (vol. 29, pp. 1–30), March 1984.

Fischel, W., *The Origin of Banking in Medieval Islam,* Journal of Asiatic Society, 1933.

Fischer, Irving, *100% Money,* New Haven, Connecticut 1945.

———, *The Theory of Interest,* McMillan, New York 1930.

Francis, Jack Clark and Stephen H. Archer, *Portfolio Analysis,* second edition, Prentice-Hall, Englewood Cliffs, N.J. 1979.

Friedman, Milton, *The Monetary Theory and Policy of Henry Simons,* published in Milton Friedman's *The Optimum Quantity of Money and Other Essays,* Aldine, Chicago 1969.

Ghazālī, Imām Muḥammad, *Iḥyā 'Ulūm al-Dīn,* translated into French by Bousquet, Paris, 1955.

———. *Book of Councel for King,* translated by F. R. C. Bagley, University of Durham Publications, Oxford 1964.

Gibb, H. A. R. and Kramers, J. H. eds., *A Shorter Encyclopedia of Islam,* Brill and Luzac, Netherlands 1961.

Gillaume, A., *The Legacy of Islam,* London 1952.

Gjesdal, F., *Information and Incentives: The Agency Information Problem,* published in *Review of Economic Studies* (vol. 49, pp. 373–390), 1982.

Glick, Thomas F., *Muḥtasib and Mustasaf: A Case Study of Institutional Diffusion,* published in *Viator* (vol. 2, pp. 59–81), 1971.

Goiten, S. W., *Commercial and Family Partnership in the Countries of Medieval Islam,* published in *Islamic Studies* (vol. III, pp. 318–319), 1964.

Golembe, Carter H. and John J. Mingo, *Can Supervision and Regulation Ensure Financial Stability?,* paper presented at the conference on the Search for Financial Stability: The Past Fifty Years, Federal Reserve Bank of San Francisco, San Francisco, June 1985.

Gulesurkhi, Riḍa, *Ṭarḥ -e Bank -e Bidūn -e Ribā,* published in *Maktab -e Islām* (vol. 15, No. 1, 4, 6, 8, 10), Qum, 1392/1972.

Gulzādeh Ghafūrī, 'Alī, *Anfāl ya Thirwat hā ye 'Umūmī,* Shirkat -e Intishār, Tehran, 1977.

Gray, Sir Alexander, *The Development of Economic Doctrine,* John Wiley and Sons Inc., New York 1931.

Green, J. and C. M. Kahn, *Wage Employment Contracts,* published in *Quarterly Journal of Economics* (vol. 98 supplement pp. 173–188), 1983.

Grice-Hutchinson, Marjorie, *Early Economic Thought in Spain 1177–1740,* George Allen and Unwin, London, 1978.

Grossman, S. S., and O. P. Hart, *An Analysis of the Principal-Agent Problem,* published in *Econometrica* (vol. 51, No. 1, pp. 7–45), 1983.

———. *Implicit Contracts under Assymetric Information,* published in *Quarterly Journal of Economics* (vol. 98 supplement, pp. 123–156), 1983b.

———. *Corporate Financial Structure and Managerial Incentive* published in the *Economics of Information and Uncertainty,* John J. McCall Ed. NBER Conference Report No. 32, 1982.

Hahn, F., *Savings and Uncertainty,* published in *The Review of Economic Studies,* (vol. 37, pp. 21–4), 1970.

Halepota, A. J., *Islamic Social Order,* published in *Islamic Studies* (vol. 14, N. 2, pp. 115–122).

al-Hamīd, Muḥammad, *Naẓarāt fī al-Kitāb Ishtirākiyah al-Islam,* Damascus, 1963.

Hamidullah, M., *The Muslim Conduct of State,* Muhammad Ashraf Publications, Lahore 1954.

Hanson, D., and C. Menezes, *The Effect of Capital Risk on Optimal Savings Decisions,* published in *Quarterly Journal of Economics,* (vol. 92, pp. 653–70), 1978.

———, *On a Neglected Aspect of the Theory of Risk Aversion,* published in *Western Economic Journal,* (vol. 9, pp. 211–17), 1971.

Haque, N. U. and Abbas Mirakhor, *Optimal Profit-Sharing Contracts and Investment in an Interest-Free Islamic Economy,* manuscript, 1986.

Haque, Z., *Ribū, Interest and Profit,* published in *Pakistan Economist,* May 24 (pp. 14–35) & May 31 (pp. 13–30), 1980.

Harris, M. and Raviv, A., *Optimal Incentive Contracts with Imperfect Information,* JET, 20, 1979.

Harris, M. and A. Raviv, *Optimal Incentive Contracts with Imperfect Information,* published in *Journal of Economic Theory* (vol. 20, pp. 231–259), 1979.

——— and R. M. Townsend, *Resource Allocation under Asymmetric Information,* published in *Econometrica* (vol. 49, pp. 231–259), 1979.

Hart, Oliver D. and Dwight M. Jaffee, *On the Application of Portfolio Theory to Depository Financial Intermediaries,* published in *The Review of Economic Studies* (vol. 41, No. 125, pp. 129–147), 1974.

Ḥasan uz Zamān, M., *The Economic Functions of the Early Islamic State,* International Islamic Publishers, Karachi 1981.

Herbo, Ibrāhīm Fāḍil Yūsuf. *'Aqd al-Muḍārabah,* Iraq 1973.

Hijāzī, Sayyid 'Abd al-Riḍā, *System -e Iqtiṣādī -e Islām* (Persian), Tehran.

Hirshleifer, J., *On the Theory of Optimal Investment Decision,* published in *Journal of Political Economy,* (vol. 66, pp. 329–52), 1958.

Hitti, P., *Islam, A Way of Life,* Oxford University Press, 1970.

Holstrom, B., *Moral Hazard and Observability,* published in *Bell Journal of Economics* (vol. 10, pp. 74–91), 1979.

———. *Equilibrium Long-Term Labor Contracts,* published in *Quarterly Journal of Economics* (vol. 98 supplement, pp. 23–54), 1983.

Ḥurr al-'Amilī, *Risālah fi anna al-Taṣarruf wa al-Yad Dalīl al-Mālikiyah,* Manuscript, Fayḍiyyah Library, Qum 1910, catalogue III, p. 148).

Ḥusayn ibn Ḥaydar al-Karakī, *Ithbāt al-Ḥaqq* (also known as *Risālah fi Jawāz Sharṭ al-Murtahin al-Wikālah li Nafsihī fi Bay' al-Marhūn,* manuscript, Malek Library, Tehran (AB, XI, p. 81)

Ḥusaynqulī al-Hamadānī, *Kitāb al-Rahn,* manuscript, Tustariyah Library, Iran (AB, XI, p. 3111)

Ibn Khaldūn, *Muqaddimah,* Translated by Franz. Rosenthal (3 volumes), Bollingen Foundation Inc. New York 1958. Revised edition Princeton University Press 1967; abridgement Princeton University Press 1981.

Ibn Taymiyah, T. A., *al-Hisbah fi al-Islam,* Dar al-Kutub al-Arabiyah, Beirut 1976.

Ibn al-Ukhuwwa, *The Ma'ālim al-Qurbah fi Aḥkām al-Ḥisbah,* Translation into English by R. Levy in *E. J. W. Gibb Memorial Series* XII (Cambridge University Press, 1938).

Itr, Nur al-Din, *al-Mu'āmalat al-Maṣrafiyah wa al-Ribawiyah,* Risalah, Beirut 1977.

Izutsu, T., *Ethico-Religious Concepts in the Qur'an,* McGill University Press, Montreal 1966.

———. *God and Man in the Koran,* the Keio Institute of Cultural and Linguistic Studies, Tokyo 1964.

al-Jarhi, Mabid Ali, *A Monetary and Financial Structure for an Interest-Free Economy,* published in Ziauddin Ahmed et al., ed., *Money and Banking in Islam,* Institute for Policy Studies, Islamabad 1983.

Jazīrī, 'Abd al-Raḥmān, *al-Fiqh 'Alā al-Madhāhib al-Arbi'ah* (5 volumes), Dar al-Ihya al-Turāth al-Arabi, Beirut.

Jensen, M. and Meckling, W., *Theory of the Firm: Managerial behavior, agency costs and ownership structure,* published in *Journal of Financial Economics,* (vol. 3, pp. 305–360), 1976.

Kahf, Monzer, *The Economic View of Taqiideen Iben Taymeyah,* published in *al-Ittihad* (vol. 18, No. 3, pp. 9–21), published by Muslim Students Association, Plainfield, Indiana 1981.

———, *The Islamic Economy,* Muslim Student Association of the United States and Canada, Plainfield Indiana 1978.

———, *Fiscal and Monetary in an Islamic Economy,* published in Ariff, Muhammad, ed., *Monetory and Fiscal Economics of Islam,* International Center for Research in Islamic Economics, Jeddah 1982.

Kahne, Yehuda, *Capital Adequacy and the Regulation of Financial Intermediaries,* published in *Journal of Banking and Finance* (vol. 1, pp. 207–218), 1977.

Kamel, Ibrahim, *Islamic Banks and Strategies of Economic Cooperation,* New Century, London 1982.

Karecken, John H. *Ensuring Financial Stability,* paper presented at the Conference on the Search for Financial Stability: The Past Fifty Years, Federal Reserve Bank of San Francisco, San Francisco, June 1985.

Karsten, Ingo, *Islam and Financial Intermediation,* published in *IMF Staff Papers* (vol. 29, No. 1), 1982.

Kazi, A. G. N., *Islamic Banking in Perspective,* published in *Journal of Islamic Banking and Finance* (vol. 1, No. 3, pp. 7–21), Karachi, July-September 1984.

Khaddouri, M. and Liebensny, H. J., ed., *Law in the Middle East,* the Middle East Institute, Washington D.C. 1955.

Khafīf, 'Alī, *Aḥkām al-Mu'āmalāt al-Shar'iyah,* Cairo 1941.

Khamenei, Seyyed Muhammad, *Insurance in Islamic Law,* Islamic Cultural Publications, Tehran 1979.

Khan, Abdul Jabbar, *Elimination of Riba From the Banking System,* published in *Journal of Islamic Banking and Finance* (vol. 1, No. 3, pp. 22–44), Karachi, 1984.

———. *Comments,* published in Ahmed Ziauddin et al., ed., *Money and Banking in Islam* (p. 254), Institute for Policy Studies, Islamabad 1983.

Khan, M. Akram, *Inflation and the Islamic Economy: A Closed Economy Model,* published in Ariff, Muhammad, ed., *Monetary and Fiscal Economics of Islam,* International Center for Research in Islamic Economics, Jeddah 1982.

———. *Issues in Islamic Economics,* Lahore 1983.

Khan, M. Fahim, *Islamic Banking as Practiced Now in the World,* published in Ahmed Ziauddin et al., ed., *Money and Banking in Islam,* Institute for Policy Studies, Islamabad 1983.

Khan, Mohsin. S. *Islamic Interest-Free Banking: A Theoretical Analysis,* published in *IMF Staff Papers,* (vol. 33, No. 1, pp. 1–27), Washington, 1986.

Khan, Mohsin, S. and Abbas Mirakhor, *The Financial System and Monetary Policy in An Islamic Economy,* International Monetary Fund, DM/85/72, Washington 1985.

Khan, Mohsin, S. and Abbas Mirakhor, *The Frame Work and Practice of Islamic Banking,* Finance and Development (Sept. 1986)

Khan, Shahrukh Rafi, *Profit and Loss Sharing: An Economic Analysis of An Islamic Financial System,* Ph.D. Dissertation, The University of Michigan, 1983.

———, *An Economic Analysis of a PLS Model for the Financial Sector,* published in *Pakistan Journal of Applied Economics* (vol. 3, pp. 89–105) 1984.

——, *The PLS System Compared to Conventional Capital Markets.* published in *Arabia* (31, pp. 48–50), 1984.

Khan, Waqar M., *Towards an Interest-Free Islamic Economic System: A Theoretical Analysis of Prohibiting Debt Financing,* unpublished Ph.D. Thesis, Department of Economics, Boston University, Boston Mass. 1983.

Khumayni, Ayatullah Sayyid Ruhullah, *al-Makāsib al-Muḥarramah,* Tehran 1381/1961.

Khumayni, Ayatullah Sayyid Ruhullah, Kitāb *al-Bay'*, Tehran

Khurrafah, A., *al-Ribā wa al-Fā' idah,* Baghdad 1962.

Kihlstrom, R. E. and J. J. Laffort, *Implicit Labor Contracts and Free Entry,* published in *Quarterly Journal of Economics* (vol. 98 supplement, pp. 55–106), 1983.

Knight, Frank H. *Risk, Uncertainty and Profit,* Sentry Press, New York 1964.

Koehn, Michael and Anthony M. Santomero, *Regulation of Bank Capital and Portfolio Risk,* published in *Journal of Finance* (vol. 35, No. 5, pp. 1235–1244), 1980.

Labib, Subhi, Y., *Capitalism in Medieval Islam,* published in *Journal of Economic History* (vol. 29, pp. 77–98), 1951.

Lane, F. C., *Family Partnership and Joint Ventures in the Venetian Republic,* published in *Journal of Economic History* (vol. 4, pp. 178–196), 1944.

Leland, H. E., *Savings and Uncertainty: The Precautionary Demand for Saving,* published in *Quarterly Journal of Economics,* (vol. 82, pp. 465–73), 1969.

Levhari, D., and T. N. Srinivasan, *Optimal Savings Under Uncertainty,* published in *Review of Economic Studies,* (vol. 36, pp. 27–38), 1969.

Levy, R., *The Social Structure of Islam,* Cambridge University Press 1958.

Lintner, John, *Security Prices and Maximal Gains from Diversification,* published in *Journal of Finance* (vol. 20, No. 4, pp. 587–615), December 1965.

Lokkegaard, Frede, *Islamic Taxation in the Classic Period,* Copenhagen 1950.

Lopez, Robert and Raymond, Irving W., *Medieval Trade in the Mediterranean World,* New York 1961.

Maliaris, A. G., and W. A. Brock, *Stochastic Methods in Economics and Finance,* North-Holland, Amsterdam, 1982.

Mao, James C. T., *Essentials of Portfolio Diversification Strategy,* published in *Journal of Finance* (vol. 25), 1970.

Mahmassani, S. *The Philosophy of Jurisprudence in Islam,* translated by F. Ziadeh, E. J. Brill, Leiden 1962.

———. *The General Theory of the Law of Obligations and Contract under Islamic Jurisprudence* (2 volumes), Beirut 1972.

Mannan, M. A., *Islamic Economics,* Ashraf Publications, Lahore 1970.

———. *Islamic Economics, Theory and Practice,* Lahore 1975.

Markowitz, Harry M., *Portfolio Selection,* John Wiley and Sons Inc. New York 1959.

al-Maṣrī, *al-Tijārah fi al-Islām,* Cairo 1976.

Mehren, A. F., *Algazel, Maqacid al-falasifah,* published in *Les Annales de philosophie chretienne* (vol. XX), Paris 1890.

Meltzer, Lloyd, A. *Wealth, Saving, and the Rate of Interest,* published in *Journal of Political Economy* (vol. 59, pp. 93–116), Chicago, April 1951.

Menezes, C. F., and G. E. Auten, *The Theory of Optimal Saving Decisions Under Income Risk,* published in *International Economic Review,* (vol. 19, pp. 253–58) 1978.

Merton, Robert, *An Analytical Derivation of the Efficient Portfolio Frontier,* published in *Journal of Financial and Quantitative Analysis* (pp. 1851–1872), September 1972.

Michaelson, Jatole B., and Robert C. Goshay, *Portfolio Selection in Financial Intermediaries,* published in *Journal of Financial and Quantitative Analysis* (pp. 166–199), 1967.

Miller, M. and Modigiliani, F., *The Cost of Capital Corporation Finance, and Theory of Investment,* published in *AER,* (vol. 48, pp. 423–443), 1958.

Milliot, L. *Introduction a l'etude du roit musulman,* Sirey, Paris 1971.

Mirakhor, Abbas, *Muslim Scholars and the History of Economics: A Need for Consideration,* Monograph Series, Institute of Islamic Economics, Islamabad 1986.

Mirakhor, Abbas, *Some Theoretical Aspects of an Islamic Financial System*, paper presented at the First International Conference on Islamic Banking, Tehran, Iran, 1986.

Mirman, L. J., *Uncertainty and Optimal Consumption Decisions, published in Econometrica,* (vol. 39, pp. 179–851), 1971.

Mirrlees, J., *The Optimal Structure of Incentives and Authority within an Organization,* published in *The Bell Journal of Economics* (vol. 7, No. 1, pp. 105–131), 1976.

Modarresi Tabataba'i, Hossein, *An Introduction to Shi'i Law, A Bibliographical Study,* Ithaca Press, London 1984.

———. *Khraraj in Islamic Law,* Archor Press Ltd., London, 1983.

Modigiliani, Franco, and Lucas Papademos, *The Structure of Financial Markets and Monetary Mechanism,* published in Federal

Reserve Bank of Boston, *Controlling Monetary Aggregates III,* Conference Series No. 23, 1980.

Mohsin, Muhammad, *A Profile of Riba-Free Banking,* published in Ariff, Muhammad, ed., *Monetory and Fiscal Economics of Islam* (pp. 187–203), International Center for Research in Islamic Economics, Jeddah 1982.

Morgan, Gerge Emir III., *On the Adequacy of Bank Capital Regulation,* published in *Journal of Financial and Quantitative Analysis* (vol. 19, No. 2, pp. 141–162), 1984.

Mossin, Jan, *Equilibrium in Capital Asset Market,* published in *Econometrica* (vol. 34, No. 4, pp. 768–783), 1966.

al-Mubārak, Muḥammad, *The State and System of al-Ḥisba in Ibn Taymeyah's Thought,* Dar al-Fikr, Beirut 1963.

Muhammad Ali, *A Manual of Hadith,* Ahmadiyah Anjuman, Lahore 1951.

Muḥammad al-Mahdī al-Ḥusaynī al-Shirāzī, *al-Bank al-Lārabawī, Kuwait.*

Muḥammad ibn 'Abd al-Aẓīm al-Mūsawī al-Khurāsānī, *Risālah fī Ḥukm al-Mu'āmalah al-Muhabatiyah,* manuscript, Danishgah Tehran Library 1136/9 (catalogue V, p. 1890).

———. *Risālah fī Hiyal al-Ribā,* manuscript, Danishgah Tehran Library 1136/14 (catalogue V, p. 1893).

Muḥammad ibn Muḥammad Khalīl al-Ḥusaynī al-Mar'ashi, *Khadimiyah dar Ḥurmat i Ḥiyal-i Shar'iyah,* manuscript, Mar'ashi Library, Qum, 234 (catalogue I, p. 260); Danishgah Tehran Library 2695 (catalogue X, p. 1578).

Muḥammad ibn Muḥammad Ṣādiq al-Mūsawī al-Khurāsanī, *Risālah fī 'Adam Jawāz al-Ḥiyal al-Shar'īyah,* Manuscript, Ustadi Library (catalogue, p. 59).

Muḥammad Hāshim al-Khurāsānī, *Risālah Ribā'iyah,* Mashad 1340, Tehran 1352.

Muḥammad Mahdī al-Ḥusaynī al-Mashhadī, *al-Ḥiyal al-Shar'iyah* (in refutation of Bahbihani's *Risālah fi Buṭlān al-Qarḍ bi Sharṭ al-Mu'āmalah al-Muhabātiyah,* Manuscript, Majlis Library, Tehran 1804/4 (catalogue IX, pp. 318–319).

Munawwar Iqbal, and M. Fahim Khan, eds. *Money and Banking in Islam,* Institute of Policy Studies, Islamabad 1983.

Munjid S. and Khuri Y., eds., *Fatāwā al-Imām Muḥammad Rashīd Riḍā* (5 volumes), Dar al-Kutub al-Jadīd, Beirut 1970.

Mushir ul-Hag, *Liberation and Justice Motifs of Islam,* published in *Religion and Society* (vol. 27, No. 2, pp. 24–31), 1980.

Muslehuddin, M., *Insurence and Islamic Law,* reprint, New Delhi 1982.

Naqvi, Syed Nawab Haidar, *Economics of Human Rights: An Islamic Synthesis,* Islamic Foundations, Leincester 1981.

———. *Ethics and Economics: An Islamic Synthesis,* Islamic Foundations, Leincester 1981.

———. *Ethical Foundation of Islamic Economics,* published in *Islamic Studies* (vol. 17, No. 2, pp. 105–133).

———. *On Replacing the Institution of Interest in a Dynamic Islamic Economy,* published in *Essays in Islamic Economic Philosophy* (III), Pakistan Institute of Developement Economics, Islamabad 1982.

Nasr, Seyyed Hossein, *An Introduction to Islamic Cosmological Doctrine,* Shambhala Publications, Boudler 1978.

———. *Ideas and Realities of Islam,* Beacon Press, Boston 1972.

———. *Science and Civilization in Islam,* New York 1970.

———. *The Significance of Persian Philosophical Works in the Tradition of Islamic Philosophy,* published in Hourani, G. F., ed., *Essays on Islamic Philosophy and Science,* p. 67–82.

Niẓām al-Mulk, *The Book of Government or Rules for the Kings (Siyāsat-Nāma),* translated by H. Rake, London 1960.

Pakistan, State Bank, *Elimination of Interest from the Banking System in Pakistan,* Karachi, 1984.

Pauly, M., *The Economics of Moral Hazard,* published in *The American Economic Review* (vol. 58, No. 3), June 1968.

Paydar, Habibullah, *Malikiyat wa Kār wa Sarmāyah az Didgāh -e Islam,* Daftar -e Nashr -e Farhang -e Islami, Tehran.

Peters, F. E., *Aristotle and the Arabs,* published in *Aristotelian Tradition in Islam,* New York University Press, New York 1968.

Phelps, E. S., *The Accumulation of Risky Capital: A Sequential Utility Analysis* in D. D. Hester and James Tobin, eds., *Risk Aversion and Portfolio Choice,* (pp. 137–53), John Wiley, New York, 1967.

Pickthal, Mohammed Marmaduke, tr., *The Meaning of the Glorious Kur'an,* Mentor Publications, New York 1953.

Postan, M. M., *Credit in Medieval Trade,* published in *Economic History Review* (vol. 1, pp. 250–), 1927.

Pratt, J. W. and R. Zeckhauser, *Principals and Agents: The Structure of Business,* Harvard Business School Press, Boston 1985.

Pringle, John J., *Bank Capital and the Performance of Banks as*

Financial Intermediaries, published in *Journal of Money, Credit and Banking* (vol. 7, No. 4), 1975.

Pryor, Fredric L. *The Islamic Economic System,* published in *Journal of Comparative Economics* (vol. 9, pp. 197–223), New York, 1985.

Pyle, David H., *Descriptive Theories of Financial Institutions Under Uncertainty,* published in *Journal of Financial and Quantitative Analysis* (pp. 2009–2029), 1972.

——— and Stephen J. Turnovsky, *Safety-First and Expected Utility Maximization in Mean-Standard Deviation Portfolio Analysis,* published in *Review of Economic and Statistics* (vol. 52, No. 1, pp. 75–81).

Qumi, *Risālah fi Mu'āmalāt al-Muhābātiyah bi Sharṭ al-Qarḍ wa bi al-'Aks* (It is included in the author's *Rasā'il*).

Qureshi, Anwar Iqbal, *Islam and the Theory of Interest,* Sh. Muhammad Ashraf, Lahore Pakistan, 1967.

Qureshi, D. M., *Instruments of Islamic Banking in the Muslim World: An Evaluation,* paper presented at the International Seminar on Islamic Banking, Islamabad, 1984.

———. *Problems of Profit Sharing,* paper presented at the Second International Conference on Islamic Economics, Islamabad, 1983.

———. *Investment Financing on the Basis of Shared Risk,* paper presented at the First Workshop on "Interest-Free Banking" organized by the Institute of Bankers in Pakistan, Karachi, 1985.

Radner, R., *Monitoring Cooperative Agreements in a Repeated Principal-Agent Relationship,* published in *Econometrica* (vol. 49, pp. 1127–1148), 1981.

Rahman, Afzalur, *Banking and Insurance,* The Muslim Students Trust, London 1979.

Rees, R., *The Theory of Principal and Agent* (Part I), published in *Bulletin of Economic Research,* (vol. 37, No. 1, pp. 3–26), 1985.

———, *The Theory of Principal and Agent* (Part II), published in *Bulletin of Economic Research,* (vol. 37, No. 2, pp. 75–95), 1985.

Rahman, Afzalur A. *Economic Doctrine of Islam: Banking and Insurance,* The Muslim Students Trust, Lahore, 1939.

Richards, D. S., ed., *Islam and Trade of Asia,* University of Pennsylvania Press 1970.

Ritter, Helmut, *Ein Arabische Handbuch der Handelswissenschaf* (for *Kitāb al-Ishāra ilā Maḥāsin al-Tijāra* of Ja'far al-Dimishqī), published in *Der Islam* (vol. 7, pp. 45–91), 1917.

Rosenthal, F., *Gambling in Islam,* Brill 1975.

Ross, S., *The Economic Theory of Agency: The Principal's Problem,* published in *American Economic Review,* (vol. 63, pp. 134–9), 1973.

Ross, Steven, *Economic Theory of Agency: The Principal's Problem,* published in *AER,* (vol. 63, pp. 134–139), 1973.

———, *The Determination of Financial Structure: The Incentive Signalling Approach,* published in *BJE,* (vol. 8, No. 1, pp. 32–40), 1977.

———, *Some notes on Financial Incentive Signalling models, Activity Choice, and Risk Preference,* published in *Journal of Finance,* vol. 33, No. 33, pp. 777–791), 1978.

Rothschild, M., and J. E. Stiglitz, *Increasing Risk II,* published in *Journal of Economic Theory,* (vol. 3, pp. 66–84), 1971.

———, *Increasing Risk I,* published in *Journal of Economic Theory,* (vol. 2, pp. 225–43), 1970.

——— and Stiglitz, J., *Increasing Risk II* published in *JET,* (vol. 2, pp. 315–329), 1979.

Roy, A. D., *Safety First and Holding Assets,* published in *Econometrica* (vol. 20, No. 3, pp. 431–449), 1952.

al-Ṣadr, Sayyid Muḥammad Bāqir, *Iqtiṣādunā,* Dar al-Fikr, Beirut 1968. Translated into Persian as *Iqtiṣād -e Mā* by Muhammad Kāzim Mūsawī, Burhan Publications, Tehran 1350/1971.

Al-Ṣadr, Sayyid Muḥammad Bāqir, Al-Bank al-lā Rabawi fi al-Islām, Kuwait, Jami'al-Naqī

Saleh, S., *Commercial Arbitration in the Arab Middle East,* Graham and Trotman, 1984.

Samuelson, Paul A., *General Proof that Diversification Pays,* published in *Journal of Financial and Quantitative Analysis* (pp. 1–13), 1967.

Sandmo, A., *The Effect of Uncertainty on Savings Decisions,* published in *Review of Economic Studies,* (vol. 37, pp. 353–60), 1970.

Sanhūrī, 'Abd al-Razzāq, *Maṣādir al-Ḥaqq fī Fiqh al-Islāmī* (6 volumes), al-Majma' al-Arabi al-Islami, Beirut.

Santomero, Anthony M. and Ronald D. Watson, *Determining an Optimal Capital Standard for the Banking Industry,* published in *Journal of Finance* (vol. 35, No. 4, pp. 1267–1282), 1977.

Schact, Joseph, *Riba*, in *Encyclopedia of Islam*, 1939.

———. *The Origin of Muhammadan Jurisprudence*, Claredon Press 1979.

Schuon, Frithjof. *Understanding Islam*, George Allen and Unwin, 1963.

Sealy, C. W., Jr., *Deposite Rate-Setting, Risk Aversion, and the Theory of Depository Financial Intermediaries*, published in *Journal of Finance* (vol. 35, No. 5, pp. 1139–1154), 1980.

Serjeant, R. B., *A Zaidi Manual of Hisba of the Third Century (H)*, published in *Rivista degli Studi Orientali* (vol. 28, pp. 1–34), 1953.

al-Sharīf, Sharaf ibn 'Alī, *al-Ijārah al-Wāridah 'Ala 'Amal al-Insān*, Saudi Arabia 1980.

Sharpe, William F., *Portfolio Theory and Capital Markets*, McGraw-Hill, New York 1970.

———. *Investments*, second edition, Prentice-Hill, New York Englewood Cliffs, N.J., 1981.

Shavell, S., *Risk-Sharing and Incentive in the Principal-Agent Relationships*, published in *Bell Journal of Economics*, (vol. 10, pp. 55–73), 1979.

Sherwani, Haroon Khan, *Studies in Muslim Political Thought and Administration*, second edition, Lahore 1945.

Shumpeter, Joseph A., *History of Economic Analysis*, Oxford University Press, New York 1954.

Siddiqui, Mohammed Nejatullah, *The Economic Enterprise in Islam*, Islamic Publications, Lahore 1972.

———. *Muslim Economic Thinking: A Survey of Contemporary Literature*, published in *Studies in Islamic Economics*, ed. by Khurshid Ahmad, The Islamic Foundation, Leicester, England 1980; International Center for Research in Islamic Economics, King Abdulaziz University, Jeddah, 1980.

———. *Banking Without Interest*, revised edition, King Abdulaziz University, Jeddah 1983.

———. *Economics of Profit Sharing*, published in *Issues in Islamic Banking*, selected papers, The Islamic Foundation, Leicester 1983.

———. *Islamic Approaches to Money, Banking and Monetary Policy: A Review*, published in Ariff, Muhammad, ed., *Monetary and Fiscal Economics of Islam*, International Center for Research in Islamic Economics, Jeddah 1982.

———. *Comments,* published in Ahmed Ziauddin et al., ed., *Money and Banking in Islam,* Institute for Policy Studies, Islamabad 1983.

Simons, Henry C., *Economic Policy for a Free Society,* University of Chicago Press, Chicago 1948.

Singh, N., *Monitoring and Hirarchies: The Marginal Value of Information in a Principal-Agent Model,* published in *Journal of Political Economy,* (vol. 93, No. 3, pp. 599–609), 1985.

Spence, M., and R. Zeckhauser, *Insurance, Information and Individual Action,* published in *The American Economic Review,* (vol. 61, pp. 380–87), 1971.

Sproule, R. A., *An Optimal Allocation of Labor Supply and Savings Under Interest-Rate Uncertainty: An Extension,* published in *Bulletin of Economic Research,* (vol. 37, pp. 115–22), 1985.

Spuler, Bertold, *Trade in the Eastern Islamic Countries in the Early Centuries,* published in *Islam and the Trade of Asia,* Richards, ed., pp. 11–20.

Stigler, George J., *Imperfections in the Capital Market,* published in *Journal of Political Economy* (vol. 75, No. 3, pp. 287–292), 1967.

Stiglitz, J., *Risk-Sharing and Incentives in Share-Cropping,* published in *Review of Economic Studies,* (pp. 219–55), 1974.

———. *Some Aspects of Pure Theory of Corporate Finance, Bankruptcies and Takeovers,* published in *BJE,* (vol. 3, No. 2, pp. 458–482), 1972.

———. *Incentives and Risk-Sharing in Share Cropping,* published in *Review of Economic Studies,* (vol. 41 (2), No. 126, p. 219–257), 1974.

——— and Weise, *Credit Rationing in markets with Imperfect Information,* published in *AER,* 1981.

Suhrawardy, A. *The Sayings of Muhammad,* J. Murry, London 1941.

Suyūṭī, Jalāl al-Dīn, *History of Califs,* translated by H. S. Jarrett, Amsterdam Oriental Press, 1970

Szego, Giorgio P., *Portfolio Theory: with Application to Bank Asset Management,* Academic Press, New York 1980.

al-Tabrīzī, Muḥammad ibn ʻAbdullāh al-Khaṭīb al-Umari *Mishkāt al-Maṣābih,* Damascus 1961, translated by J. Robson, Muhammad Ashraf Publications, Lahore 1965.

Ṭaleqāni, Sayyid Maḥmūd, *Islam wa Mālikiyat,* Book Distribution Center, Houston, 1978. Translated into English as *Islam and Ownership* by Ahmad Jabbari and Farhang Rajaee, Mazda Publishers, Lexington, Kentucky 1983.

Telser, Lester, *Safety First and Hedging,* published *Review of Economic Studies* (vol. 23, No. 1, pp. 1–16), 1955.

Thomson, *Practical Philosophy of Muhammedan People,* London 1839.

Tobin, James, *Liquidity Preference as Behaviour Towards Risk,* published in *Review of Economic Studies,* February 1958.

———, *The Theory of Portfolio Selection,* published in Hahn, F. H. and F. P. R. Brechling eds., *The Theory of Interest Rates,* Macmillan, 1966.

———. *A General Equilibrium Approach to Monetary Theory,* published in *Journal of Money, Credit, and Banking,* February 1969.

Toutouchinan, I., *Towards a Theory of Muslim Consumer Behavior,* Open Press, London, Forthcoming.

Tuma, Elias, *Early Arab Economic Policies (1st/7th–4th/10th Centuries,* published in *Islamic Studies* (vol. 6, No. 1. pp. 1–23) 1965.

Udovitch, Abraham L., *Commercial Techniques in Early Medieval Islamic Trade,* published in *Islam and the Trade of Asia,* Richards, ed., pp. 37–62.

———. *Credit as a Means of Investment in Medieval Islamic Trade,* published in *Journal of the American Oriental Study* (vol. 87, pp. 260–265), 1967.

———. *Labor Partnership in Early Islamic Law,* published in *Journal of Economic and Social History of the Orient* (vol. 10, pp. 64–80), 1967.

———. *Partnership and Profit in Medieval Islam,* Princeton 1970.

Uzair, Mohammed, *Interest-Free Banking,* Royal Book Company, Karachi 1978.

———, *Central Banking Operations in an Interest-Free Banking System,* published in Ariff, Muhammad, ed., *Monetory and Fiscal Economics of Islam,* International Center for Research in Islamic Economics, Jeddah 1982.

Vesey-Fitzgerald, S., *Muhammadan Law,* Scientia, Germany, reprint, 1979.

Weitzman, M. L., *Some Macroeconomic Implications of Alterna-*

tive Compensation Systems, published in *Economic Journal,* (vol. 93, pp. 763–83), December, 1983.

———, *The Share Economy,* Harvard University Press, Cambridge, Massachusettes, 1984.

———, *Profit Sharing as Macroeconomic Policy,* published in *American Economic Review,* (pp. 41–45), May 1985.

Weston, J. F., *The Profit Concept and Theory: A Restatement,* published in *Journal of Political Economy,* 42(2):152–170.

Wickens, G. M., *Al-Jarsifi on Hisba,* published in *Islamic Quarterly* (vol. 3, pp. 176–187), 1956.

Wilson, C. A., *A Model of Insurance Markets with Incomplete Information,* published in *Journal of Economic Theory,* (vol. 16, pp. 167–207), 1977.

Wilson, R., *The Theory of Syndicates,* published in *Econometrica,* (vol. 36, pp. 119–132), 1968.

Yaḥyā ibn Ādam al-Qurashī, *Kitab al-Kharāj,* edited and translated by A. Ben Shemesh, Leiden 1958.

Yazdi, Ibrāhim, Iqtiṣād -e Islāmī, Maktab Mubarez vol. 1–4. Europe, 1974.

Zanjānī, Sayyid Abu al-Faḍl, *Balāy -e Ribā.*

Zarqa, Mohammed Anas, *Stability in an Interest-Free Economy: A Note,* published in *Pakistan Journal of Applied Economics* (vol. 2, pp. 181–188), Winter 1983.

———. *Discussion,* published in Ariff, Muhammad, ed., *Monetory and Fiscal Economics of Islam,* International Center for Research in Islamic Economics, Jeddah 1982.

de Zayas, F., *The Law and Philosophy of Zakat,* al-Jadidah Press, Damascus 1960.

Zaydān, 'Abd al-Karīm, *Aḥkām al-Dhimmiyah wa al-Musta'manin,* Baghdad 1963.

Zaydān, Abu al-Makārim, *Binā al-Iqtiṣād fi al-Islām,*

Zeckhauser, R., Medical Insurance: A Case Study of the Trade-Off Between Risk-Spreading and Appropriate Incentives, published in *Journal of Economy Theory,* (vol. 2, pp. 10–26), 1970.

Ziadah, Nichola, *al-Ḥisba and al-Muḥtasib in Islam,* Catholic Press, Beirut 1962.

Index